POLICING AFGHANISTAN

ANTONIO GIUSTOZZI
MOHAMMAD ISAQZADEH

Policing Afghanistan

The Politics of the Lame Leviathan

HURST & COMPANY, LONDON

First published in the United Kingdom in 2013 by
C. Hurst & Co. (Publishers) Ltd.,
41 Great Russell Street, London, WC1B 3PL
© Antonio Giustozzi and Mohammad Isaqzadeh, 2013
All rights reserved.
Printed in India

The right of Antonio Giustozzi and Mohammad Isaqzadeh to be identified as the Authors of this publication is asserted by them in accordance with the Copyright, Designs and Patents Act, 1988.

A Cataloguing-in-Publication data record for this book is available from the British Library.

ISBN: 978-1-84904-205-5

www.hurstpublishers.com

This book is printed on paper from registered sustainable and managed sources.

CONTENTS

Acknowledgements ix
Glossary xi

1. Introduction 1
   Policing as the object of study 1
   Policing in the context of state formation and state-building 2
   Policing in history 5
   Throwing light on the mystery of institution building 7
   The Afghan context 10
2. Background: history of police in Afghanistan 13
   The origins 13
   To 1978 14
      Structural development 14
      Territorial and population control 15
      Command and control 19
      Rule of law and professionalisation 21
   1978–2001 24
      Politicisation and the first assault on meritocracy, 1978–9 24
      A new institutional order, under Soviet patronage, 1979–92 26
      State collapse and the second assault on meritocracy, 1992–6 32
      Policing under the Taliban 34
3. Afghanistan's police in 2002 37
   A new year zero of policing 37
   The early post-2001 political economy 39
4. The changing post-2001 operating environment 41
5. The uncertain impact of external assistance 47
   Financial assistance 47

CONTENTS

Training, mentoring and advising	48
The beginnings	48
The American wave	50
Impact of assistance	52
6. Internal organisation and reorganisation	55
Structural development	55
Professionalisation	59
Local/non-local	59
Indiscipline	64
Cooperation with other government institutions	68
Investigative capabilities	69
Reporting and record keeping	70
Pay and retention	72
Education	74
Competence and motivation	76
Corruption	78
The corruption landscape	78
Case study: the ANP and illegal tolls	84
Counter-narcotics	89
Ghost police	91
Fighting corruption	93
7. Recruitment and retention	97
The scarcity of professionals	97
Charismatic officers and patrons	100
Provincial dynamics: Balkh's most durable stationary bandit	102
Façades of reform	103
Purges, clean-ups and patronage	105
Ethnicity	105
Political affiliation	108
Professionalism	110
Lobbying	112
Criminal networking and corruption	113
8. The ultimate test of functionality: the paramilitary dimension	115
Commanding and controlling the police	115
The early days	115
Impact of improvement efforts	116
Persistent patrimonialism	119
Collaboration with the enemy	120
Alternative models?	123
Control of territory and population	124

CONTENTS

The early days	124
Persistent weakness	125
Wasteful use of human resources	128
Reduction of coverage faced with the insurgency	128
Reporting	130
Logistics	130
9. The ambiguous impact of reform	135
The first wave of reforms and the difficulties of re-centralisation	135
Nature of the reforms	135
The centralisation effort vis-à-vis the strongmen	136
Provincial dynamics: Faryab province, 2004	137
Provincial dynamics: Kandahar province, 2005	139
Reform, counter-reform and external scrutiny	140
The Trojan horse which was not	140
The lone reformer at the top	141
Thermidor: from reform to technical improvements	143
The debate over paramilitary or civilian policing	145
Gender issues	147
Pay and rank reform	150
The rule of law	151
The Afghan Leviathan and the rule of law	151
External oversight and accountability	152
The foreigners' influence	153
Abusive and arbitrary behaviour	154
Torture	155
Illegal detention	155
Arbitrary executions	157
Riot control	158
Community demands and rule of law	159
10. Provincial dynamics: a case study of Herat	165
Historical background	165
Police during Ismail Khan's first rule over Herat (1992–5)	166
Police under the Taliban's Emirate	167
Police during Ismail Khan's second rule over Herat (2001–4)	168
Building a loyal police force	168
Command and control of the Police	169
Police corruption	171
Police in post-Ismail Khan Herat	172
Police and politics	173
Command and control	175

CONTENTS

Political economy		176
Police corruption and criminal behaviour		177
Oversight of the police		178
11. Conclusion		183
Notes		187
References		219
Index		225

ACKNOWLEDGEMENTS

The authors' interests in policing in Afghanistan had different origins. Antonio Giustozzi started dealing with Afghanistan's police when working in UNAMA and maintained this interest as an academic. In 2010–11 he was repeatedly involved in studies on the Afghan Ministry of the Interior. Eventually, after carrying out work on the police for years, he began to think that the development of policing is a crucial aspect of state-building. Particularly during his involvement with the Crisis States Research Centre (LSE), Giustozzi had the opportunity to spend time and energy thinking about statebuilding in its various aspects.

Mohammad Isaqzadeh's interest in conducting research on Afghanistan's police started with his fieldwork in Afghanistan in 2008. Interested in studying post-conflict state-building in Afghanistan from an institutional perspective, he noticed that the police play a key role in enhancing, or undermining, the legitimacy of a new political system due to the frequent interactions between citizens and the police. Since then he has taken part in various studies on the Afghan police and has interacted with police officers and officials from the Ministry of the Interior through offering public policy workshops at the Ministry, which have given him invaluable insights into policing in Afghanistan.

Eventually the two authors' interests in Afghan policing converged in 2010, when they realised by chance that they had been working at similar topics. In 2011 they decided that it was about time to write a book together on the subject.

The authors wish to thank all those who gave interviews for the book or for any of their several projects related to Afghanistan's police. They are highly grateful to the officials in the Ministry and to the police officers who shared with them their experiences and showed courage in discussing sensitive issues. Mohammad wishes to thank particularly those in the provincial police force in Herat. Since some of the material contained in the book might be considered somewhat controversial, we cannot name them here as we would

ACKNOWLEDGEMENTS

have liked. We can however thank those who made the book possible by either contributing funding or working on its technical aspects. We therefore thank the Afghanistan Analyst Network (Berlin), which paid for a report which was then integrated into this book. We also thank Michael Dwyer and his team at Hurst & Co for quickly processing the book and publishing it in good time.

GLOSSARY

AACP	Afghan Anti-Crime Police
AIHRC	Afghan Independent Human Rights Commission
ABP	Afghanistan Border Police
ALP	Afghan Local Police
ANA	Afghan National Army
ANAP	Afghan National Auxiliary Police
ANP	Afghan National Police (incorporating all police forces)
ANSF	ISAF acronym for Afghan National Security Forces
APPF	Afghan Public Protection Force
AUP	Afghan Uniformed Police
ATA	Afghanistan Transitional Authority
CID	Criminal Investigation Department
CM	Capability Milestones, an ISAF assessment tool
CoP	Chief of Police
CSTC-A	Combined Security Transition Command—Afghanistan
DoD	Department of Defense (US)
DoS	Department of State (US)
EUPOL	European Union Police Mission
FAS	Federation of Atomic Scientists
FDD	ISAF acronym for Focused District Development
GAO	Government Accountability Office (US)
HDK	Hizb-i Demokratik-i Khalq (People's Democratic Party)
Hizb-i Islami	Islamic Party
Hizb-i Wahdat	Abbreviation for Hizb-i Wahdat-i Islami Afghanistan

GLOSSARY

	(Islamic Unity Party of Afghanistan, a Shi'ite, Khomeinist organisation)
Hizbullah	'Party of God', a Shi'ite organisation closely linked to Iran
ICPC	Interim Criminal Procedure Code
IDLG	Independent Directorate for Local Governance
IJC	Integrated Joint Command (ISAF)
INL	Bureau of International Narcotics & Law (US)
ISAF	International Security Assistance Force
Junbish-e-Mili	Abbreviation for Junbish-i Milli-ye Islami Afghanistan, National Islamic Front of Afghanistan
Kalantars (muhassils)	An armed militia assigned to each provincial governor
KhAD	Khadamat-e Aetla'at-e Dawlati (State Intelligence Agency) in 1980–6
Khalq	'Masses', a wing of the HDK (see above)
Kotwali	The security branch of the police in its early days
LOFTA	Law and Order Trust Fund for Afghanistan
MoF	Ministry of Finance
Mujahidin	Literally 'holy warriors', the armed opposition to the HDK regime in 1978–92
Mustufi	the MoF representative at the provincial level
NDS	National Directorate of Security (Resayat-i Amniyat-i Milli)
NTM-A	NATO Training Mission—Afghanistan
Parcham	'Flag', a wing of the HDK (see above)
Sarandoi	The name of the police in 1978–92
SIGAR	Special Inspector General for Afghanistan Reconstruction
SN	Saronwali Nezami (Military Attorney Directorate)
Taliban	Shorthand for Harakat-i Taliban or for Islamic Emirate of Afghanistan
Tazkira	ID
UNAMA	United Nations Assistance Mission to Afghanistan
UNDP	United Nations Development Organisation
UNODC	United Nations Organisation for Drugs and Crime

1

INTRODUCTION

Policing as the object of study

Policing is not a popular topic of research among scholars. Although a vast literature exists, it is mostly technical in nature and only rarely analytical. Even the police forces of Western Europe and North America have rarely been investigated in depth as far as their history and functioning is concerned. In particular, the politics of policing and its political economy have been largely neglected. If that is the case in the West, logically little better should be expected of developing countries, where archives often do not exist and in any case are almost never accessible. However, one advantage of studying police forces in developing countries is that we can see the police in the course of its early evolution towards professionalism, including aspects often neglected in the European chronicles and documentation of the modern age.

For personal and professional reasons, the authors of this book have chosen to study Afghanistan's police for an in-depth study. This choice, inevitable as far as the authors are concerned, comes with advantages and disadvantages. The most obvious advantage, as mentioned above, is the possibility of observing the development of a police force from its early stages, starting from what was a very primitive, militia-based organisation. As a post-conflict country for a few years after 2001 (until the Taliban insurgency took off in 2006), Afghanistan has been a particularly privileged observation point for this evolution of policing, which in one form or another has taken place in any country which now has a sophisticated police force. The other advantage is that the huge external intervention in the country has multiplied the potential sources of information available, an important consideration in field research when local archives are not accessible and much information is not recorded by local sources.

POLICING AFGHANISTAN

The massive external intervention in Afghanistan, including in the field of policing, is at the same time the main disadvantage of Afghanistan as a case study of police development. External intervention 'pollutes' internal political developments, twists them, accelerates them (or tries to), with the result that what happened in Afghanistan after 2001 can only with great caution be taken as a hint of wider processes of police development. However, imitation has been a factor in police development since the nineteenth century at least, so we should not overstate the impact of the stream of donors, advisers and mentors visiting Afghanistan and trying to drive the development of its police force in one direction or the other.

Carrying out research in a country like Afghanistan, particularly in the middle of a conflict, presents a number of limitations as well. Access to documentation has been limited, for example, although this is not much of a disadvantage as, even in developed countries at peace, documentation about the inner workings of the police is hard to obtain. Facts and figures have also proved difficult to confirm or verify; truth is the first victim of war. Much of the information was obtained through interviews and most informants requested anonymity. Whenever possible, we tried to confirm the information provided with alternative sources, but inevitably this was not always possible. We used cross-checks to establish the reliability of sources and once convinced that a particular source was reliable, we also used single source information. Much of the information we obtained could not be used because it was insufficiently reliable, particularly concerning issues of corruption and wrong-doing, where allegations of all kinds were flourishing.

In summary, this book aims to throw light on the development of policing in Afghanistan and through that contribute to the wider understanding of 'police-building'. The literature on policing in Afghanistan is scant and largely focused on recent reform efforts. One exception is the authors' 'Afghanistan's paramilitary policing in context', published as a paper in 2011 by the Afghanistan Analyst Network, on which some of the chapters of this book are based, in particular those dealing with paramilitary policing. Even when we look at the wider literature on policing, national case studies are lacking. We hope, therefore, that this book will be of help to the wider community of scholars working on the development of policing, as we believe that without a granular understanding of the political dynamics surrounding policing, the understanding of these processes can only be very limited.

Please note that the Afghan Year calendar and the Gregorian calendar are often used alongside each other in the text.

Policing in the context of state formation and state-building

A study of the development of policing needs to be supported by clear concepts of state formation and state-building. Policing is clearly about the management of violence and rules imposed by a particular government, but where does policing end and the military start? In principle it is possible to

INTRODUCTION

distinguish between the military as an organisation specialising in the monopoly of large-scale violence (the first step towards state formation) and the police as an organisation specialising instead in the management of small-scale violence, a later concern of state-makers. While the army conquers and holds the monopoly of large-scale violence, policing is a specific strategy of consolidation of the monopoly of violence. A state needs a strategy towards small violent actors, even if they did not represent a direct threat to the large scale monopoly of violence of the regime in power. There are several reasons for this:[1]

1. Small violent actors have to be monitored and kept in check, lest they develop the capacity or willingness to challenge the core of the state.
2. Perpetrators of small-scale violence may disrupt specific interests of the state, such as taxation and the mobilisation of human resources. However, it is important to consider that claiming a 'monopoly over theft' might be very expensive, depending on such factors as geography, the capacities of the state and its agencies, etc., and therefore a strategy of monopolisation of theft might well be economically unsound. Furthermore, a policy of further centralisation of the means of coercion may also run the risk of non-state armed groups coalescing, by giving them a shared enemy to fight against, namely the state itself. This helps to explain why rulers often have chosen to ignore this option.
3. The ruling elite might see some advantage in improving the conditions of internal order for the population in general. In other words, it could offer policing as a service provided by the state to its subjects in order to win their gratitude, and more importantly to make them more dependent on the state. The provision of state policing often went hand-in-hand with the at least partial and gradual disarmament of the population and/or the disbandment of non-state armed groups, which in turn resulted in the inability of local communities to police themselves.
4. The commitment of the state, or of influential lobbies around it, to specific aims of economic and social development. In this case the state would have to develop policing as a response to growing social differentiation or to regiment the population.

It is clear that several rationales for the development of a civilian police force exist. It should also be clear how the factors driving the development of such a police force can vary in strength from situation to situation and from country to country, depending on whether those factors are all in play or not. The actual shape of the police force of a country depends on other factors as well: even if a civilian police does emerge and develop, it may co-exist with an army which plays a similar role or with a paramilitary police force. In Europe, these paramilitary forces have evolved to the point where they can barely be distinguished from the civilian police, except for the fact that they remain under military discipline and that they tend to devolve a greater share of their resources to anti-riot units of counter-terrorism.

3

It was not always like that, however. In the presence of a threat to the monopoly of large-scale violence, a civilian police force or even a tame form of paramilitary police is not sufficient to handle it. Even in Europe's recent history, when insurgencies took off and became a serious threat (in Northern Ireland for example), the army had to intervene and a paramilitary force put in charge of the repression. In practice, therefore, where the monopoly of large-scale violence is still uncertain, policing is going to be carried out by a mixed civilian and paramilitary force, if a civilian police even exist, or sometimes by the army as well.

However confused real life situations might be, the distinction between civilian police and paramilitary or gendarmerie forces is nonetheless of primary analytical importance. While the former deals with the monopolisation (or at least management) of small-scale violence, the latter deals with the monopolisation of large-scale violence. As a result the two tend to have remarkably different characteristics, which can be summarised as follows.

Civilian police
1. in charge of enforcing law and order;
2. it operates in small and very small units, often individuals and pairs; it does not have the capability to operate in a coordinated fashion in units larger than tens of men;
3. it has no heavy weaponry and little logistical capacity, it sometimes even makes limited use of light weapons;
4. in principle use of force has to be authorised externally, by the judiciary or the executive;
5. it has well-developed investigative capabilities;
6. its command structure might be monolithic or decentralised, but individual units are generally assigned to specific areas and do not rotate;
7. it has limited or no long-range mobility;
8. supervision is in principle strong and multi-layered and is both internal and external.

Gendarmerie
1. it has some capability for large-scale violence, although not for sustaining long battles or for massing thousands of troops;
2. it has a hierarchical structure and is based on military discipline;
3. it deals primarily not with ordinary crime, but with internal threats to state security;
4. it has little or no investigative capabilities;
5. it is cheaper to maintain than an army, although it is more expensive than the police;
6. it is more heavily armed than the civilian police, often with armour and a generous supply of military weapons (in modern terms: assault rifles and machine guns);

INTRODUCTION

7. it is permanently based in localities, so it can develop local knowledge;
8. its operational command and logistical structure exist mainly at the local level, although a central reserve force may also exist, and it cannot usually operate in a coordinated fashion beyond the local level;
9. supervision is bureaucratised and stronger than in the army, but not as strong as in the police as the emphasis is on eliminating direct threats to regimes and quality control of rule-of-law enforcement is not as important;
10. because of their military background and organisation gendarmes may be useful in tasks such as crowd management, where discipline and hierarchy have to take over once disorder has broken out.

Civilian policing and paramilitary policing should be treated therefore as two ideal-types in the Weberian sense: as models not as realities.

Policing in history

Before being incorporated in a state, local communities typically made some arrangements to maintain order among their members. The actual nature of such arrangements varied from community to community. Egalitarian communities such as tribes, led by councils of elders, would entrust the council with the ability to call into service young members of the community to enforce the decisions of the council on matters such as disputes, crimes, etc. Hierarchically structured communities would rely on the armed retinue of the local 'big man' to do the same; in this case the community would of course be dependent on the willingness of the 'big man' to enforce some definition of 'justice'. What neither the big man nor the council could easily do was enforce order across communities.[2] These community-based forces could already be described as militias, although they might not be permanently mobilised unless the big man was wealthy enough to pay his recruits a salary.

With the incorporation of communities into the state, a process started of expropriation of their ability to administer their own justice (in the case of egalitarian communities) or of co-option (in the case of many big men). Because new states typically relied on limited revenue, militias, that is irregular volunteer forces recruited locally, continued to be used to maintain law and order for a long time in European history. In the absence of institutionalised police, early rulers had to rely on local leaders, buying their loyalty with lavish gifts, honour and titles. Because such forces tended originally to reflect partisan political interests, arguably they lacked general legitimacy.[3]

Historically, the extension of moral consensus to the state and the development of police as instruments of legitimate coercion went hand-in-hand. The quality of coercion (that is also its accurate targeting) was a major factor in determining the success or failure of coercive legitimation. In other words, the legitimacy of the state was at stake whenever the army was unable to coerce in a carefully targeted and restrained way. Specialised policing could be described as a specific strategy for maintaining internal order and responding to changes in society in a creative way. Such social changes, however, have as yet been far from universal, posing the question of whether 'modern' policing is appropriate for late developing countries. Nor can every ruler be assumed to have the capability to implement sophisticated models of policing. Even if able, some rulers might be unwilling, particularly if free from pressure coming from constituencies and lobbies promoting specialised policing.[4]

One important aspect of the development of specialised policing is that it is expensive, not only in terms of direct financial costs but also of longer-term investments. For example, it requires the training and education of substantial numbers of staff. As this is also and perhaps foremost an exercise in institution-building, it implies political sacrifices for the rulers, who might have to sacrifice some of their own arbitrary prerogatives as well as some clients and constituencies to make space for a professional police.

Even when a political decision is made to develop specialised policing, several strategies are always available to policy makers. An incomplete list of them could look like this:

1. Centralisation: maximises government control, but sometimes at the expense of effectiveness, flexibility and the ability to match policing to local realities; might imply a significant political cost in marginalising local power players;
2. Co-option: allows the incorporation of local leaders within the regime; implies renouncing direct control; is inexpensive, but largely incompatible with professionalisation;
3. Devolution: allows for a degree of local influence and participation, maybe through co-option, but not necessarily; is compatible in principle with professionalisation; implies to some degree the renunciation of the centre to exercise strategic direction;
4. Militarisation: maximises the ability of the centre to use a 'suppression' strategy; hampers the adoption of alternative strategies; ensures strict control from the centre and high discipline; is incompatible with devolution or co-option; does not work well as a 'service';
5. Civilianisation: maximises the ability of adopting a 'criminalisation' strategy; is not the most effective way to implement 'suppression'; is bureaucratised; is usually subject to external supervision (judiciary, executive, parliament), which might limit its (or the centre's) room for manoeuvre;
6. Party control: (a variant of the bureaucratisation/professionalisation model); requires a certain degree of efficiency and the existence of a widespread/pervasive structure, maximises control from the government and loyalty to it; is unresponsive to local concerns; risks suffering delegitimisation if party rule enters a crisis;
7. De-factionalisation: removes any party or factional control over the police, ensuring a greater acceptability of police to all sections of society; is also a precondition of full professionalisation; however makes control from the

INTRODUCTION

centre more difficult and turns the police into a relatively independent force, controlled mainly bureaucratically;
8. Patrimonialisation: makes some degree of indirect control possible at low cost; causes inefficiency and is difficult to micro-direct towards specific security strategies; might make matching local realities easier on condition of selecting appointees carefully;
9. Privatisation: is expensive when funded by the state, but removes from the shoulders of policy-makers the burden of carrying out difficult reforms of a police force; can offer quick solutions to the problem of delivering policing services to impatient constituencies; is flexible as there are several options, ranging from simply allowing private companies to offer their services to private firms and citizens, to contracting out public policing; reduces the degree of control over policing by the authorities;
10. 'Democratic policing': maximises the ability of the centre to adopt an 'accommodation' strategy; greatly reduces the ability to adopt strategies such as 'suppression' and to some extent 'criminalisation' too; exposes policing to the internal political debate, with potentially demoralising effects on rank and file in specific circumstances;
11. Professionalisation/bureaucratisation: reduces freedom in making appointments as meritocratic/bureaucratic procedures are used; most effective at implementing strategies like 'criminalisation' and 'accommodation', not suitable for 'suppression'; is expensive to put into practice; has a political cost because it might require the marginalisation of important players within a given regime.

Sometimes these strategies are complementary, sometime in opposition to each other. Graph 1 illustrates this and the process of development of 'legitimate coercion', which is what mature policing is.

Throwing light on the mystery of institution building

We have highlighted above how different strategies of policing exist and have been used in different contexts, depending on what the aims of a particular ruling elite were. The literature, although limited, tends to support the case that in abstract certain approaches to policing are more effective; like in state-building in general, institution-building pays considerable rewards in terms of a more stable system, more effective in containing crime and corruption within the police, and in insulating the political elite from failures and shortcomings.[5]

However, the real question however is why, if institution building is such an obvious blessing, it has not been universally adopted in every country of the world. In other words, what drives the adoption of institution-building strategies by a ruling elite? In this book, a political economy framework is adopted to provide an explanation of processes of state consolidation. In Olson's analysis, the stationary bandit represents a ruler who is able to consol-

Graph 1: The development of policing.

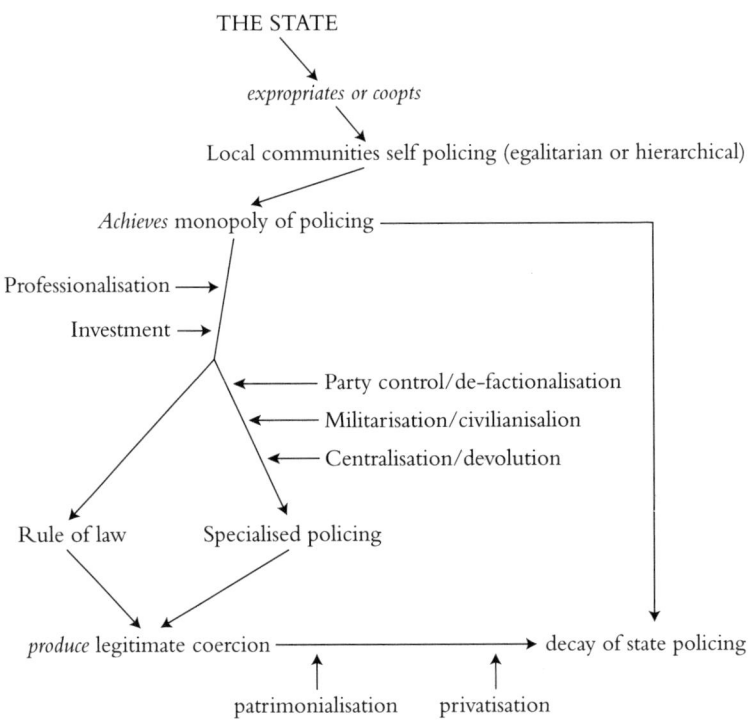

idate his control over a territory and expects to remain in control of that territory for a period of time. Such a ruler has the incentives to set up a limit on how many resources he would extract from the territory under his control since over-extraction would undermine the prosperity in his territory and would decrease the total resources that he could extract. Stationary bandits are not institution-builders (yet), but their strategy of investing in the consolidation of the polity under their control is susceptible to evolving into institution building at some stage. These patrimonial and personalistic regimes at least have a chance of consolidating the monopoly of violence in their hands, the first stage of state formation.[6]

In this book some examples of stationary bandits are discussed. The problem lies in explaining why monopolisation and violence are a preliminary conditions of institution building, but the latter does not necessarily follow from the former. One major factor to consider is what drives efforts to build institutions: the demand of specific constituencies of the state, the need to improve effectiveness vis-à-vis internal challenges or the requests of foreign supporters? Depending on the answer, the success of institution-building

INTRODUCTION

might vary. Institution-building of some sort will start if there is pressure from some quarter for it to start, but building a system does not guarantee that the institution thus created will function. Endowing a complex bureaucratic system with functionality is a difficult task as bureaucratic systems tend towards dysfunctionality, particularly when they are very complex, because they are difficult to manage and management skills are always scarce.

The recent example of China is useful for explanatory purposes: police reform there was clearly the result of decisions taken at the centre, to allow professionalism and autonomy to grow: 'the nature and functions of the police are being shifted from police suppression under a dictatorship to law enforcement and public services'. The police increasingly came to be seen as playing 'a supporting role in protecting economic development'. Apart from the strategic decisions taken at the centre, other factors favouring police reform in China were the growing middle class and a vibrant society that 'demands rights' and 'international pressures, through the mechanism of the World Trade Organization (WTO), International Covenant on Civil and Political Rights (ICCPR)'.[7]

Dysfunctionality occurs when a system is not fulfilling the purpose for which it was established. Therefore, a police force might be corrupt but still be functional, if asking for money to top up the salaries of the policemen does not divert them from their tasks. Some forms of corruption, however, breed dysfunctionality: when bribes are taken not to fulfil a task, when appointments are sold for cash, when political patronage overrides meritocratic considerations and appointees are short of the qualifications and skills required for the job.[8]

How a system gets to become dysfunctional can be illustrated by the case of Pakistan. The weak centralisation of Pakistan, the prominence of local elites in the elite bargain at the centre and the lack of political will in shaping a more effective police force all seem to have been major factors in the decay of Pakistan's police, as 'the political masters who are mainly interested in bending the laws to favour their party men and to hound the opposition'. During 1985–92 Pakistan's police seem to have touched rock bottom, as politicians were recruiting many officers among protégés with a criminal record. Political protection destroyed the chain of command, as subordinates refused punishment by appealing to their patrons. The lack of interest in controlling the countryside and challenging the hold of the landlords was visible in the abolition of the office of the village chowkidar, which was only replaced by two or three detective constables per police station, far too few to tour the villages and pick up information, particularly now that the landlords, sensing the weakening of the central government, became more active and interested in asserting themselves in national and local politics.[9]

If it easy for an elite to sabotage the functionality of a police force, so how does a ruling elite instead ensure that the investment it makes in a bureaucratic system of policing pays off and dysfunctionality is avoided? Multiple layers of bureaucratic supervision must be created. Without those, a system is

9

bound to be dysfunctional because nobody will even know what is going on within it. An alert and dynamic political leadership might be able, at least in the short term, to ensure functionality by exclusively relying on these layers of internal supervision. In general, however, and particularly in the long term, external oversight is indispensable to maintaining the functionality of a system. The supervision of the political leadership is unlikely to remain focused for very long. External oversight can be exercised by a variety of sources: other branches of government, parliaments, political parties and organisations, civil society organisations, and so on.[10]

Vice-versa, dysfunctionality occurs when a political leadership does not judge that it needs a system to be functional, or when there is a gap between the model of system adopted and the human and/or financial resources available to realise it, or again when the system design is defective and either supervision or oversight are insufficient.

Once dysfunctionality affects a system, it might still be possible to restore its functionality. In practice, any effort to change a system or build a new one from scratch, that is in other words to 'reform' a system, is subject to controversy and political friction. The reformers will face opposition from conservative elements, who think the reforms are not necessary or even damaging, as well as from other reformers who will disagree on how to actually carry out the reform. Reformers, in order to have a chance to succeed, have therefore to be tactically aware: they need a fine political sense of what the opportunities are. Otherwise they will crash against a wall of resistance. The reformers have to crush their enemies early and make it clear who the beneficiaries of reform are, in order to gain support. It is always a matter of fine political judgement in such cases whether the purity of reform should be defended or whether compromise should occur.

The example of Ghana is useful to explain this point. President Rawlings' approach in the early 1980s was highly controversial and completely opposed to the international consensus on police development. Ghana's police had serious problems of corruption and management. He abolished altogether the division of labour between police, army, intelligence and paramilitary, mainly due to resource constraints and a bureaucratic crisis but despite the obvious risks, including the militarisation of the police, the system worked reasonably well from his perspective and it was retained. Rawlings could do that because he had seized power in a military coup as it is highly unlikely that he would ever have overcome opposition to his reform plan if he had been democratically elected.[11]

The Afghan context

A discussion of policing in Afghanistan must start from the transition, briefly discussed above, from private or semi-private militias to a state-controlled, disciplined police force. Such transition occurred for the first time between 1880 and the 1920s, although little is known about it. It started again in 2002, as

INTRODUCTION

policing in Afghanistan had nearly reverted to the pre-1880 status quo as a result of twenty-three years of war. This more recent transition is easier to study, because much more information is available.

Famously, the Afghanistan Compact envisaged a rapid transition for Afghanistan's police:

By end-2010, a fully constituted, professional, functional and ethnically balanced Afghan National Police and Afghan Border Police with a combined force of up to 62,000 will be able to meet security needs of the country effectively and will be increasingly fiscally sustainable.[12]

Although quantitative growth was actually faster than initially planned, on any other account the police of 2010 still looked far from the target of professionalism and functionality stated in the Compact. This is not surprising as the Compact was very ambitious in its aims, as was to be expected from a document that was meant to raise support from donors.

The debate about success and failure in reshaping or reforming Afghanistan's police after 2001 therefore risks being too narrow. It is of much greater importance to explore the developments of 2001–11 to see what political processes were going on and where they were pointing at in terms of the role of policing within the wider context of state-building. Rarely, in fact, have professional police forces emerged out of straight processes of reform. More complex and tortuous political processes were usually at the roots of police development, although as professional police forces were becoming more common around the world in the nineteenth century, imitation also started which might in some cases have speeded up and even simplified change in policing.

The political fights that characterised police development in Afghanistan after 2001 were not unique in history, perhaps not even exceptional. The strategies described in the previous section were often considered, but not in a vacuum where policing per se was the only concern. The variety of economic, social and political interests that affected decision making (or the lack thereof) need to be factored into the analysis of policing. The political economy of police development in Afghanistan is also far from unique in some of its extreme characteristics, which will be reviewed in detail in the text below.

This volume tries to be as comprehensive as possible in the treatment of police development in Afghanistan. Although historical sources are limited, a history of policing in Afghanistan from its origins is provided in Chapter 2. From the 1970s onwards, information becomes more abundant and so our analysis get richer. The focus is, however, inevitably on the post-2001 period, both because of the relative richness of sources and the expected greater interest among readers.

As mentioned already, international intervention after 2001 (and in the 1980s) has been a very important aspect of police development in Afghanistan, which is one of the few aspects of Afghan policing that has attracted attention and has been the object of several published analyses. Although this book cannot avoid discussing the issue, it is not going to be focused on this aspect, both because it is already understood comparatively better than other aspects of policing in Afghanistan and because of an explicit choice to focus on *Afghan* policing. Advising and mentoring of Afghan police are dealt in greater detail in another, forthcoming work, *Missionaries of Modernity*. This book only deals with external assistance to the extent that it is necessary to explain and understand developments internal to Afghanistan's police (Chapter 5), but the role of foreign advisers is considered throughout the book when necessary (in particular concerning reform efforts).

Chapter 3 discusses how Afghanistan's police looked in 2002 and how it changed, when it did. It is necessary to take into account how the operating environment post-2001 differed from that of previous years, as well as from other international contexts: Chapter 4 deals with this aspect. There is no question that much changed between 2001 and 2011, as detailed in Chapters 6–9. However, to paraphrase Italian novelist Tomasi di Lampedusa (author of the *Gattopardo*), change sometimes occurs in order to maintain the status quo as much as possible. Throughout Chapter 9 we debate the issue of how deep change has been. It is possible to anticipate that change was driven by external pressure and that Afghan policy makers were mostly half hearted at best in promoting it.

The predominant concern of those policy makers who were investing genuine effort in improving Afghanistan's police became, from 2003 onwards, the effectiveness of paramilitary policing. Chapter 8 deals with this aspect and shows how, despite what should have been the self-preservation instinct of the post-2001 elites, the paramilitary capacity of Afghanistan's police still left much to be desired by 2011. In a sense the effectiveness of paramilitary policing is the litmus test of state functionality (or lack thereof): if a state is unable to effectively defend itself in the presence of a clear challenge, then there can be no question that it is indeed dysfunctional. The policy of appointments is dedicated a particular attention (Chapter 7) because it appeared to be the most solid way of testing information provided by interviewers and matching it with verifiable data.

The volume is equipped with plenty of empirical material, both for the purpose of documenting assertions and views and for the purpose of illustration. The empirical material is distributed throughout the book, but a few expanded case studies have also been inserted to give a flavour of what policing in Afghanistan looks like at the provincial level. The largest and most comprehensive case study is Herat's which deserved a dedicated chapter (10). Faryab and Kandahar in 2004–5 have also been dedicated relatively long case studies (9.1.3 and 9.1.4).

2

BACKGROUND

HISTORY OF POLICE IN AFGHANISTAN

The origins

Urban police systems have existed in Afghanistan's main cities for a long time; for example, in the mid-nineteenth century, Kandahar city had a small police force consisting of two officers, four NCOs and thirty-one patrolmen, mostly focused on protecting the bazaar, financed by the municipality. The first signs of the emergence of a centralised and specialised policing system in Afghanistan date back to the reigns of Abdur Rahman (1880–1901) and Habibullah Khan (1901–19). Abdur Rahman realised that tribal 'police' forces were not suitable for enforcing taxation and started developing his own police.[1] The khassadars (muhassils), whether mounted or on foot, were assigned to each provincial governor but did not have any specific training as police: they were in fact an armed militia. The system worked in practice using tax farming, with khassadars being allowed to extract revenue on top of what they were supposed to collect on behalf of the government.[2] During this period the kotwali, which roughly translates as Ministry of Interior, assumed wider powers. It had the power of ruling in small criminal cases, while major criminal cases were to be referred to the amir himself. Abdur Rahman's efforts were mainly focused on the development of a political police and little is known about the organisation of the kotwali, except that it was certainly very active in arresting people. Torture and executions were common, as were abuses by self-interested and perverse officials.[3] In the cities, the local kotwal units relied on elected kalantars (a kind of sheriff) to control the neighbourhoods.[4] The system grew under Abdur Rahman's son Habibullah, who also established a system of IDs (tazkira) for the first time.[5]

Under Abdur Rahman and his successors, order was primarily maintained through the principle of collective responsibility. Even reformist King Amanullah (1919–29), who succeeded Habibullah, found that he had no realistic alternative but to keep the system in place given the weakness of his police.[6] Amanullah however did try to 'modernise' (i.e. to bring closer to the European and Turkish standards) the policing system of Afghanistan. The Ministry of the Interior as such was first established in 1299 (1920/1921) under the name 'Domestic Management', which in 1301 (1922/1923) was changed to 'Ministry of Interior' (MoI). However, the MoI during this period was mostly dealing with sub-national administration and did not have a policing role.[7] Such a role pertained instead to the Public Security Ministry, which was divided into two main directorates, urban police and rural police (kotwali). This ministry also incorporated political policing and intelligence functions. It had authority to sentence those responsible for 'minor crimes' without involving the judiciary in the process at all, with the possibility of appeal to the provincial governor. Only major crimes were to be transferred to the courts (and no longer to the King as under Abdur Rahman) after preliminary police investigation. Training took place in a Police and Kotwali School and in a Kotwali Cadet School, located in Kabul.[8] During the reign of Amanullah, different rules and regulations also started being developed, including guidelines for the preliminary investigation of crimes and a general penal code.[9]

Under Nadir Shah (1929–33) the Public Security Ministry was incorporated into the MoI and renamed the Security Department.[10] During the late 1930s a wave of translations from Turkish of police manuals and criminal codes took place, giving the Ministry a 'software' to run its operations more effectively.[11] A police law was only approved in 1973, however.[12]

To 1978

Structural development

Throughout the periods of the monarchy (1880–1973) and of Daud's republic (1973–8), one can speak of an evolutionary process of change, with the MoI developing an increasingly sophisticated structure as well as taking on more tasks along the way. By 1312 (1933/1934) the structure of Interior Ministry had taken the shape shown in Figure 1.

The road toll directorate had just been added in 1311 (1934/1935). It was the first directorate to employ a foreign advisor: Mr. 'Tema', a German architect.[13] At the same time, training abroad also started and in the 1930s some officials were sent to Birmingham to train as police administrators. As seen in Figure 1, the structure of the MoI was initially quite basic. In the course of the following decades, it became gradually more sophisticated.[14] In 1318 (1939/1940), 1319 (1940/1941) and 1337 (1958/1959) a few new directorates were added, as shown in Figure 1.[15] In 1346–7 (1967–9) the whole organisation of the MoI was overhauled and ended up looking as in Figure 2.

BACKGROUND: HISTORY OF POLICE IN AFGHANISTAN

Figure 1: Structure of the MoI in 1934 and subsequent changes.

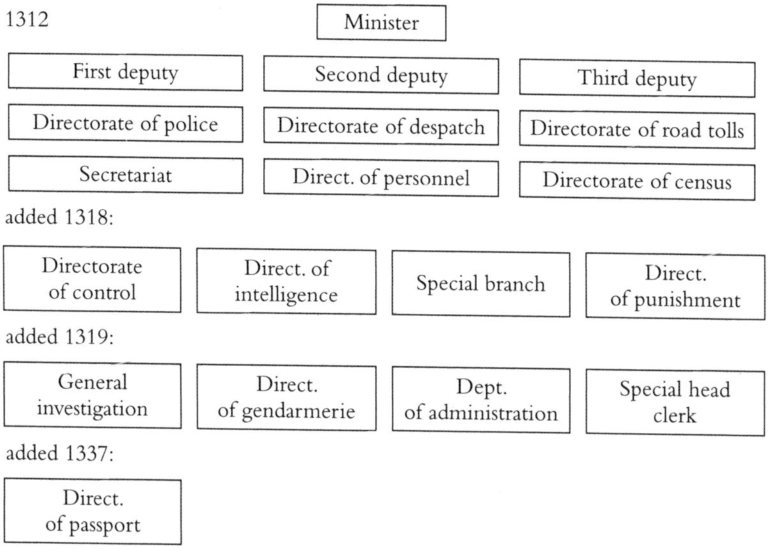

1312

Minister

First deputy	Second deputy	Third deputy
Directorate of police	Directorate of despatch	Directorate of road tolls
Secretariat	Direct. of personnel	Directorate of census

added 1318:

Directorate of control	Direct. of intelligence	Special branch	Direct. of punishment

added 1319:

General investigation	Direct. of gendarmerie	Dept. of administration	Special head clerk

added 1337:

Direct. of passport

Because information about the period is scant, the exact line of responsibility between general directorates and directorates is uncertain.

By 1355–6 (1976–8) the structure of the Ministry had undergone yet another restructuring and had turned into something like Figure 3.[16] Initially many sub-units of the MoI were extremely modest in size: when the traffic directorate was added to the structure of the Ministry, it just counted on six staff members and the head of department, a colonel.[17]

The structural development highlighted above shows that there was a trend towards an increasing sophistication of the Afghan policing system, even if by 1978 the capacity of the police was still limited in most regards, as will be discussed in the following paragraphs.

Territorial and population control

The development of an increasingly sophisticated ministerial structure was mirrored with some lag in the provinces. The Kabul police station led the way in developing a more sophisticated organisation, adding department after department. Initially the structure at the provincial level was extremely basic. For example the intelligence branches only started being activated in the provinces in 1332 (1953/1954).[18] Until 1349 (1970/1971) only Kabul, Kandahar, Herat, Balkh and Kunduz provinces had criminal investigation departments.[19]

15

Figure 2: Structure of the MoI in 1969.

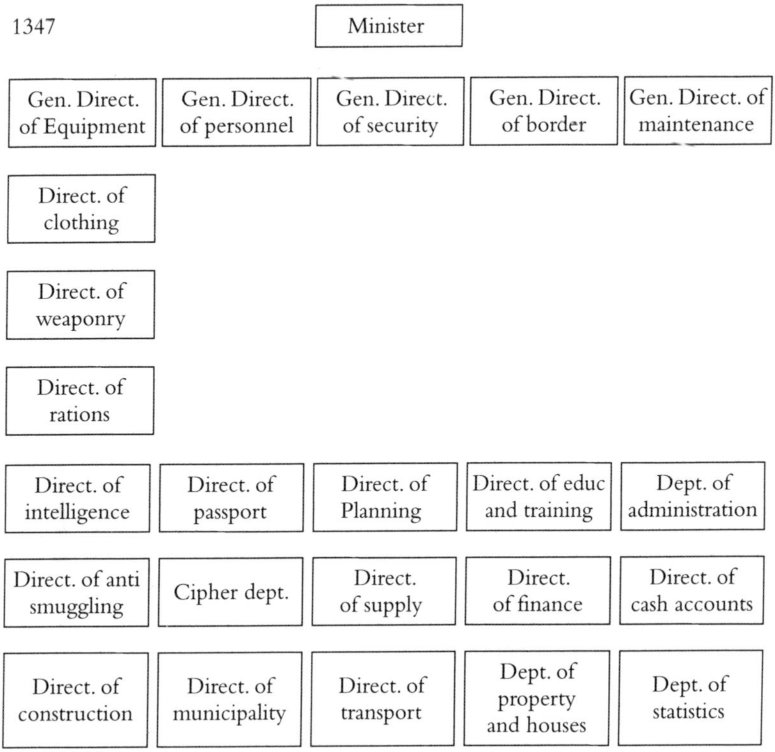

1347

| Minister |

| Gen. Direct. of Equipment | Gen. Direct. of personnel | Gen. Direct. of security | Gen. Direct. of border | Gen. Direct. of maintenance |

| Direct. of clothing |

| Direct. of weaponry |

| Direct. of rations |

| Direct. of intelligence | Direct. of passport | Direct. of Planning | Direct. of educ and training | Dept. of administration |

| Direct. of anti smuggling | Cipher dept. | Direct. of supply | Direct. of finance | Direct. of cash accounts |

| Direct. of construction | Direct. of municipality | Direct. of transport | Dept. of property and houses | Dept. of statistics |

The extension of the presence of the police in the rural areas happened through the establishment of smaller and smaller administrative divisions (provinces, districts and sub-districts), each having a police garrison, and through the strengthening of MoI staff at each level of the structure. In 1315 (1936/1937), for example, Shamali, Logar, Nuristan, Katawaz and Ghazni saw their own detachments being formed.[20] In every province the kotwali commander was placed in charge of overall security matters and was hence called the Security Commander. For a while the kotwali relied on a kind of village militiamen, called Kotwali deh bashis, in practice civilians wearing a particular attire, whose salary was paid half by the kotwali and half by the villagers. Soon, however, they were replaced by state-paid security personnel.[21]

Initially totally reliant on the army for support in the event of serious trouble, the MoI gradually developed some autonomous capacity to intervene. In 1314 (1935/1936) for the first time a central reserve police consisting of volunteers was established and organised in three battalions.[22] More battalions

BACKGROUND: HISTORY OF POLICE IN AFGHANISTAN

Figure 3: Structure of the MoI in 1978.

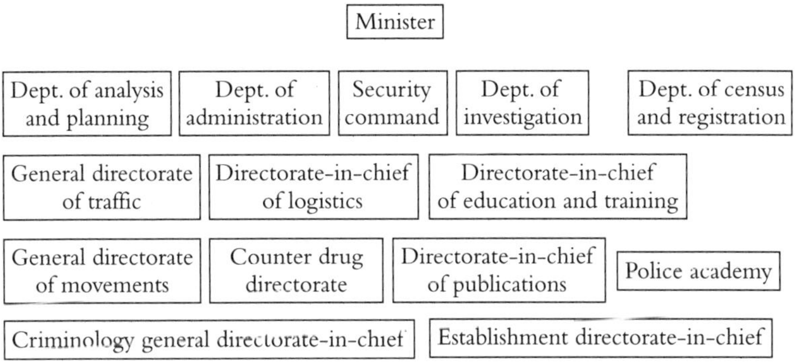

```
                              Minister
   ┌──────────────┬──────────────┬──────────┬──────────────┬───────────────┐
Dept. of analysis  Dept. of      Security   Dept. of       Dept. of census
and planning       administration command   investigation  and registration

General directorate   Directorate-in-chief   Directorate-in-chief
of traffic            of logistics           of education and training

General directorate   Counter drug           Directorate-in-chief   Police academy
of movements          directorate            of publications

Criminology general directorate-in-chief     Establishment directorate-in-chief
```

were established in 1316 (1937/1938): one mobile and one infantry battalion, as well as bicycle and horse units. In 1317 (1938/1939) the process of developing an autonomous paramilitary capability reached a milestone with the creation of a gendarmerie, which incorporated the border police: the first brigade of the gendarmerie was established in 1318 (1939/1940).[23] By the 1960s the gendarmerie appeared to be mostly a mobile force, on horses but with a few vehicles as well.[24] Later some of the mobile reserve force was deployed away from Kabul: one mobile battalion was created in Kandahar in 1350 (1971/1972).[25]

All in all, however, the sense is that the degree of control over territory and the population by the central government was still very modest in the 1970s. Official statistics for 1349 (1970/1971) showed only a handful of murder incidents throughout the country,[26] as well as 735 incidents of banditry and seventy-one of smuggling. It is not credible that a country of the size and population of Afghanistan might have experienced such negligible levels of criminal activity: simply very few crimes were being reported. Control over the population was so weak that the government was never able to carry out a proper census. The Census Department of the Ministry had a primary duty to collect conscripts for the army but its failure to fulfil this role successfully led to its abolition in 1330 (1951/1952). It was replaced by the Directorate of Census Data and Personal Registration.[27] The importance of this Directorate can be gathered from the fact that it was the first Afghan state institution ever to send staff for training to the Soviet Union: in the 1940s four officials were sent there to acquire new skills.[28]

Control over the tribal areas was particularly weak and reliant on tribal militiamen; as late as 1345 (1966/1967) tribesmen were still being recruited into a system of check posts which covered several provinces.[29] The tribal areas were left to their own devices as far as crimes and disputes were concerned.

17

The police were instead instructed not to allow the communities to handle their own justice affairs in the north. Although the police cooperated with the elders, it did not allow them to administer justice as in the Pashtun areas.[30] The MoI was able to enforce compliance when needed and with minimal effort. Former police officers and elders agreed that the appearance of a lone policeman armed with a stick was enough to prompt villagers into cooperation and suspects would be handed over without resistance. Even khans could be arrested peacefully, including sometimes in places like Kandahar where even in the 1970s they had retinues of armed men around them. The khans never challenged the police and relied instead on negotiations and political patronage to get out of prison.[31]

However, this was not so much the result of respect or fear of the police per se, but of the knowledge that resistance would lead to the intervention of the army. Sub-district police stations never had more than fifteen policemen and often as few as three, with a few bolt-action rifles and pistols: they were not able to handle serious opposition. The districts had a maximum complement of thirty-six. Apart from the fear of army repression, the villagers were also aware that they would be expected to feed army detachments at their own expense. As Glatzer observed about Jawand (Baghdis) in 1970:

A nomad camp and a peasant village clashed over access to a pasture. […] When the conflict turned violent the elders of both groups worried that it could get out of control. […] Over the following days peasants and nomads frequently visited each other […] and an agreement was formulated on how the pasture would be used by both parties in the future. The fear was repeatedly expressed: 'we must come to an agreement, otherwise we will have to pay […] and we will also have to feed the army if it intervenes'. […] In fact the sub-governor and his police chief (qumandan) only had two soldiers under their command, but the people's knowledge that somewhere there was a central government and a national army, no matter how distant from Jawand, created a potential threat to keep local conflicts under control, while also creating a feeling of security appreciated by almost everyone among the rural population.[32]

Much of the role of the MoI was indeed in resolving disputes among individuals and groups or forcing them to resolve the dispute themselves. This was a task of the sub-national administration, with police back-up, but also of the administrative section of the MoI, which in the 1960s acquired a Property Directorate to handle property disputes.[33] The local CoPs had the authority to mobilise tribesmen as auxiliary police as needed (one out of every eight weapon-bearing males).[34]

The role of a solid, credible backup from the army in keeping the system of territorial and population control together is highlighted by the fact that every time the monopoly of violence by the state was in doubt, the government's hold over the country rapidly disintegrated. The 1928–9 civil war was the first instance of post-Abdur Rahman widespread disorder in Afghanistan. It is likely that the inability of Amanullah's army to suppress the 1924 revolt in Khost (a

BACKGROUND: HISTORY OF POLICE IN AFGHANISTAN

negotiated settlement was reached after tribal levies were mobilised by the government) might have encouraged the 1928 tribal uprisings, which in turn encouraged others to rise. After the civil war, the new King, Nadir Shah, was careful to ruthlessly repress any challenge to his government. The army was then regularly called in throughout the 1930s–1950s to crush local revolts, making sure that King Abdur Rahman's lessons not to challenge the state were not forgotten. The army was also often called in to assist the police in clashes with the 'armed guards of smuggling caravans'. Much of the effort to create a gendarmerie was focused on handling the armed smugglers.[35]

The system was however fragile due to the bluntness of the army as a repressive tool and the weakness of the police as an institution more specialised in internal order. As is usually the case, the police had more local knowledge than the army and could be more discriminatory in repression, but was poorly staffed (particularly in the provinces) and too thinly spread to be able to handle more than low-scale banditry. It worked more like an early warning security system than as a real internal security force: it had the ability to detect trouble at the sub-district level and identify what could be sorted out locally and what could not. The principle of collective responsibility worked effectively when communities were rising up, but not as well against organised dissent which had an ideological base and some social base, as well as an ability to operate underground. The appearance of politicised gangs linked to the Maoists from 1976 onwards in the mountains north of Kabul already tested the capacity of the police, even if only tens of individuals were involved.[36]

The number of police during the monarchy and Daud's republic was estimated by officers serving at that time as 15–30,000, plus the militias of the border police.[37] Of these, about 7,500 were officers.[38] It was a thin layer of policing overall.

Command and control

Under the monarchy and President Daud the police was headed by a general and the next layer contained colonels, mostly taken from the army.[39] The patrolmen were largely recruited locally, but were under the orders of officers despatched from the centre and serving in a province different from their own.[40] The officer system guaranteed discipline, but the ability to exercise direct command and control of the MoI structures in the provinces suffered from technical limitations: only in 1350 (1971/1972) did the MoI acquire twenty-one fixed wireless communication sets and a mobile one from West Germany.[41] Horses, cars and other vehicles were always available in limited numbers and mostly in the rapid intervention battalions. The HQ was better-equipped, but each province would not have more than one to two vehicles, mostly used by the Chief of Police (CoP).[42] By 1978 the police only had fifty patrol cars in all of Afghanistan and only seven were equipped with radios: there were also 100 motorbikes.[43]

19

The recruits, who made up the bulk of the police (the patrolmen) were mostly taken from what the Army had left behind after having been given the first choice. However, recruits whose families were well-connected politically often chose to serve in the police because it was less demanding than serving in the army. Under Daud, high-school graduates started being often sent to the police, improving as a result the quality of human resources available.[44]

In the early 1970s the patrolmen were paid the negligible amount of 80 US cents a month and were therefore not very motivated. The literacy rate was then barely 2 per cent and record keeping 'virtually non-existent', according to US government sources. In the provinces, 'lack of authority, know-how, initiative, and equipment reduce[d] the police virtually to a token presence'.[45] However, at least the police were well disciplined and were taking their job seriously: they asserted their authority 'energetically and positively'. They seemed 'to carry out their duties conscientiously in accordance with the orders of their superiors. They apparently treat[ed] high and low alike for similar infractions if they [felt] they [had] the support of their superiors.' People seemed to obey the police, 'perhaps more from fear [...] than from respect'.[46] The insertion of army officers at the top was one of the factors behind the high level of discipline and among the conscripted patrolmen discipline was maintained by the MoI's ability to extend their period of service as a punishment. Even today (2011) many police officers who trained in the 1970s believe that in a system where so many patrolmen are illiterate, military discipline was necessary and good.[47]

With its limited means, the MoI managed therefore to maintain a degree of functionality in the system. By Daud's time, patrols were enforced through a system of check-posts and logs, which certified that patrolmen had carried out their tour as required. However, most villages only saw traces of the police once every several months, if not even less often. It was on the whole rare for the police to visit villages and this mostly occurred when a crime or a clash was reported.[48] Under President Daud (1973–8) the system of internal reporting improved and at least some paperwork started being used to keep track of events. Bureaucratic supervision improved. Senior officers were effectively controlling their subordinates and levels of reporting were high. Every three to six months a delegation would visit the provinces, to check what was occurring.[49] The cooperation between the governors and the police was very close and the relationship between the two was clear: the former was in charge of the latter.[50]

Corruption might have not been very high by South Asian standards, but it was certainly felt. As Kakar noted in the early 1970s:

As representatives of the state in the rural areas, government officials (tax assessors, tax collectors, mirzads [junior bureaucrats], district and provincial governors, even the police and gendarmerie) have openly and ruthlessly squeezed the poor peasants, often in collaboration with village and community elders [...]. This is not to suggest that all government officials are corrupt. One can sometimes find God-fearing, incorruptible

BACKGROUND: HISTORY OF POLICE IN AFGHANISTAN

men among them, especially among the judges. But the hard fact is that it is impossible for officials to live decently on the salaries they receive, which must be shared with their superiors, especially on their appointment.[51]

Anecdotal evidence suggests that extortion from the police occurred in the early 1970s too: people were saying 'If we go [to] the police they will beat us until we pay money to them'.[52] It was possible to get out of prison by paying bribes, and have a sentence reduced.[53] Road tolls were common also at that time and it was not always clear whether they were legal or not, and smuggling of hashish with the complicity of police was also reported. As mentioned already, the strongmen had an impact on policing, being often able to secure their own release, although mostly in Kandahar only, where tribal leaders had close connections with the government.[54]

Corruption was limited by the fact that there was little opportunity for it in the country. Although salaries were low, few jobs were paid better in Afghanistan at that time. The economy was stagnant and mostly state-controlled and in the rural areas the use of cash was limited. Expatriates felt particularly vulnerable, mostly because of the lack of clear rules, which allowed manipulation by government institutions.[55] The fact that the few foreigners working in the country in the 1970s were targeted by the police in various scams, usually centring around allegations of involvement in road accidents (for those who were driving cars), seems to confirm that the lack of opportunity might have been an important factor in keeping corruption low.[56] Police were also reported to harass traders whenever the law was not clear or some excuse could be found, as in the case of currency exchange dealers in the 1960s and 1970s, a time when tourists started flocking to the country.[57]

Whatever the case, until 1978 Afghanistan's police was on the whole functional, even if limited in its capabilities. Corruption and favouritism existed, but not to the extent of creating major dysfunctionalities in the system. By South-Asian standards, this was no small achievement.

Rule of law and professionalisation

The ability of the police to carry out professional investigations was initially almost non-existent, as would be expected. Only in 1317 (1938/1939) were specialist photographers hired for the first time to work in some of the larger police units,[58] a sign that the acquisition of the relevant skills had begun. Then in 1332 (1953/1954) an attorney general within the ministry structure was appointed.[59] In 1337 (1958/1959) the MoI also started hiring graduates from the public services department of the faculty of law of Kabul University, initially a group of forty.[60]

The formation and development of training institutions is an important indicator of patterns of professionalisation. In 1315 (1936/1937) it was decided to establish a police training centre, with teachers being taken from the officer corps. In 1935 it was upgraded to a school of gendarmerie and

21

police. In 1316 (1937/1938) the first German adviser to the police training centre was appointed. A second German instructor arrived a year later.[61] Turkish instructors also started being appointed. In 1337 (1958/1959) the former school of gendarmerie and police was changed into a high school of police, offering a baccalaureate in policing, and a few students started being sent to Germany for further qualification. From 1340 (1961/1962) the school turned into a Police Academy and started offering Bachelor degrees.[62] In 1346 (1967/1968) for the first time women started being accepted into the Police Academy. In 1350 (1976/1977) police training centres in Kandahar, Herat, Balkh and Nangarhar were also established.[63] By the time of Daud's republic, the professionally trained NCOs were beginning to play an increasingly important role within the police: most professional police were in fact NCOs.[64]

The types of course being offered at the Police Academy increasingly diversified, coming to include short and long courses for the updating of professional knowledge and specialist officer courses to be imparted to the newly promoted. Training in the various branches of police specialisation was also developed. A forensic laboratory was established within the academy in the late 1960s. The Germans were out by 1941, after their number (together with a few Italians) had peaked at maybe 200, but the Turks stayed. The MoI then sent 200 officers for training in British India, but this programme also ceased with the British withdrawal and partition. The Germans were back in 1953, this time not from the Third Reich but from the Federal Republic.[65] Their presence was modest compared to what happened after 2001: five instructors and one adviser.[66] In 1957 an agreement was signed with the US, featuring training for police officers in the US and transfer of equipment to the police in Afghanistan, but the programme was soon discontinued as the Americans decided to let the Germans fully manage police training in Afghanistan.[67]

The standards for admission to the courses were quite high, considering the very low level of education in the country overall. The basic courses for constables were open to students already having undergone six years of education and lasted one year plus two years of further training while serving in the reserve. NCO courses required the candidates for admission to have studied to ninth class and lasted three years. Each year twenty to thirty high-school graduates with high marks were accepted for the officer courses.[68]

The criminal investigation component of the MoI also developed noticeably over the years, particularly from the 1960s onwards, acquiring specialised sections on identity verification and chemistry. In the 1950s three new foreign advisers were recruited into the criminal investigation branch.[69] In 1347 (1968/1969) the training of police dogs was established.[70] The fact remains, however, that the top ranks of the MoI remained staffed by military officers until the end of the monarchy in 1973 and that no professional police officer could reach above the rank of captain.[71] This indicates clearly that the priority remained paramilitary policing and civilian policing was subordinate.

BACKGROUND: HISTORY OF POLICE IN AFGHANISTAN

By the late 1970s the rule of law had therefore established itself in Afghanistan only to a limited degree. Even individuals of modest social standing in Kabul, but connected to the Royal Government, were often in a position to dictate to the MoI officials on the ground and avoid punishment for themselves and their relatives.[72] As Weinbaum comments:

In practice, the prosecutor writes his report based on a file prepared by the police, and with the knowledge that poorly educated and trained police personnel are rarely even-handed in securing facts about a crime. It is very seldom that a prosecutor will return to the police an incomplete or inadequate file. The prosecutor himself has little or no experience in gathering and evaluating evidence and no staff to undertake an independent investigation. Despite this, the prosecutor's report, based on a file over which he has exercised so little independent judgement, forms the scenario for most trials; and its recommendations ordinarily presage their outcome.[73]

It was common for people to be sentenced to prison and for no record to be kept of the length of their term or of the expected date of release.[74] The system was very rigid and bureaucratic, hampered by the limited capabilities of the average patrolman. Expatriate Janice Minnott, who lived in Kabul for two years in the 1960s, recounts how, in the second half of the 1960s, she was almost arrested by a patrolman because her car's number plate almost matched that of another car, involved in an accident.[75] An official document of the US Department of State (DoS), written in 1964, described Afghanistan's police as 'illiterate, underpaid and hopeless' and advocated the establishment of an elite unit to handle special situations such as riots.[76]

As already hinted above, an improvement in the effectiveness of the police was noticed in the early years of Daud's republic, under a proactive Minister like Nuristani, not least because the new government allowed promotions of professional police to ranks above captain.[77] Abdul Qadir, another of the leading figures in Daud's government, presided over a commission which met every week for several hours, reviewing all the security issues.[78] Until the establishment of Daud's republic, the government had paid little attention to issues such as the protocol and the proper keeping of documents. The protocol could be manipulated relatively easily and this changed somewhat under Daud.[79] However, by the second half of the 1970s, cronyism was predominant again, as Daud became more worried about disloyalty: the head of police Mohammed Issa, was reportedly appointed as a result of his loyalty to Daud, not because of his capabilities.[80] Professional police officers who served at that time also recall how Daud started the practice of appointing loyalists in positions of power.[81]

Favouritism of Pashtuns seems to have existed to some extent before 1978: the Police Academy, for example, had a teacher of Pashto, but not a teacher of Dari.[82] Foreign eyewitnesses reported frequent harassment of Hazaras by the police in the 1970s.[83] However, the ethnic composition of the police in those years is not known. In general the policing system of the monarchy and Daud could be described as moderately meritocratic. Although it was not equally open to all strata of society and appointees had to show at least formal loyalty to the regime, merit was taken into account when appointments were made and there were efforts to improve the professionalism of the police. Discipline was strictly enforced and even occasional deviations from strict respect of the chain of command and control (political interference) did not disrupt the functionality of the system more than to a limited extent.

Up to 1978 policing in Afghanistan seemed to be evolving along the patterns described in 1.3: gradual expropriation of the policing capacity of the communities, a slow growth of civilian policing to cater for the needs of the growing business and middle classes, a gradual increase in the specialisation of the police, and so on. The central government was not very responsive to the demands of the more dynamic sectors of the population, but it did deliver some improvements in policing and a process of institution-building was in place. In addition, the government was very keen to ensure that the police were functional enough to guarantee the security of the state and it achieved this aim.

1978–2001

Politicisation and the first assault on meritocracy, 1978–9

A major restructuring of the police took place in the late 1970s and early 1980s, with the change of regime in Kabul and the coming to power of Khalqi leaders Taraki and Amin initially (1978–9) and of Parchami leader Karmal afterwards (1979–86). The most important feature of this change, apart from a further growth in sophistication, which reflected the expanding size of the MoI, was the creation of an area for political affairs within the Ministry. In a way the politicisation of the police had already started during Daud's republic (as opposed to nepotism under the monarchy), when he promoted close political associates to the key positions,[84] but it escalated to unprecedented heights in 1978–9. As the new regime took charge, the police force was seen as predominantly pro-Daud and pro-King, with just three to four Parchamis and a couple of Khalqis among the leading officers. 'Synchronisation' of the police with the new regime started soon with the input of 160 party volunteers, mostly by transferring people from the army to the top positions and recruiting party members from outside the security establishment. In Takhar, for example, it was the governor who, in 1979, invited party members to accept appointments as police officers.[85]

The officers trained by the Germans were either demoted or left the police. Initially the Khalqis tried to retain the teachers at the Police Academy, but also started training party loyalists as replacements: they gathered support, however, among the youngest teachers. After a few months the Parchamis started being purged too, with high profile officers like Gen. Nabi and Gen. Miakhel even being imprisoned.[86] As most high-ranking officers were

BACKGROUND: HISTORY OF POLICE IN AFGHANISTAN

replaced by members of Khalq, regardless of their lack of any professional expertise, the professional effectiveness of the police quickly declined.[87] The kidnapping and killing of the American ambassador, A. Dubs, on 14 February 1979, highlighted the level of inefficiency and incompetence to which the police had fallen. Dubs was kidnapped by a group of leftist radicals and was killed in a botched rescue attempt.[88]

Infighting disrupted the functionality of the MoI. While Minister of Interior Watanjar (until September 1979) was aligned with President Taraki, the head of the police Paiman was closely linked to Amin and the two were often at loggerheads. After Watanjar's flight, even Paiman fell out of favour with Amin and was sacked.[89] The purges and the gradual slide towards civil war led to defections from the police and declining recruitment, so by late 1979 there might have been only 5–6,000 police left, according to one estimate, from as many as 30,000 at the beginning of the crisis. By the end of 1979 in many provinces the staffing of the Sarandoi was down to 10 per cent of their personnel charts.[90] Even where the situation was not too bad, the strength of the police was inadequate: in a province like Takhar there were 300 policemen in late 1979 but they were still equipped with bolt-action rifles and unable to control the situation.[91] The out-dated equipment of the police was a factor in the rapid loss of control, but once the Soviets started supplying more modern equipment it was already too late.

It is therefore hardly surprising that once a serious insurgency gradually developed after 1978 the police (and the army) were rapidly overwhelmed. Efforts to set up a department for the fight against 'banditism' were half-hearted. In the provinces companies dedicated to fighting banditism were created, but the department in Kabul barely existed: its head Azim Zurmat had no administration under him, just ten soldiers and two sergeants to help, and simply transmitted orders received from above. The training of the troops was very poor, anti-guerrilla manuals were lacking and the companies had no more advanced skills than the rest of the police: the officers were also poorly prepared.[92]

The police was not professional enough even as a paramilitary force and was too weak to cope. The army moved in with characteristic bluntness against an elusive enemy and the only achievement was to demonstrate that the principle of collective responsibility was no longer effective. Sometimes the MoI showed some ability to cope flexibly with difficult situations on the ground. In Surkhi Parsa of Parwan in 1979, the arbitrary arrest of eleven individuals caused riots and the MoI reacted by replacing the whole Sarandoi garrison to pacify the population.[93] Even the police engaged in erratic repression and committed massacres; one episode in December 1978 ended in the arbitrary execution of about 100 prisoners.[94] In general, the Sarandoi implemented the arrests decided by the political police, a fact which did not earn them sympathy.[95]

25

A new institutional order, under Soviet patronage (1979–92)

The arrival of the Soviet Army at the end of 1979 and the change of the guard between Amin and Karmal was followed by a mixture of change and continuity. The MoI had almost to be rebuilt from scratch, even if the wave of deserters in January and February 1980 was modest compared to the army: 150 deserters to the army's 1,620.[96] The February 1980 riots in Kabul demonstrated how ineffective the police had become: the army had to intervene heavy-handedly and about ninety civilian lives were lost.[97] The Karmal government tried to replenish the ranks and increased the quota of recruits allocated to the MoI to 40 per cent of total conscription, at the expense of the army, even if overall recruitment levels were low and desertions high. The MoI was also the first among the armed services to offer incentives for people to volunteer and by 1984 about a third of the force was composed of volunteers.[98] The police was better supplied than the army and the general conditions of service were also better, not least because Minister of Interior Gulabzoi managed the logistics directly and used his political weight to force other ministries to deliver.[99]

The very weakly organised Sarandoi gradually developed a more sophisticated organisation and management, with the help of a few hundred Soviet advisers, who however also faced considerable resistence in exporting new organisational techniques to the Afghans.[100]

The politicisation of the police continued, although it was systematised and rationalised. Importantly, under Gulabzoi the promotion of party stalwarts was subordinated to the possession of the relevant qualifications.[101] While in 1980 just 5 per cent of the Sarandoi were members of the HDK, by 1982 the number had gone up to 12 per cent, plus another 16 per cent in the party youth; by the mid-1980s about 35 per cent of the MoI staff carried the membership card of the HDK and every unit of the MoI had party organisations. By 1988, 46 per cent of the Sarandoi had a HDK membership card and another 20 per cent was in the party youth.[102]

The politicisation went beyond party affiliation and the competition between the two wings of the party was another aspect of it. Some of Amin's supporters were purged and some of the military whom he had transferred to the police were transferred back.[103] The MoI remained a Khalqi stronghold under Gulabzoi, although of a different brand of Khalqis (the old supporters of President Taraki). Under the new regime, the rival Parchamis insisted upon having their men in the structure, appointed not by Gulabzoi himself but by the Revolutionary Council: the head of Political Affairs was a Parchami, as was the Head of Logistics and the Head of the Revolution Defence Groups. The middle ranks were 30–40 per cent Parchami, according to the estimate of an Afghan official, but below the district level the members of the party were overwhelmingly Khalqis. Clashes between Khalqis and Parchamis sometimes affected the ability of the MoI to operate and had to be resolved with sackings: this was the case with Faruq, head of the political affairs department,

BACKGROUND: HISTORY OF POLICE IN AFGHANISTAN

a Parchami who clashed with Gulabzoi and was eventually removed. Another case was that of Asgar, the head of the Sarandoi, another Parchami who often clashed with Gulabzoi and was then sacked under the accusation of having passed weapons to Parchami cadres.[104] Some Khalqis appointed by Gulabzoi proved particularly difficult to digest for the Parchamis: Sultaeddin Asos had served under Amin and been placed in the reserve before Amin's fall, but had never showed any disloyalty to him before Gulabzoi appointed him as head of the political department.[105] Khalqis were transferred into the MoI from all ministries, but Gulabzoi was particularly good at recruiting non-politicised Pashtuns as well. Gulabzoi and his Khalqis had broad support even among the large number of MoI staffers who were not members of the party or had joined for opportunistic reasons.[106]

The occasional factional friction was not enough to turn the MoI into a dysfunctional organisation, as Gulabzoi always had full ownership. His former officers describe Gulabzoi as in full control of the MoI. Nobody was able to challenge him and those who tried were all removed or posted to 'bad' regions such as Panjshir or Kandahar. Always well-informed and organised, he was ready to defend his men against the government and even the Soviets, in turn winning over the loyalty of most of them.[107] After Gulabzoi was forced to leave in 1988, the MoI lost political clout: the difficult military situation also offered an objective incentive to prioritise the army in terms of quota of conscripts. By 1990 the MoI ranks were filled only to 56 per cent.[108]

The structural organisation continued to evolve in Karmal's time, with a reduction in the responsibilities of the MoI. Figure 4 shows how the structure looked like in 1359 (1980/1981). Noteworthy changes included the transfer of Border Affairs to the Ministry of Defence, while sub-national government was also taken out of the MoI and placed in an independent department under the Presidency.[109] In part these amputations of important responsibilities of the MoI were due to political balancing within the uneasy coalition in power: President Karmal had conceded the MoI to his Khalqi allies, but did not want their influence to expand too much. He advocated to himself the control over the sub-national administration, while the border guards, which expanded greatly in terms of human and material resources, came under a Ministry of Defence which Karmal's Parchamis were trying to bring under their own control.[110] It is also worth noting the establishment of two more deputy ministerial positions, on top of that of deputy for security, and the creation of eight zones grouping the provinces into larger units.[111]

In other regards, by contrast, the expansion of the MoI capabilities continued, fuelled by generous Soviet support. Among the early gains of the MoI was a new command of Highway Police, created under a deputy minister.[112] In 1364 (1985/1986) the structure underwent significant modifications again, with the Personnel Department being upgraded to a deputy ministerial office and also taking census, communication, fire brigade and passports under its responsibility. New directorates such as Health, Construction and Supply were formed under the Deputy Minister for Logistics.[113]

The gendarmerie component of the MoI benefited from most of this investment, re-deploying wholly re-equipped 'operational' battalions in 1358 (1979/1980), creating new battalions and then brigades and even a division, with light artillery and light armour in abundance. The decision to form operational battalions was taken on 3 December 1979, still under Amin, but Gulabzoi moved very quickly with its implementation as he became minister. Twenty-six battalions and one regiment were originally planned, but later they grew to eleven regiments and sixty battalions of various types.[114] Village militias called 'Defenders of the Revolution' were also placed under the MoI control starting from March 1980, with a creation of a dedicated department and a structure based on battalions under that.[115] Self-defence militias were also organised under the MoI in order to protect public installations in urban areas.[116] Together with militias of party activists, these irregular forces eventually had a total of over 80,000 men, who were paid by the MoI and responded to it. Counter-terrorism unsurprisingly also grew, the high staff turnover slowed growth and the habit of VIPs to insist on being assigned bodyguards taken from the counter-terrorism department also represented a waste of the skills accumulated.[117] From mid-1981, the Sarandoi started taking part in offensive operations against the insurgents alongside the Afghan and Soviet armies.[118] A major task of the MoI was protecting objects of economic interest and it dedicated a large portion of its force to this, initially with four dedicated regiments which grew into a full division organised into one brigade, three regiments and one battalion, with a total of 13,500–14,000 men.[119]

In part at least because of the extremist policies of 1978–9, the Karmal (1979–86) and Najibullah (1986–92) regimes faced very unfavourable odds in its effort to stabilise Afghanistan between 1980 and 1992. The countryside was now armed and under the influence of a variety of opposition groups and the constant inflow of weapons eventually led to the armed opposition counting hundreds of thousands in its ranks. The police had little contact with the people outside the cities: they were even instructed not to accept food because of some cases of poisoning.[120] In order to bring some MoI influence into the villages and resolve the problem of mujahidin intimidation of families who had men serving in the Sarandoi, it became common practice to recruit villagers hostile to conscription or even previously aligned with the opposition, on the basis of the promise of letting them serve in their village, although under the command of officers dispatched from the centre. In this way the MoI was able to expand its presence to a few thousands of villages (out of 44,000), even if the remaining over 80 per cent remained outside its influence throughout the 1980s and early 1990s. It was also able to fill its ranks, after attempts to extend the length of service backfired disastrously: after the first decision to extend service by six months, meetings of Sarandoi opposed to the move were reported around the country.[121]

A system of vetting for recruits was established, where elders and HDK members would be asked to recommend conscripts.[122] The purpose was to avoid infiltration by mujahidin and contain desertions, but few elders would

BACKGROUND: HISTORY OF POLICE IN AFGHANISTAN

recommend the best youth for the task of serving in the armed forces. Still, collaboration with the enemy was not so infrequent as one Soviet adviser reported several cases even on the basis of his limited experience in Charikar.[123]

Minister of Interior Gulabzoi at least succeeded in the 1980s to maintain effective command and control over his force, despite the difficult communications. Arguably command and control over the police reached its apex during this period because of Gulabzoi's charismatic leadership and *cart blanche* from the party in running the MoI. His ability to recruit many fellow Khalqis into the MoI, discussed above, was a key enabling factor. He and his aides would share the same food as the rank and file, a display of egalitarianism which seems to have been appreciated.[124] Anecdotes about his incorruptibility are still told by his former officers. In one instance a police officer who reportedly used the service car to help Gulabzoi's father was punished by the Minister as a warning to all who would think of not sticking strictly to the rules.[125] Under Gulabzoi the old practice of officers being entrusted with the money for their subordinates, a source of much corruption, was abandoned and replaced with commissions of Sarandoi which took responsibility for making sure that the money reached the troops.[126] Significant investment went into improving the conditions of the troops and periods of leave were instituted for the first time.[127]

The Sarandoi under Gulabzoi were also better than their predecessors in sticking to institutional practices when enforcing 'revolutionary legality'. They assisted the political police (KhAD) in carrying out arrests, but otherwise stayed relatively clear of the political repression. Even individuals critical of the regime believe that the police during those years was perceived by the majority of the population under the control of the government as a professional force.[128] As long as Gulabzoi was there, he tried to resist the ever expanding militias (the 'tribal regiments') recruited by KhAD as an essential part of the counter-insurgency effort but notorious for their indiscipline. He always refused to allow the militias into the cities and particularly Kabul, sometime clashing with them openly. In the provinces, his CoPs were struggling to contain the militias; as Gulabzoi himself put it, they could succeed if they were 'strong and effective'.[129]

The phenomenon of ghost police, which would plague the MoI after 2001, was hardly ever encountered in the 1980s. In 1360 (1981/1982) an abuse was discovered in Kunduz, where the governor and the CoP colluded in inflating the number of Defence of the Revolution militiamen whom they were recruiting. Although the scale of abuse was limited (thirty ghost militiamen in all), Gulabzoi claims that he cracked down and prosecuted both officials. The episode played a role in his decision to bring the Defence of the Revolution groups under the administrative control of the MoI in the following year.[130] According to officers serving at that time, the MoI during this period had a solid grip on its logistics and kept good track of its equipment.[131]

Apart from the consequences of politicisation, the war effort had a negative impact on the professionalisation of the MoI, as multi-year courses for the training of officers could no longer be afforded. 'Educational brigades and regiments' were set up in 1983 aside from the Sarandoi Academy to impart quick training to thousands of recruits every year. Nonetheless the Sarandoi Academy continued to expand and restructure, mirroring more general changes in the MoI. A political school was established alongside four more usual ones: security, criminology, communication and traffic. In addition, West German advisers were replaced by Soviet and Warsaw Pact ones during 1979. More specialist faculties were established in 1981, including criminal investigation and border policing. Students were also sent abroad for further study in numbers greater than ever, particularly to the Soviet Union, but also Czechoslovakia, Bulgaria, Hungary and the German Democratic Republic.[132]

During the 1980s and early 1990s the concept of rule of law inevitably acquired a new meaning: revolutionary legality as conceived by the new regime does not fit well with today's prevalent understanding of the rule of law.[133] When assessing the functionality of the system, however, the question to be asked is whether the new regime was able to stick to its own rules and proclaimed aims. Under the Taraki and Amin regimes (1978–9) the police was acting in an arbitrary way, as was the rest of the state apparatus, and indiscriminate killings became common.[134] From 1980 onwards, however, the picture changed in that the repression became more carefully targeted, although still falling well below contemporary human rights standards as set in the West. Among other things, during the 1980s, thanks to the massive Soviet training programme, the availability of trained investigators reached a level where even districts had the capability to investigate criminal cases.[135]

One accusation coming from the military was that Gulabzoi sheltered the Sarandoi from the fight, a fact which facilitated his task of maintaining discipline and capacity.[136] The limited data available on the desertions and casualties suffered during the war do not seem to confirm this (see Table 2): the Sarandoi were taking more casualties, but suffering fewer desertions. Another accusation was that under Gulabzoi the MoI became a Pashtun feud (the Khalqis being in their majority Pashtuns). Even in this case the data does not seem to support the argument without further qualifications: even if the smaller minorities were under-represented (in particular Hazaras), Tajiks were over-represented and the representation of Pashtuns was about fair if the population as a whole was considered (although many had fled to Pakistan; see Table 3). Gulabzoi even claims that he introduced a policy of positive discrimination in favour of regions which were particularly poor or had marginal representation within the state apparatus. Badakhshan province, for example, was reserved 120 posts within the MoI.[137] However, Pashtuns did dominate the gendarmerie branch of the MoI, where volunteers mostly served, suggesting that the MoI was attracting mostly Pashtun volunteers (see Table 3).

In sum, from the perspective of policing, the 1980–92 period was in some regards a return to the pre-1978 attitude: moderate meritocracy. Merit was considered in making appointments, but so was political loyalty. Once appointments were made, strict adherence to a code of conduct was expected

BACKGROUND: HISTORY OF POLICE IN AFGHANISTAN

and enforced. Efforts to improve the professionalism of the police were resumed and received larger investment than ever before. Territorial and population control remained priorities, but not without some consideration for other aspects of policing. The type of political loyalty and the way it was supposed to be expressed, of course, differed compared to Daud's republic and the monarchy, the party organisation being the cornerstone of it. However, as we have seen, inter-party personal and factional loyalties mattered more than simple party membership. Although the MoI under Gulabzoi was functional, this is not to say that it was effective, as the wider political environment made interaction with Afghan society difficult and limited. The implicit lesson here is that an improvement in the functionality of the police has to develop in parallel with the ability of the government to reach out politically to the village communities, or risk resulting in the 'splendid isolation' of a bureaucracy which cannot relate to society.

To some extent after 1979 the MoI leadership seems to have been aware that challenging even the worst habits prevailing in Afghan society would bring no benefits. A Soviet adviser to the MoI noted the unwillingness of the anti-smuggling department to actually do much against the smugglers, despite

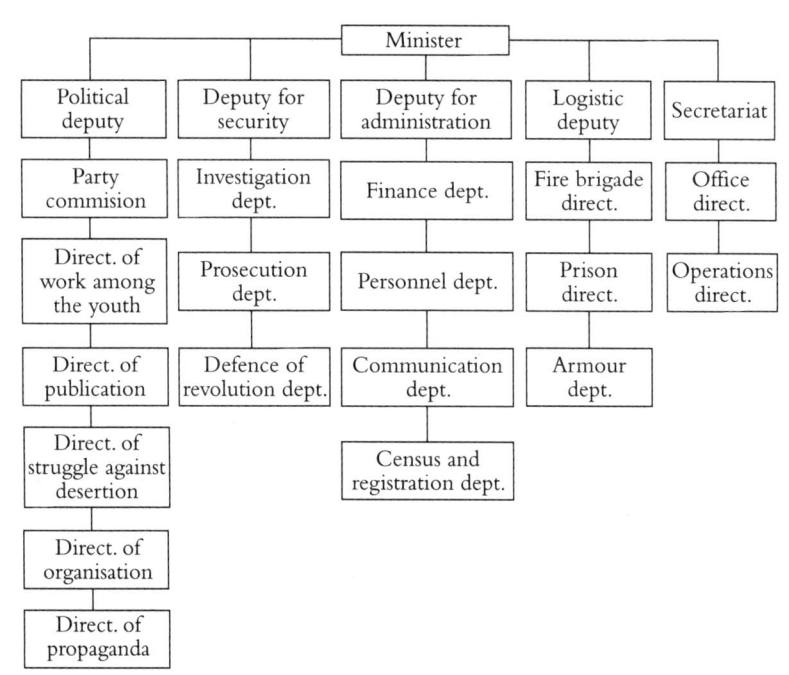

Figure 4: Organisation of the Ministry of Interior in 1359 (1980/1981).

```
                                Minister
        ┌──────────┬──────────────┼──────────────┬──────────┐
   Political    Deputy for    Deputy for       Logistic    Secretariat
   deputy       security      administration   deputy
        │            │              │              │            │
    Party       Investigation   Finance dept.   Fire brigade   Office
    commision   dept.                           direct.        direct.
        │            │              │              │            │
   Direct. of    Prosecution    Personnel dept.  Prison       Operations
   work among    dept.                           direct.      direct.
   the youth
        │            │              │              │
   Direct. of    Defence of     Communication   Armour
   publication   revolution dept. dept.         dept.
        │                           │
   Direct. of                   Census and
   struggle against             registration dept.
   desertion
        │
   Direct. of
   organisation
        │
   Direct. of
   propaganda
```

Soviet insistence that the smuggling routes be sealed. Officials responded that 'this is not human because people live off that'. They argued that compensation was needed before any action could be taken.[138] Some successful operations were carried out on difficult ground through a negotiating approach, such as in Paktika in the early 1980s.[139]

Table 1: Staffing levels of the police/Sarandoi.[140]

	Tash kil	Staffing (%)	staffing
1960s–1970s	20–30,000	–	–
1978	–	–	28,000
1979	50,000	40	20,000
1979 end	50,000	16	8,000
1980 beg	50,000	27	13,400
1980 end	50,000	60	29,600
1981	90,000	36	32,100
1982	100,000	54	54,300
1983	100,000	75	74,800
1984	100,000	80	79,500
1985	100,000	90	90,200
1986	115,000	80	91,700
1987	160,000	62	98,700
1988	60,000	60	96,700
1989	160,000	61	97,000
1990	160,000	58	93,000
1991	160,000	63	100,000
1996	140,000	22	30,000
1997	75,000	–	–
2001	30,000	33	10,000

State collapse and the second assault on meritocracy, 1992–6

Inevitably, with the collapse of Najib's regime and the international neglect of Afghanistan which followed, the huge structure which developed in the 1980s could not be sustained. Although the structure per se was not immediately dismantled, staffing levels collapsed quickly (see Table 1). All activities of the MoI were paralysed during this period and the new mujahidin appointees could not even manage the release of passports.

The fate of the Police Academy was characteristic of what was going on in those days. Its activities were completely suspended from 1992 onwards, as Kabul turned into a battleground for mujahidin factions. The teachers' salaries were still being paid, but the students all left the premises. Many of the

BACKGROUND: HISTORY OF POLICE IN AFGHANISTAN

Table 2: Desertions in MoD and MoI forces, 1980s. Monthly rates as % of total force.

	Desertions: Sarandoi	Desertions: Army	KIAs and WIAs: Sarandoi	KIAs and WIAs: Army	KIAs: Army	KIAs: Sarandoi	KIAs: KhAD
1984	0.67	1.52	–	–	–	–	–
1985	0.37	0.87	–	–	0.11	0.16	0.21
1987	0.08	0.86	0.13	0.13	–	–	–
1988 spring and summer	0.53	0.83	0.60	0.14	–	–	–

Source: Giustozzi, 2000, tables 19 and 35. KIA, killed in action; WIA, wounded in action; KhAD, political police.

Table 3: Ethnic composition of Sarandoi, 1980s %.

	1980s	1987	1990
	All	Officers and NCOs	Gendarmerie
Pashtuns	52.0	46.9	90
Tajiks	40.0	41.0	–
Hazaras	3.0	–	–
Uzbeks	3.4	5.7	–
Turkmens	0.2	–	–
Nuristanis	0.2	–	–
Baluchis	0.2	–	–
Others	0.5	6.40	10

Source: Giustozzi, 2000, table 43; personal communication S.M. Gulabzoi, Kabul, April 2008.

teachers left after having been mistreated and humiliated by the militias which had occupied the Academy. Three or four months into the new regime, an agreement was reached for the running of three-month courses to train the new mujahidin officials who were taking over the MoI: 1,050 were admitted to the courses and some very basic functionality was restored to the MoI. The beginning of the civil war in 1993 threw even these modest efforts into the air.[141]

As a result the police became largely de-professionalised. Few stayed on. The police was used as a source of patronage and nepotism, and the number of generals started proliferating in the hundreds, despite the reduction in the ranks. Occasionally in the 1990s policemen wearing uniforms could be spotted, but largely discipline was not enforced and recruitment of party/faction loyalists became the rule. In areas outside Kabul's control either no police existed or local arrangements were made, where some police forces would be maintained by local councils.[142] Where the police continued to operate it does not appear to have been particularly corrupt. At least in Mazar-i Sharif under Gen. Dostum they appeared to content themselves with taking some apples from the traders but at the same time they did nothing to prevent abuses by the warlords, which were very frequent.[143]

Policing under the Taliban

By the time of the Taliban regime, the police was little more than a branch of the army and had a very low grade of specialisation. Training had almost been completely abandoned and purge after purge meant that few professional officers were left in the system. Some professional police stayed in the job, at least for some time. They were then often accused of being infidels and communists and were sometimes purged or arrested. Mostly they left the job because of the humiliations they were suffering.[144] The only professional police officers, who had received official training under Najib's rule and were not dismissed by the Taliban, were working at the Passport Department and ID Issuance Department. The few police officials who were allowed to wear uniforms were the traffic police officers who were stationed on the streets to manage the flow of traffic. In sum, the little that has remained of a professional police force was lost under the Taliban's rule.[145,146] Even in the later years of the Taliban regime they could at least be found among the traffic police: in one incident, a German NGO employee was rescued from an aggressive Talib 'policeman' by some old professionals.[147]

The Taliban regime made its own effort to re-launch the Police Academy and in 1997 courses for police officers with 100–120 students took off. The curriculum was modified with the injection of high doses of shari'ah and several mullahs were integrated in what was left of the teacher corps. None of the students managed to graduate before the collapse of the Taliban regime, but they joined the police force of Karzai's interim government.[148]

By and large the police as an institution collapsed as the Taliban dismissed the bulk of the police force and placed their fighters in police stations.[149] The Taliban regime ignored the criminal procedure code and eliminated the function of public prosecution (attorney general) and to a great degree also ignored many provisions of the penal code.[150] The police stations, now manned by young fighters without any uniform and mainly from Pashtun regions, operated almost autonomously. The Taliban fighters occupying the police stations would not open a file or record of the petitions or the cases. They would not refer the criminal cases to the Criminal Investigation Unit of the Provincial Police Directorate or even report to it. The Taliban abandoned the bureaucratic rules and procedures of the police completely (see also section 10.3 for the case of Herat province).

BACKGROUND: HISTORY OF POLICE IN AFGHANISTAN

In its own way, the Taliban policing system was more functional than the Rabbani regime's. They made no pretence of sticking to the system developed until the 1980s and replaced it with one of their own concept of policing: very basic but functional in its own terms. Everybody in Afghanistan, even the most bitter adversaries of the Taliban, seems to agree that they were successful in maintaining security in the areas under their control, and crime almost disappeared. Although the international press in those days focused on the draconian punishment inflicted by Taliban courts, the real strength of the system was the ability of the system to apprehend most criminals and to enlist or coerce the cooperation of the population for that purpose. The Taliban relied also on a vast network of informers and on the willingness of their 'policemen' to pursue the culprits relentlessly. The Taliban's 'intelligence' was closely linked to the police and the Taliban's army, as these were not yet consolidated in separate bureaucratic organisations. What we see here is a system which was opposite to that operating in the 1980s: instead of a 'splendid bureaucracy', it featured a very weak bureaucratic component, but was deeply embedded in society, particularly in the rural communities. This does not necessarily mean that the Taliban were always popular, but it does mean that they were not isolated from society.

A new development under Taliban's rule was the establishment of a religious police. The Taliban created the Ministry of Enforcing Virtue and Preventing Vice. The Ministry had directorates in every province which functioned as religious police. Their men patrolled the city quite often and forced people to close down their stores at the time of the daily prayers and attend mosques. They also punished women who attended public spaces without an accompanying male. Furthermore, they arrested the men who had shaved or trimmed their beards or did not wear turbans. The religious police would punish those recalcitrant and detain them for days. In practice, the level of staffing of the ministry (in the low thousands) was insufficient to implement the Taliban's mores effectively throughout the country and the new police force was mainly active in Kabul, where the moral attitudes of the population were more suspect.[151]

Overall, Taliban policing relied largely on the deterrent impact of harsh punishments, which were in fact rarely implemented. In practice, negotiations with the elders and among the families of the victims and of the culprits resulted in alternative solutions, such as blood price being paid.[152]

In sum, the 1978–2001 period was one of extreme turmoil. The development or reshaping of policing in this period was driven by the security concerns of the regimes in power. The actual shape taken by the police also depended on the availability of resources. None of the regimes in power had constituencies which demanded civilian policing, but these regimes tried to develop effective paramilitary policing and saw it as instrumental to the survival of the regime. Within the context of a civil war, these systems centred on paramilitary policing were functional in their own way: the leftists' in the 1980s and the Taliban's in the 1990s.

3

AFGHANISTAN'S POLICE IN 2002

A new year zero of policing

As Afghanistan emerged from the Taliban regime and entered a new phase of its history, little was left of any state institutions as they had existed until 1992. A few officials who had managed to serve all the regimes from the 1970s onwards stayed on and many others who had left came back and re-occupied their posts. Almost no equipment was left at the beginning, not even chairs and desks. Uniforms were not available, nor vehicles. The few vehicles available were reserved for the CoP. One example illustrates this predicament:

in Paghman, Kabul, the only car available was for the police chief, thus making it very difficult for the police to patrol, respond to requests, or visit the scene of a crime. The Paghman shura has mandated that local people with private cars (e.g., those who drive transport routes to Kabul) must provide their car for the night-time use of the police for a rotating period of three to four months. The police can use this car at night to respond to emergencies.[1]

In these conditions, the prospect seemed necessarily one of rebuilding everything from scratch. A debate started over which model the new MoI should follow. Most Afghan players either had no particular model in mind, or were inclined to stick to the models of the past: typically Daud's or Gulabzoi's. The donors and the intervening powers (which in part coincided) were instead inclined to bring Afghanistan's policing more in line with policing in the western hemisphere, that is moving towards a civilian model of policing. However, they differed among themselves about what particular model of 'western' policing was to be adopted (see Chapter 5).[2]

Recruitment was fully decentralised and self-appointed CoPs (usually strongmen linked to the anti-Taliban factions) were recruiting officers and patrolmen as they pleased, with no oversight. The anti-Taliban factions were however wary of supplying weapons to the police, even when staffed by their own men, and for years after the fall of the Taliban it was common to have shortages of weapons in the police stations. Among everything else, this signalled their weak sense of ownership of the MoI and commitment to it. A few professional police were brought back into the force in order to handle whatever little administration was there, some logistics and communications; some also made it to the CID. A Tufts report dating back to those years describes their plight as follows:

> In most cases, the few trained police officers in the system serve as clerks who mainly push paperwork, write minutes of meetings, schedule appointments, and formalize the informal (and sometimes unlawful) activities of the higher ranking officers. […] Trained and experienced police officers often approached the Tufts team to voice their frustration over serving under high ranking officers who lack training and experience.[3]

The weapons were usually worn-out Kalashnikovs or cheap copies made outside Russia and maintenance was non-existent. Salaries were very low and rarely paid on time: allowances, prizes and even part of the salaries themselves were often embezzled in Kabul or locally by corrupt officers. The intelligence department's budget was so small that it could not deploy even a single officer in every district.[4]

As a result of all this, discipline within the police force was very poor. Internal affairs hardly operated, while the investigative capability was minimal everywhere or even non-existent in some provinces. Ghost police, discussed in detail below (section 6.3.4), was a widespread problem, eating away much of the meagre resources allocated to the MoI. Whole sections of the population were excluded from any benefit deriving from policing because they could hardly approach the police directly. This was in particular the case of women, who had to rely on their male relatives to contact the police, but also of most of the villagers: without vehicles the police could not reach out to them. On the other hand, given the level of corruption of the police, its indiscipline and incompetence, and the links between CoPs and strongmen or factions, not many Afghans were too keen to see the police at all.[5]

The command and control structure of the police was very weak at the national level and relied on the top ministerial staff contacting the provincial CoPs and persuading them to take a particular course of action: hardly anything that could be described as command in any proper sense. Even at the national level, personal relations, usually along factional lines, determined the responsiveness of the system to orders coming from the top. At the provincial level, command and control again depended on the personal status of the CoP. In areas where he had full control, he could issues orders and expect obedience in the districts, assuming he was able to communicate, because in 2002 the police was not equipped with UHF radios. If the police force at the provincial level had itself been divided up among factions and strongmen as part of the division of the spoils which followed the collapse of the Taliban, then even the provincial CoP would not be able to exercise much control and friction could often occur.[6]

At least in 2002 Afghanistan seemed to be at peace, apart from a few pockets of residual activity by the Taliban and its allies and some activities along the border with Pakistan. As shown by the casualties of 2002 (see below) the police was at this time hardly engaged at all in the 'counter-terrorism' effort. Fighting crime was not much of a concern either, not because crime did not exist, but because the police let the communities deal with it or simply tolerated the criminal activities of the strongmen and the militias to which it was connected: in fact the police itself was a major source of criminal activity (see section 6.3 below). This easy environment was however not to last.

The early post-2001 political economy

In late 2001 the MoI, like other institutions of the Afghan state, was used in the distribution of the spoils to pacify all the different anti-Taliban factions. The basic formula used during the negotiations which led to the Bonn agreement was to assign each ministry to a leading faction, which would then distribute spoils within the ministry after having served itself first. In the case of the MoI, provincial and district CoPs had either appointed themselves or had been appointed by the various anti-Taliban factions in control of the different provinces. The political/factional appointees then surrounded themselves with their likes in subordinate positions, privileging factional loyalty and sometimes ethnicity over merit and qualifications.[7]

They did not really respond to the MoI, nor did the MoI have a say in their appointments. The process largely took place under the sponsorship of the party which had received the Ministry among the spoils of war, Jamiat-i Islami. The top positions and many of the intermediate and lower positions were also filled with Jamiati loyalists. An estimated 80 per cent of the police force were former militiamen.[8] With Yunis Qanuni as Minister of Interior, the 'Panjshiri' network was dominant in the MoI in Kabul. The Panjshiri network was formed of militia commanders closely linked to the now defunct Ahmad Shah Massud, Minister of Defence of the Rabbani government in 1992–2001. It mainly recruited in the districts of the Panjshir valley, although its base of recruitment was not strictly geographical but was founded on personal loyalty and the comradeship forged in many years of fighting side-by-side. The 'Panjshiris' also took control of most of the north-east, sometimes in alliance with smaller networks of commanders, such as the Andarabis in Baghlan province, or in uneasy power-sharing arrangements with not-so-friendly groups such as Hizb-i Islami in Badakhshan and Junbesh in Takhar. Political patronage was common within the MoI, going all the way from the top to the bottom: the people at the bottom were connected to someone at the top for protection.[9]

Allied networks such the 'Parwani' and Atta Mohammed's received shares of the spoils in Parwan and parts of the north. The Parwanis were an alliance of militia commanders who had worked with Massud, but had maintained a degree of autonomy and controlled almost all of Parwan province. Most of the north went to Gen. Dostum and his associates, who maintained an uneasy relationship with Atta Mohammed; the two groups often fought each other in 2003. Small networks of commanders and individual allies of the Panjshiris also established themselves as the police, somewhat more precariously, in the region of Kabul (Kapisa, Wardak, Logar, Kabul province) as well as other areas of the country: Laghman, Nangarhar, the centre of Paktya province and Kandahar.[10]

In the south it was mostly individual strongmen centred around President Karzai and his local allies who empowered themselves: Uruzgan, Zabul, Helmand, parts of Kandahar. In the West, Herat's strongman Ismail Khan tried to dominate the scene and succeeded in Herat province, though he had to rely on local allies in Baghdis and Ghor. Farah was shared between allies of Ismail Khan and of the Karzais. In Nimruz a local strongman, Karim Barahui, took over. In Hazarajat, the Khalili faction of the Hizb-i Wahdat party/militia seized control of police positions. Finally, in the rest of south-east Afghanistan no faction was able to assert clear control, leaving a confused situation on the ground with various weak factions sharing the appointments.[11]

This situation hardly changed throughout the tenures of Qanuni and Wardak as ministers. In fact neither of them tried seriously to change the situation as both were linked (to different degrees) to one of the anti-Taliban factions which had taken charge. At the same time the MoI was doing very little in terms of offering support to the police stations in the provinces, leaving the least resourceful strongmen struggling to cope with a deteriorating security situation.[12] Changes in the political alignment of provincial police forces occurred in 2002–3, but largely as a result of local conflicts. In Paktya, for example, the thin layer of Panjshiri control was quickly wiped out by a Pashtun tribal alliance. The Panjshiri powerbase had been a small cluster of Tajik villages and their local militia commanders in the surroundings of Gardez but their alliance with the Ahmadzai tribe was not enough to prevent change.[13]

One important aspect of the situation to keep in mind is that the new crop of former militiamen who came to staff the police after 2001 had no understanding of the meaning of institution building. The policemen trained by the Soviets might often have been as corrupt, but generally they had a concept of institution building.[14] When different political factions and groups nationally and regionally started competing for influence over the police, they faced little resistance within the organisation of the MoI.

4

THE CHANGING POST-2001 OPERATING ENVIRONMENT

After 2001, Afghanistan entered a period of rapid social change and of a fast-evolving political landscape, which made any prospect of re-establishing the pre-1978 or even the pre-1992 status quo unrealistic. The massive expansion of Afghanistan's cities and the inflow of migrants from rural areas changed the policing environment in Afghanistan. To the extent that the MoI had a policy, it was focused on re-establishing the status-quo of the 1970s.[1]

The long years of war and the general mobilisation of anti-Taliban groups in late 2001 left behind an environment populated by illegal armed groups. According to the DIAG database, maintained by ANBP and the Disarmament Commission, there were 5,557 illegal armed groups as of late 2006, almost certainly an underestimate.[2] Although a few hundred illegal armed groups were claimed to have been disbanded from 2006 onwards, from 2009 onwards it is likely that the generation of new armed groups largely exceeded the number disbanded. As rising insecurity lead to the multiplication of armed gangs roaming the Afghan countryside, many decided to organise themselves in armed groups. According to NDS sources, just in Wardak province alone there were 600 such gangs in early 2010.[3]

The other big change, compared to the 2002 assumption of a peaceful Afghanistan, was of course the rising insurgency. Already by 2003–4 some provinces were seriously affected. The police in insurgency-affected districts like Maruf (Kandahar) were having a hard time under relentless pressure from the Taliban.[4] By 2007 it was estimated that 70 per cent of Afghan National Police (ANP) time was spent fighting the insurgency as opposed to law and order tasks.[5] The spread of the insurgency meant that whereas it had previously been possible to patrol the rural areas in small groups of one to two policemen, it became very difficult to carry out any patrol afterwards. Most police stations in the affected areas could only patrol within a range of a few kilometres from the district centre, particularly if not assisted by ISAF.[6]

The police was already stretched thin without the insurgency. By 2008 a typical police station in northern Afghanistan, where the insurgency was only beginning to raise its head, divided its limited human resources of nineteen policemen as follows: one cook, one CoP, eight guards of station, two bodyguards of district governor, four available for patrols and three engaged in other duties.[7] The ability of the police to cope with the challenges was reduced by weak paramilitary preparation. For example, despite the military focus of training and mentoring, few Explosive Disposal experts were available, were trained in very short three-week courses and were not even used in their role due to a manpower shortage.[8]

Because the police were more often on the defensive than not, the manpower available on paper was halved, as in the provinces police worked on twelve-hour shifts. Only on very special occasions was it possible to mobilise the full manpower for operations.[9] By mid-2009 the distribution of police forces and the intensity of its engagement in the counter-insurgency looked like that shown in Map 2.

The recognition of the insufficiency of manpower eventually led to the start of a new debate from 2008 onwards over the size of the police force. In the early post-2001 years, the tendency had been to argue for fewer but bet-

Map 1A: Areas affected by insecurity in 2003.

THE CHANGING POST-2001 OPERATING ENVIRONMENT

Map 1B: Areas affected by insecurity in 2010.

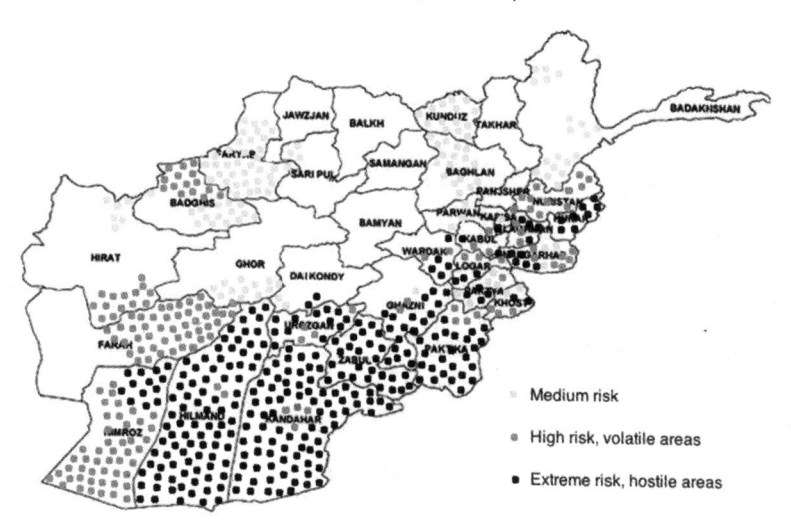

- Medium risk
- High risk, volatile areas
- Extreme risk, hostile areas

Graph 2. Police losses.

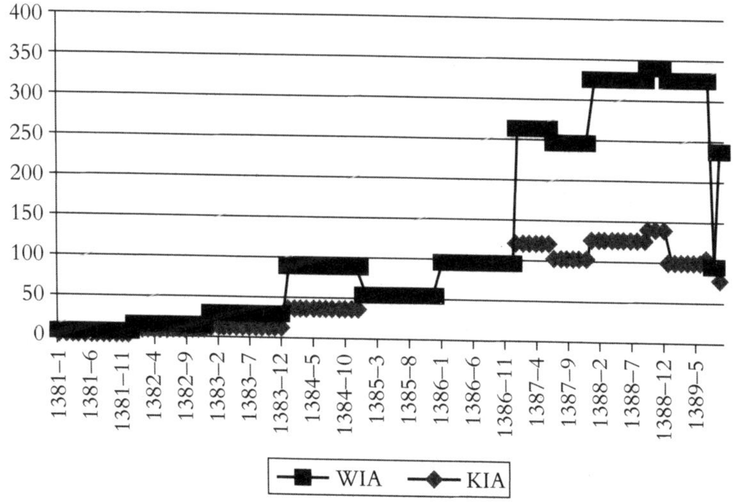

WIA   KIA

POLICING AFGHANISTAN

Graph 3: Wounded in action/killed in action ratio for the police.

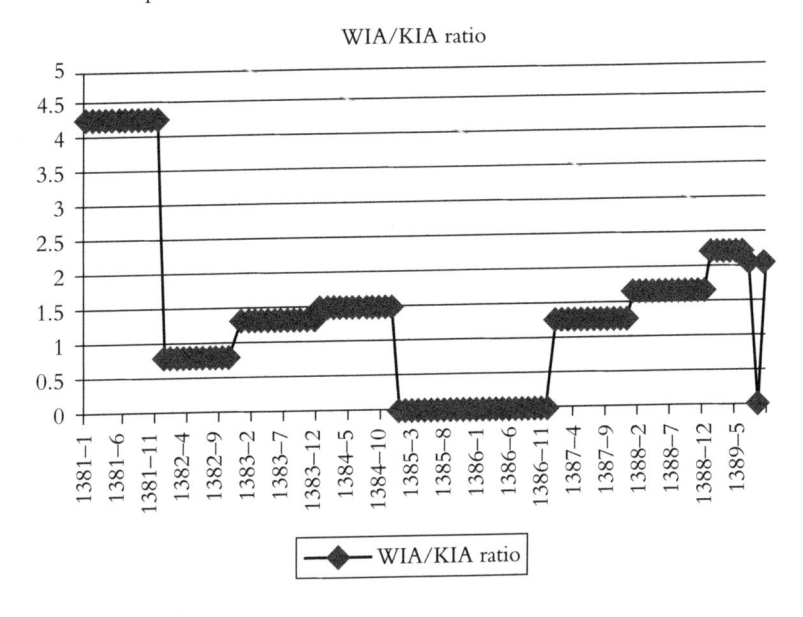

Map 2: Police deployment and casualties first half of 2009.

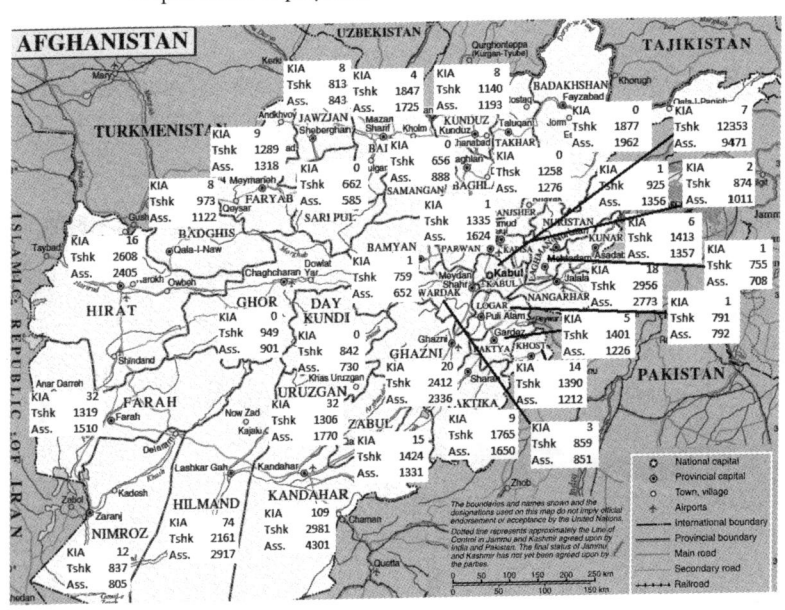

Source of data: Chilton et al.

THE CHANGING POST-2001 OPERATING ENVIRONMENT

ter quality police, particularly among donors. From 2008, the consensus increasingly was that more police were needed and as quickly as possible, with an inevitable impact on quality, as the following sections will discuss (see section 6.2).

5

THE UNCERTAIN IMPACT OF EXTERNAL ASSISTANCE

Financial assistance

As shown in Table 4, international expenditure on Afghanistan's police started picking up in 2004, after a slow start in 2002–3. Even in 2002–3 such contributions were not negligible when compared to the Afghan government's own resources, which at that point did not exceed a few tens of million of dollars of tax and customs revenue. The money was however not spent according to anything resembling a coherent plan until 2005, when the US Department of Defense (DoD) took over. Even then the implementation of the plan adopted was questionable, particularly until the improvements decided between the end of 2009 and the beginning of 2010. However, by 2005, expenditure on the police was already higher than the whole ordinary budget of the Afghan state and by 2010 it was exceeding the entire state budget by several times. Much of the money was spent at western cost rates, rather than Afghan rates, because of the employment of thousands of trainers, advisers and mentors and because of the contracting of non-Afghan companies to provide services and deliver projects. Even taking this into account, it is inconceivable that such a massive investment (by Afghanistan's standards) would not have a significant impact on Afghanistan's police. The issue is whether the impact was positive and whether it was proportionate to the scale of the resources committed. In subsequent paragraphs, the impact of external assistance will be discussed, while the proportionality of the results will be left aside as it is not pertinent to the topic of this study.

Efforts by donors to stimulate their Afghan counterparts into taking over a greater share of the burden of funding the MoI met little enthusiasm in Kabul. In 2010 the donors had demanded that the MoI take over 5 per cent of the salary costs of the police, on top of providing food to 82,000 policemen. The MoF, however, eventually only agreed to take over only 3 per cent of the salary costs (US$10.4 million of US$355.3 million).[1]

Table 4: External assistance to Afghanistan's police.

Million Euros	2002	2003	2004	2005	2006	2007	2008	2009	2010	2011
Germany	10	12	12	12	12	12	36	53.7	77	
EUPOL								64	17.4	54.6
USA, Million US$	25.5	5	223.9	837.9	1300	2701.2	1105.6	1500	3500	4100
LOFTA			120	89.5	109.5	146.4	185.3	258.6	390.3	

Notes: USA 2011 is only budgeted expenditure; LOFTA 2004–8 refers to Afghan years March to March; LOFTA 2004 refers to the period November 2003–March 2005; LOFTA 2010 is a provisional figure to the end of September; EUPOL 2009 refers to June 2007–November 2009; EUPOL 2010 refers to December 2009–May 2010; EUPOL 2011 refers to June 2010–May 2011; US, EUPOL and German data also include LOFTA contributions, so there is some overlap in the figures.
Sources: German government; GAO and FAS; LOFTA.

Training, mentoring and advising

The beginnings

The rationale for the assistance in general was that the Afghans would not have been able to reorganise the MoI themselves, for a number of reasons. The first was the lack of human resources, itself in part the result of a lack of political will to bring back as many former policemen as possible (see Chapter 3). The second was that presumably it would have been politically embarrassing for the intervening coalition if Afghanistan had adopted a policing system not in line with western standards, particularly as far as the rule of law and human rights were concerned. Later a third factor came into play, which is the low grade of effectiveness of the MoI in containing the Taliban insurgency.

Even as far as mentoring and advising were concerned, the international assistance programme to Afghanistan's police started on a very modest scale, with the partial exception of the Police Academy, where a team of German trainers and advisers was posted relatively early. The Police Academy started taking in trainees and by 2007 it had graduated 1,000 lieutenants and almost 2,400 NCOs.[2] The curriculum used at the Academy from 2002 onwards was still the old one dating back to the King's time and the teachers themselves were often the old ones too: there was little injection of new techniques and technologies.[3]

THE UNCERTAIN IMPACT OF EXTERNAL ASSISTANCE

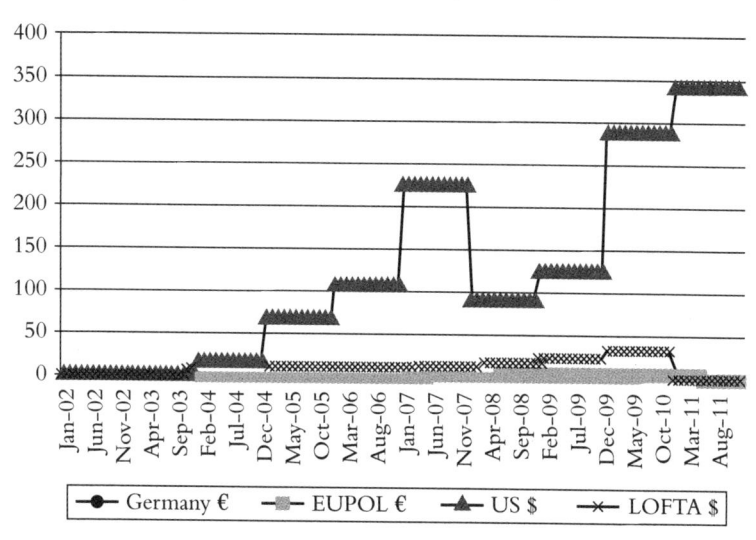

Graph 4: External assistance to Afghanistan's police.

Sources: see Table 4.

The MoI itself only received a single German adviser in 2003[4] and German impact on the MoI as a whole was almost negligible. As one non-German adviser later commented, in their years of leadership the Germans had not even managed to get the Afghans to produce a policy, or guidance on how to use vehicles and weapons.[5] On the basis of what happened later, however, it is not immediately obvious that the small-scale presence of advisers in 2002–3 represented an obstacle. It could also have worked out as a way to let or stimulate Afghans take ownership of the MoI reconstruction process.

Worse than the small numbers was the fact that the first crop of German and European advisers were noteworthy for their naivety: in some cases they even argued that Kalashnikovs should be replaced by pistols or even that weapons were not necessary, completely failing to take into account the reality of Afghanistan.[6] The US DoS got involved in 2003 in order to prepare the police for the forthcoming electoral process. It brought more resources, but its lack of capability and experience in the field of training foreign police forces prevented it from achieving more then the Europeans. All it could do was contract out to a private company, Dyncorp, to provide basic training of questionable quality. In 2005, the US government decided to transfer responsibility to the Department of Defense, which established a new unit called the Office of Security Cooperation-Afghanistan, renamed CSTC-A in 2006, but the state remained involved with the training, holding the contract with Dyncorp.[7]

The American wave

The growing American involvement had a major impact in some of the key debates discussed in section 3.7. In reality the DoS was a supporter of civilian policing and resisted the DoD tendency to militarise the programme and its officials accused the DoD of not understanding the rule of law. The compromise which was worked out allowed a DoS representative to retain oversight over the ANP within CSTC-A, but strong friction persisted over what to teach to the police and other issues. With the DoD in charge, resources became plentiful, but the effectiveness of the programme hardly improved, perhaps in part due to this friction between DoS and DoD. The conflict also contributed to delay the launch of a mentoring programme for the police, which only started in 2007 and is still on a much smaller scale than the one which was proceeding for the army.[8]

The cornerstone of the new police training plan became in 2007 the Focused District Development (FDD), which involved taking whole police units away from their base, retraining them and then bringing them back accompanied by a mentoring unit. Trainers and mentors were supposed to weed out corrupt police in the process as well and offer new equipment, including better weapons, radios and bullet-proof vests.[9] The plan was immediately recognised as flawed by some of those involved in it, in part because it was very manpower-intensive as it required twelve to eighteen trainers for each unit of 100–120 policemen, at a time when such human resources were not available. The result was that the mentoring team were mostly formed parcelling out mostly US Army units without any selection and little preparations. Another acknowledged flaw affecting FDD was the short training course provided, as eight weeks were not enough to leave much of a mark on the trainees.[10] The programme was also criticised for being 'too quantitative and narrowly focused on creating immediate results and [for not incorporating] the need for community policing or its own long-term sustainability'.[11] Finally, in 2008 doubts were already being raised concerning its seriousness, as despite the high levels of corruption and abuse in the police units subjected to FDD only 5 per cent of the FDD trainees were failing to pass the screening.[12] Moreover, in the run-up to the 2009 elections, the courses were cut down to three weeks in order to cover as many districts as quickly as possible.[13]

By 2010 FDD was seen as a disappointment, if not a complete failure.[14] In some cases, when the mentoring team did not manage to find the right approach, whole police stations were deserted after the FDD training, as in Sangin (Helmand).[15] Often the retrained units were found to be slipping back into their old habits and improvements were short term. This was particularly the case when mentoring teams were no longer present.[16] An additional problem that emerged was the low degree of commitment of the Afghan officers themselves. After completing FDD, police officers often tried to transfer to the provincial centre, particularly in dangerous areas such as Kandahar province.[17] Not everybody assessed the programme negatively: some believed that FDD

THE UNCERTAIN IMPACT OF EXTERNAL ASSISTANCE

training at least allowed the police to improve its fighting skills. The police to ANA casualty ratio reportedly halved from 5 to 1 to 2.5 to 1;[18] however, as Graph 2 shows, the actual reduction in police casualties only occurred in 2010 and was modest. What really happened was that an expanding army took over a greater role in the conflict and suffered correspondingly higher casualties.

The combination of basic training by CSTC-A and the FDD of deployed units was replaced in 2010 by a new mix of improved basic training, leadership development and mentoring: FDD was quietly shelved away. While basic training was overhauled quickly, leadership development could necessarily only be implemented gradually. It was planned to involve managerial training, seminars and courses for newly promoted officers. The number of advisers at the ministerial level was increased and reached about 260, of which 160 were just for administration and support, with a total of 2,000 advisers and interpreters being deployed in all of the MoI structure.[19]

Basic training is where NTM-A focused its early efforts. Until the end of 2009, when the change of management occurred, CSTC-A's training courses were regularly passing all trainees. Attendance of the course was not even compulsory and indeed many trainees seem to have been present only on the first and last day of the course, that is for induction and graduation. This led Cordesman to write of 'false training standards'. The quality of the training imparted was in general very poor even as far as military skills were concerned.[20] All recruits were sent to a standard course regardless of their qualifications.[21] In principle, the recruits were being vetted before signing up to a three-year contract: two individuals were also required to vouch for the character and good conduct of each recruit. However, the regional training centres managed by CSTC-A did not always comply with this procedure. Politicians and officials at various levels were also able to interfere with the procedure and recommend protégés.[22] The absence of a national criminal database also contributed to making vetting ineffective.[23]

In February 2010, after improvements to the basic training course had started, even the 5 per cent of recruits who failed the firearms tests were issued a weapon and posted to their units.[24] The priority was still filling the personnel charts.[25] It can be assumed that policing skills fared even worse in the training imparted by the military. Subtleties such as taking people away from the road before handcuffing them in order to avoid humiliating them in public were not understood.[26] On the other hand, the tightened training standards led to a 67 per cent drop-out rate among recruits in early 2010.[27] Although there is no objective measurement of NTM-A's success in turning basic training around, at least the tighter rules signal a greater seriousness of effort.

The existence of different and sometimes incompatible training standards among the countries involved was another problem. Only in March 2011 was a new, standardised basic Patrolmen Basic Program of Instruction approved by NTM-A and EUPOL and distributed.[28]

By 2010 EUPOL was completely marginalised by CSTC-A's successor, NTM-A, which had much greater financial resources. Moreover, Minister in

51

charge Mohammadi had much stronger pro-US leanings than his predecessor Atmar. It became common for EUPOL officials to see their meetings with the Minister and other top officials terminated as soon as the Americans turned up for a visit, regardless of schedule.[29]

Minister Atmar had advocated the extensive training abroad of Afghan police officers, preferably in developing countries like Jordan, Turkey and the UAE, in the range of 2,000–3,000 each year.[30] With his departure, pressure on this front relented and only in March 2011 was an agreement signed with the Turkish government for the training of Afghan police officers in Turkey, with 500 officers scheduled to undertake a six-month course. However, soon allegations of favouritism and bribe-taking in the assignation of the scholarships emerged: a disproportionate number of those assigned to the course in Turkey were from Logar.[31] In June 2011 the Spanish government also agreed to train a small number of Afghan police in Spain on custom and fiscal control.[32]

Impact of assistance

In the field, the indications are that many of the Afghan police officers were not enthusiastic about getting trained by the Americans or anybody else and were only going along because they wanted US or NATO support in battle.[33] This reliance got to the point where police units were falsely claiming to be under attack in the middle of the night, allegedly in order to sleep while the ISAF soldiers stood guard in their place.[34] In other cases police officers justified their inactivity with the lack of the same equipment which western armies use, such as night-vision goggles.[35] Arguably, fighting side-by-side with the best equipped armed forces in the world had a demoralising impact on the Afghans, who felt they were being used as cannon fodder and asked to take risks that their foreign partners would not take themselves. At the same time, the police's capacity for absorbing and accounting for sophisticated equipment was very low, which provided a justification for the Americans to withhold it.[36]

Coordination between the MoI and advisers was often complicated and weakly institutionalised:

> Most strategic and tactical level liaison seems to build on personal relations more than official connections. This was illustrated during a visit by the author to Regional Command South in Kandahar. A decision to increase the ANP in the most insecure provinces by some 10,000 personnel had been made. However, ISAF at Regional Command South was not informed about the decision, even though it has an important role in tactical-level police mentoring. Only because of the close personal relations between the CSTC-A representative and a higher-level ISAF staff officer was the information made available to ISAF. As was remarked during an interview in Kandahar, '[t]here are no official communications structures. It is all about personal relations, and this has to be solved if unity is to be achieved.[37]

The tendency of trained and mentored units which reach the highest rating (CM1, see 6.2) to fall back once the mentoring stops begs the question

THE UNCERTAIN IMPACT OF EXTERNAL ASSISTANCE

of how genuine the claimed achievements were in the first place. Mentors often talked about the need for post-CM1 mentoring 'to sustain training results and stave off regression'. Personnel attrition and reassignments also contributed to the loss of capacity. Worse still, the SIGAR came to the conclusion that the CM rating system:

> created disincentives for ANSF units to make progress toward a CM1 rating and, thereafter, to become independent of Coalition support. Mentor/partner support for ANA units at the top rating level has been minimized to re-prioritize support for lower-rated units; in the case of ANP units, it is withdrawn entirely. Not surprisingly, ANSF units dislike the prospect of losing US and Coalition mentors and partners who bring with them force protection, expertise, supplies, funding, and prestige. According to ANSF mentors and partners and IJC officials, the potential loss of US and Coalition support has been a direct disincentive to improvement on the part of Afghan units.[38]

Very rarely police units have made it to CM1 status: the first of them, the Baghlan Jadid police station, turned into an exemplary story of regression.[39] In mid-2010 it was reported that 66 per cent of police districts had regressed in their capabilities, according to adviser ratings.[40] Some mentors also believed that the rating system was constructed to systematically over-rate the condition of police units.[41] Anecdotal evidence suggests that mentoring really had an impact only in the presence of capable and motivated counterparts. One reported example was that of the strategy and policy department, where MPRI (a security contractor company) mentorship achieved results because the head of department, Sadiqi, was already educated and capable, as well as ready to appoint subordinates on the basis of merit-based selection.[42]

Otherwise, the perverse side-effects of a pervasive mentoring and advising presence could take different shapes. Even the MoI's production of internal documents appears to have been more a result of the need to pay lip service to the demands of foreign donors than of genuine conviction. The advisers convinced the Afghan counterparts that a whole set of documents had to be produced in order for the MoI to function effectively. Again the Afghans were often doing little more than paying lip service to the idea. For example, in 2008 the National Threat Assessment being used at the MoI was still the 2005 one, despite the dramatic change in the security landscape.[43] Another perverse effect was the tendency of many MoI officers to shelter behind their mentors and rely on their support for career advancement. It was not uncommon for police officers to claim to have been 'appointed by the US', an additional way to avoid accountability.[44]

6

INTERNAL ORGANISATION AND REORGANISATION

In early 2002, the MoI was in a state of disarray. Together with the demands of the international community for the reorganisation of the MoI and the restoration of basic functionality within it, this disorganised state took several dimensions, ranging from structural development to professionalisation, to the fight against corruption. External pressure was meant to push the MoI along a path of transformation into something more like the Weberian model of the 'modern state'. This pressure managed to move the MoI from its early tolerance of undisciplined behaviour and lack of professionalism, but inevitably interacted with a range of other sources of pressure, pushing the MoI in different directions. Some criminal networks quickly established roots within the MoI and either resisted or coopted reorganisation efforts, while external interest groups were often as effective as the international community in pushing their agendas, if not more. Professionalisation and the fight against corruption turned out to be not politically neutral at all: in fact they became the scene of major political battles fought inside the MoI over several years.

Structural development

The MoI structure adopted after the fall of the Taliban regime is shown in Figure 5. The main features were the return of sub-national administration to the MoI and the creation of a National Command Centre, which was meant to exercise direct command and control over police units spread around the country, through the provision of communication technology by foreign donors. Some elements of the old structure acquired new functions. For example, the political officers established in the late 1970s were given media and communication tasks.[1]

The structure was soon to change again with the establishment of the Independent Directorate of Local Governance (IDLG) in August 2007, which took the sub-national administration away from the MoI once more. Several other changes occurred in 2007–8, of which the most noteworthy ones were a new department of gendarmerie called the Afghan National Civil Order Police (ANCOP) and the creation of the Afghan Anti-Crime Police (AACP), bringing together all investigative capacity within the MoI: counter-terrorism, counter-narcotics, intelligence, criminal investigation, major crime task force, special units and forensics.

ANCOP was the successor to the Stand-by Police, created shortly after the inception of the new government (see section 9.1). The Stand-by Police was supposed to be a mobile reserve force, but in reality the provincial detachments refused to travel to other provinces and were ridden with corruption: out of a force supposed to number 11,000, only 3,000 were estimated to exist. They were also poorly equipped, usually having to hitch-hike in order to deploy, and were not selected particularly carefully.[2]

ANCOP was initially seen as the great hope of an improved MoI performance, but has in part at least turned into a disappointment as signs of corruption, drug taking and less then competent leadership emerged.[3] Many important MoI players did not particularly appreciate the idea of establishing ANCOP. The original proposal for ANCOP featured a mobile, elite force of 20,000, but in the initial debate a ceiling of 5,000 was agreed. Deputy Minister Hadi Khalid argued in favour of a large ANCOP, while Minister Zarar tried to protect the Stand-by Police and then, once that appeared to be a lost cause, tried to place his own men in the new ANCOP.[4]

By the end of 2008 the structure of MoI looked like that shown in Figure 6. Finally in 2009 a new Department called the Afghan Public Protection Force (APPF) was established, in charge of locally recruited militias, under the Deputy Minister for Security and Police. This latest addition raised concerns, given that the MoI was already struggling to exercise some kind of control over the uniformed police and that APPF units were meant to be activated in the most difficult districts.[5] The decision to create the Afghan Local Police (ALP) further complicated the picture. As of late 2010, after some discussions of a possible merger of the two, it appeared that APPF would take over the former private security companies and provide a state-sponsored protection service instead. The ALP would instead focus on the local militias. ALP reportedly was supposed to have two commanding officers, one reporting to district police stations and the other reporting to APPF in the MoI.[6]

The structural changes of this period were the result of a number of factors. The will and determination of Afghan political players, particularly within the MoI, played some role. For example, Minister Atmar (2008–10) strongly supported some changes, even when he had not initiated them. ANCOP was one of them. But as a rule, structural change was rather driven

INTERNAL ORGANISATION AND REORGANISATION

Figure 5: MoI structure in 2005.

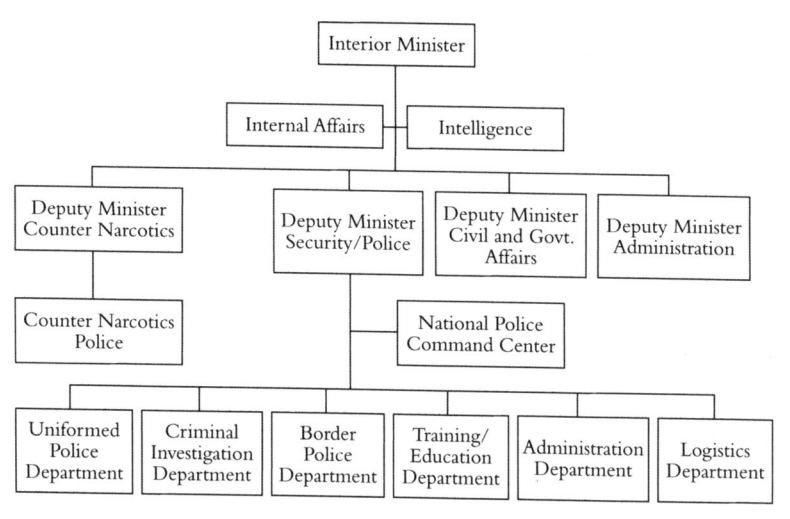

```
                          Interior Minister
                                 |
                  Internal Affairs — Intelligence
                                 |
   ┌──────────────────┬──────────────────┬──────────────────┐
Deputy Minister   Deputy Minister   Deputy Minister   Deputy Minister
Counter Narcotics Security/Police   Civil and Govt.   Administration
                                       Affairs
        |                 |
Counter Narcotics     National Police
    Police            Command Center
                          |
   ┌────────┬────────┬────────┬────────┬────────┐
Uniformed Criminal  Border  Training/ Administration Logistics
 Police  Investigation Police Education  Department  Department
Department Department Department Department
```

Source: German Embassy, 2006.

Figure 6: MoI structure in 2008.

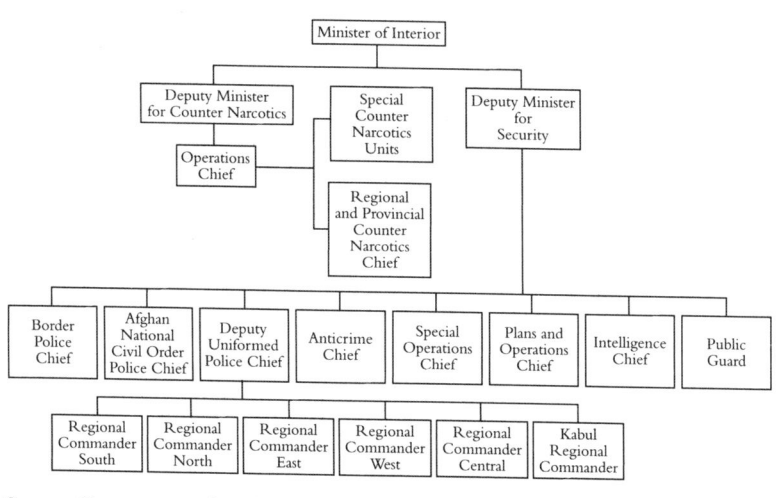

```
                      Minister of Interior
                             |
   ┌─────────────────┬──────────────────┬─────────────────┐
Deputy Minister   Special            Deputy Minister
for Counter       Counter            for
Narcotics         Narcotics          Security
     |            Units
Operations           |
  Chief          Regional
                and Provincial
                Counter
                Narcotics
                Chief

Border | Afghan    | Deputy   | Anticrime| Special  | Plans and | Intelligence | Public
Police | National  | Uniformed| Chief    | Operations| Operations| Chief       | Guard
Chief  | Civil Order| Police  |          | Chief    | Chief     |             |
       | Police Chief| Chief  |          |          |           |             |

Regional   Regional   Regional   Regional   Regional   Kabul
Commander  Commander  Commander  Commander  Commander  Regional
South      North      East       West       Central    Commander
```

Source: Department of Defense.

57

by the demands of donors. In fact Afghan initiatives were often stymied. When the head of CID and counter-terrorism Jamil Junbesh proposed to merge the two departments, he faced a US veto and the proposal was blocked.[7] A small but significant example of foreign-driven innovation is when EUPOL sponsored the formation of mobile units in the provincial centres, replacing the system in use where in case of alarm everybody available would jump on trucks and leave.[8]

Another obvious example is that of 'institutional reform', the plan to separate police bureaucracy and operational command. By 2010 the belief was gaining ground within the ranks of EUPOL and NTM-A that the structure of the MoI itself was not conducive to the recruitment of the necessary management skills. At the Kabul conference (2010) it was agreed that the MoI needed an institutional reform. The plan sponsored by the Canadians was aimed at separating police bureaucracy and operational command and depoliticising the former, which would then be in charge of overseeing the latter. That would imply the filling of 6,000 civilian positions, of which just sixty were already filled as of November 2010, most being menial jobs. The MoI was tepid about the plan and Minister Mohammadi (2010–) delayed his response. One of the implications of the plan was that the Minister would no longer be involved in making appointments and that a bureaucratic process would instead be in place.[9]

The hostility to bringing civilians into the MoI reached the point that even the appointment of a civilian legal adviser to the MoI proved to be a matter of controversy, as the MoI countered that by appointing a Chief of Law who was a police officer. As a result, little power or influence was then left to the legal adviser.[10] Institutional reform's trouble was not just due to MoI resistance: the Canadians admitted that there would be a shortage of skills if the plan was to be implemented. Indeed by March 2011 problems were already emerging in hiring civilian employees, so the Human Resources Department had to be established from scratch.[11] One of the few MoI civilian officials recognised that the MoI had a bad reputation among civil servants, while better opportunities elsewhere contributed to making an MoI job an unattractive proposition. The MoI preferred to think in terms of bringing in fresh Police Academy graduates to take over a growing portion of the administration. In 2011, 105 such graduates were assigned as permanent staff of the MoI.[12]

In other cases one can speak of a convergence of interests between Afghans and foreign donors. This is for example the case in counter-narcotics, which after 2002 was paid a particular attention, particularly by the British, but also by the Americans. As a result the department's HQ capabilities were in 2010 higher than the MoI average: at least they had somewhat better financial management and higher quality human resources. The role of Deputy Minister Daud (2005–10) was to bolster the process, by lobbying actively in order to build up his 'small empire', with a perceivable impact down to the district level.[13]

INTERNAL ORGANISATION AND REORGANISATION

The MoI could hardly have taken the lead in determining the need for structural change. As of the end of 2010, there was still nobody in the MoI to determine policy, such as how to organise training.[14] The repeated changes in the personnel charts (tashkil) were recognised to be disruptive but continued nonetheless, a fact that seemed to suggest improvisation, as if nobody knew what the needs were.[15]

A potentially key development was the establishment in January 2010 of a Recruitment Command within the MoI, which once activated later in the year took the responsibility of recruiting away from the CoPs and gave it to a centralised system under direct MoI control, as it had already been the case with ANCOP. The system, however, was still unable to track where the recruits were being deployed.[16] In March the staffing of the Command was increased from 300 to 1,000, substantially enhancing its capacity, and provincial offices started opening up.[17] Another positive development was the establishment of a Training Command, expected to lead to the strengthening of training. Most CoPs had shown little interest in training, despite lobbying by NTM-A. With training and operations being separated, it became easier to allocate resources and time to training and avoid diversion.[18] Under the new rules, the vetting of new recruits in 2010 was taken more seriously and implemented, although the criteria used by the officers in charge to judge suitability were different from those advocated by the mentors: people had to belong to the 'right family'.[19]

Professionalisation

Local/non-local

The debate about local and non-local policing is easily simplified and ideologised as one pitting a benign central government against local strongmen or, vice versa, as one pitting benign communities versus a malign central state. In reality there are benefits and disadvantages both in centralisation and local policing. Military mentors accompanying Afghan police in mission quickly realised that the lack of contacts and relations with the local population was a major handicap for the police. Often the police would be totally unaware of who was who in their area, or of what was going on: in such conditions, doing anything more than merely guarding posts was not possible. It is worth mentioning that the rapid rotation of police units in certain areas contributed to compounding the problem.[20] The essential local knowledge and relationship with (at least part of) the population can be ideally achieved through some form of community policing in the case of a professional and motivated police force. A cheap surrogate of this is recruiting police locally, or posting them to an area for long periods of time, if they are willing (which is a rare occurrence, at least as far as the rural areas are concerned).

Because of the limited capabilities of Afghanistan's police after 2001, the 'cheap surrogate' became the only viable option if local knowledge had to be available. The MoI tried to do its own semi-local recruitment, taking recruits from one district or province and sending them to a neighbouring district or province, so that they would be out of their own area but at the same time not too far from their families. For example, in 2007 most of the police of Garmser (Helmand) were from another district of the same province, Nawa.[21] This worked only to a limited extent, because the salaries were too low to justify serving in a district other than their own.[22]

Sometimes local recruitment did create at least a bond with the local population, or part thereof. In at least one district of Parwan the police did not seem to be seen as an authoritarian force, according to an MoI advisor. The population did not seem to live in fear of the police and policemen could often be seen chatting with locals.[23] A line of thinking picked up by western officials was that the CoP had to be local also because of their role in dispute resolution.[24]

The risks of locally recruited police forces are however obvious. In particular, local police forces seem to have become obviously involved in local conflicts, at the expense of some of the communities. Squabbles among policemen in some cases even led to armed clashes and loss of life: a dozen policemen were killed in a series of clashes among police groups in Kandahar province in 2007–8.[25] In Shindand district in 2007 the police split along tribal lines, Barakzani versus Noorzai, and they began fighting each other.[26]

The original post-2001 division of the spoils was often based on a precarious balance of power among a variety of characters and factions. As a result, altering the balance between two such factions could be destabilising. This was in the case of two Pashtun tribes in Uruzgan province in June 2010, when demonstrations took place against the alleged favouritism of the provincial police chief in favour of the Popolzais at the expense of the Barakzais, involving the disarming of policemen at four check-posts. The CoP maintained that the sacked policemen had been involved in the sexual molestation of a woman.[27] Another example comes from Kandahar, where the appointment of a new governor closely linked to the Karzais, Assadullah Khalid, in 2006 brought much turmoil as he tried to bring a police force previously controlled by strongmen Gul Agha Shirzai and Mullah Naqib under his own control. The power struggle might have facilitated the emergence of the Taliban as a serious insurgent force. Gul Agha Shirzai had a system of incentives which topped up the salaries of the patrolmen: the system was abolished with his departure, damaging the morale of the rank-and-file.[28]

As of 2010, the varying willingness of the strongmen to support the district stations was still linked to political relations. In Dand, for example, the police benefited from the help of Gul Aga Shirzai's militias, after a deal in which Shirzai was promised that some of his militiamen would be recruited into the police.[29]

The problem was compounded by the fact that in some areas the modest complement of police was supplemented by men loyal to the local strongman and not registered with the MoI, usually not having even been issued a

INTERNAL ORGANISATION AND REORGANISATION

uniform. In Herat, for example, the typical twenty-five registered policemen of a district were supplemented by another ten to fifteen loyal to Ismail Khan, even long after he had been removed as governor (2008).[30] Another example is that of Baghlan, where under Sayyed Khel's authority at least thirty-five men were using police uniforms and vehicles without being registered as police.[31] The risks associated with this practice became evident when in Herat province a number of violent attacks on the police were attributed by provincial police officers to local 'unregistered' police, who were trying to keep official police out of sensitive areas.[32]

The police officers recruited on the basis of patronage and local influence proved often impossible to control. Wilder reports one episode in which a provincial CoP who was given 900 weapons by the Americans and then distributed 700 of them to his tribesmen after having temporarily dressed them up as police.[33] Moreover, while locally recruited police had better local knowledge than police coming from outside, that would not necessarily result in a willingness to take on criminals and insurgents. It could equally easily result in collaboration with them (see also 8.1.4 below).[34]

In short, there are trade-offs between local and non-local police forces as the former have local knowledge, but are also entangled in local power struggles. The latter are usually free of such entanglements, but lack local knowledge. In Afghanistan, community policing was a completely alien concept until 2008 at least, when the first experiments and pilots started being carried out. In the early post-2001 days the lack of a centrally recruited police force left little option but to rely entirely on locally raised forces (see also 6.2.1 below). In 2002, virtually all the CoPs were from the province where they served, as were the large majority of the officers. In practice, therefore, policing was local and decentralised even if in theory the structure remained very centralised.

The practice was the object of much criticism since these local policemen tended to get involved in local feuds and took sides in local conflicts, in other words they usually lacked impartiality. The demand for out-of-area police seemed to be gaining ground within the MoI for several years after 2001, as the central recruitment of officers and the establishment of a few mobile police units started making headway.

Among the population, support for both local and centralised policing can be found. For local policing, the example cited above about Parwan is valid and the same can be said of places like Panjshir and some others. Heratis by contrast complained of the police being local and therefore being involved in local factional and ethnic struggles, as well as being constrained by connections with relatives and communities. In practice little could be done in this regard, so the new CoP appointed in 2009 started bringing Hazaras into the police, in order to rebalance it ethnically and ensure that each community was represented.[35]

On the whole, the balance of anecdotal evidence seemed to go towards distrust being more common. The potential of the police to collaborate with communities and local authorities was further reduced by lasting disagreement over who was ultimately in charge of the provincial police: the governor or the provincial CoP. It remained a point of contention also in recent years between the MoI and the IDLG.[36]

By the second half of the decade, in some areas a portion of the provincial police force was now loyal to the centre, rather than to local strongmen and factions. This had some enabling impact for those CoPs or governors who were themselves inclined to improve law and order. In Helmand, for example, Governor Daud estimated in 2007 that of 1,700 police in the province, 250 were loyal to him and to the central government.[37] Similarly, after 2004, Herat's police was divided between supporters of the central government and supporters of local strongman Ismail Khan, whereas until 2004 it had been entirely dominated by the former.

By 2006–8 the debate among donors and within the MoI over centralised versus local police was taking on new shapes. Instead of opposing supporters of local strongmen and their adversaries, proponents of village-based police forces and those who believed such forces could never be controlled by the centre were increasingly pitted against each other. Successive experiments with local police forces (Auxiliary Police, Afghan Public Protection Force, Afghan Local Police), mostly confirmed the fears of the pessimists.[38]

The first experiment with the creation of 'integrated' militias, dating back to 2006, but planned already during 2005, was the formation of the Auxiliary Police (ANAP). With an authorised strength of over 11,000, the ANAP was supposed to deliver community policing in areas beyond the reach of the AUP. The recruits were supposed to be recommended by elders and then vetted by MoI and NDS but in practice this seems to have rarely happened. Despite the claim that ANAP units would come under the control of local MoI structures, the latter were too flimsy to represent an effective chain of command. Dressed in ANP uniforms, they were perceived by the population as ANP. In fact the ANAP were basically tribal/personal militias with an official stamp and were used mostly in a counter-insurgency role. Due to their affiliations, the ANAP were even less impartial towards other ethnic/tribal groups than the regular ANP. The beginnings of the insurgency in Badghis province, for example, might owe much to two ANAP units which harassed the Pashtun population there. Most of these ANAP formations were outside any control mechanism and functioned basically on personal loyalty. The programme was perceived as such a failure than it was shut down in May 2008, following criticism by the UN and others, as well as negative press reporting.[39]

As the ANAP experiment was folding up in a failure, the idea of forming community militias went through a phase of re-elaboration, taking into account the opposition to the formation of 'militias' among Members of Parliament and the population, as well as the diplomatic corps. The product of long negotiations between the Afghan government and ISAF, the Afghan Social Outreach Programme was launched in 2008 featuring the formation of 'community guards', recruited by new village shuras established by IDLG,

INTERNAL ORGANISATION AND REORGANISATION

which would also be in charge of paying them. The Afghan government wanted militias that would be 'relatively formal bodies more akin to a locally recruited police force. In many cases, such local forces would not even be armed'. A pilot project started at the beginning of 2009 in Wardak province. It was supposed to entail the recruitment of 100–200 militiamen per district, to be screened by 'local leaders', who would then receive a short training course.

Not many Afghans were however convinced by the new plan, mainly because the IDLG shuras are not universally accepted as representative. The Social Outreach plan took 'community militias' as a model, aiming to form small village militias which are not integrated into larger militia structures, thus preventing the formation of a truly 'parallel security structure', which some commentators feared could ultimately represent a direct threat to the residual integrity of the Afghan state. However, commentators highlighted the drawbacks of such a fragmented structure (involving hundreds of small, separate militias, supervised only by their elders and hence hard to monitor), namely the risk of 'shifting loyalties' and 'local deals'. Central government was to have no direct control over these small militias, which some observers view as a positive aspect of the plan given the dysfunctional nature of the government. In any case the Social Outreach plan, which turned into the APPF once the MoI moved in to claim ownership, was widely recognised as a failure and never moved beyond its pilot in Wardak province. In order for it to take off and achieve an impact in terms of counter-insurgency, it proved necessary to appoint Ghulam Muhammad Hotak in December 2009 as a commander and de facto 'owner' of the force, having mobilised his old retinue of fighters (dating back to the 1980s and 1990s) into the force. He refused to place himself and his men under the authority of the CoP and maintained a large degree of autonomy.[40]

Paradoxically, however, the same arguments (how to fight the insurgency more effectively) which had driven the debate towards a near consensus on a para-militarised and centralised police force resurfaced in 2009 to argue in favour of the creation of a local police force, based among the local communities. The decision to form the ALP was driven by a convergence of interests between ISAF and the MoI, both desiring to integrate into some kind of framework pro-government armed groups which were emerging in the rural areas in reaction to the expansion of the insurgency. Originally meant to number 10,000 and to be based in the districts, where a lack of uniformed police was most evident, the plans rapidly became more ambitious and soon the talk was of a final size of 30–50,000.[41] Evidence on the ground suggests that the ALP in its early days was quite effective at securing patches of territory and its population from the influence of the insurgents, but at the price of compounding the already existing problems of command and control within the police (see Chapter 8). The ANP officers in charge of supervising the ALP often found it difficult if not impossible to play the role assigned to them.[42]

Among Afghans too the arguments pro and con local and non-local police have been often used instrumentally: strongmen appointed as governors away from their home turf became supporters of non-local police, having resisted it previously, because they wanted to get their retinue of armed men with them in their new post.[43] Often the non-local element of the police forces in the provinces was not centrally appointed, but handpicked by the CoP, usually from among his own circle of loyalists and cronies. When Sayyid Khel was appointed CoP of Baghlan, for example, he appointed twenty-five of thirty-two officers in the Provincial HQ from his own Parwani retinue.[44] Another example is that of Takhar CoP Mamozai, who when appointed in 2004 brought a lot of former members of Hizb-i Islami and even Taliban with him.[45]

In sum, as of 2011 the MoI had not yet managed to find a balance between local and non-local policing. The problem is essentially that local policing is unlikely to work in the interests of a central government unless it is strictly supervised and monitored. For such supervision to occur, a capable central bureaucracy is necessary and the MoI had not been able to develop it in the first ten years of the post-Taliban regime.

Indiscipline

In 2002–3, even the most basic features of discipline were missing from Afghanistan's police, despite its paramilitary character. It was common for the police not to wear uniforms even in the cities.[46] Table 5 illustrates this.

One of the causes of pride of the top officials of the MoI in 2010 was to have standardised the uniforms utilised by the police, which in 2002 did not exist or belonged to different types supplied by different countries.[47] As late as 2008–10, however, if all police in Kabul were wearing uniforms, even in a big city like Kandahar it was common to see policemen wearing ordinary clothes. The resistance to using uniforms was strong and weak officers would not enforce the regulations.[48,49] In the provinces it was still common to find policemen wearing tunic and baggy pants instead of their uniform.[50] Often the police refused to wear uniforms for fear of reprisals from the insurgents, particularly when not accompanying ISAF units.[51] Where the governors and the CoPs insisted, policemen started wearing uniforms in the provincial centres at least, even in remote provinces like Uruzgan.[52] An assertive and professional CoP in Khost, for example, managed to reduce the number of policemen in civilian clothes to an estimated 5–10 per cent in the provincial centre. Outside Khost, however, few followed the orders of their chief.[53]

Another example of basic indiscipline was the displaying of symbols of affiliation with factions on their cars or in their offices. The most classical example of his was commander Massud's pictures displayed by police in Kabul and in the north-east. Initially this was tolerated by the MoI, itself badly factionalised. When an MoI keen to show at least some outer signs of de-factionalisation at various stages ordered the removal of these symbols, success was partial at best if the orders had to be repeated periodically.[54] Yet another basic example of indiscipline was that often the police were not wearing the

INTERNAL ORGANISATION AND REORGANISATION

bullet-proof vests handed over by the Americans, although this was in part justified by the fact that the old model, low-grade vests were not really strong enough to resist the 7.62 mm bullets of the Kalashnikovs.[55] More serious forms of indiscipline have been rather common occurrences as well. There have been cases of police refusing to deploy for operations, particularly in the most dangerous areas.[56] Sending them to do the holding job after an ANA/ISAF clearing operation was the least popular job and here insubordination could be a serious problem.[57]

Table 5: Percentage of district police forces in uniform with uniforms distinct from military, proper registration of firearms, secure location of stored firearms, and composition of police force, by province, 2003. Based on Tufts University study data.

	Badghis	Balkh	Herat	Kabul	Kandahar	Nangarhar
Majority of Police Force	Former Mujahideen	Former Mujahideen	Former Mujahideen	Former Mujahideen	Former Mujahideen	Former Mujahideen
Some Police in Uniform	50%	20%	75%	25%	0%	0%
Police Uniform Distinct from Militaty	50%	0%	75%	25%	0%	0%
Proper Registration of Firearms	50%	0%	75%	50%	0%	0%
Secure Location of Firearms	0%	0%	0%	75%	0%	0%

Source: Afghanistan's Systems of Justice, cit.

Perhaps the greatest constraint in enforcing discipline within the police was the constant failure to prosecute deserters. Absence from duty was a widespread problem, estimated by then Minister Atmar at 20 per cent in 2008.[58] One mentor observed that despite being a militarised force, there was a lack of rules and discipline in the Border Police as they quit the force with uniforms and discipline, often in whole groups, even ten at a time in the east.[59] Absence without leave was still in 2011 a major problem within the police. In February 2010–January 2011 more than 13,000 policemen were officially reported as absent, or well over 10 per cent of the average personnel charts of the police during the period. The tolerance for absence without leave in all likelihood encouraged this type of behaviour and from March 2011 it was decided to drop from the rolls all those remaining absent for more than twenty (officers) or thirty days (NCOs and patrolmen).[60] Under Minister Mohammadi, a new Act of Duty was introduced in 2010, which asked the new police officer to commit himself to ten years of service, while NCOs were asked to serve five years and patrolmen three years. With the approval of the Act of Duty, they could be prosecuted if they left earlier. The punishment was however not specified and President Karzai appeared to be on a different track as he kept proclaiming amnesties for deserters.[61]

A peculiar aspect of police indiscipline which attracted attention was underage recruitment for purposes that had little to do with policing. In May 2010 a decision (taken under pressure from UNAMA) to ban recruitment of under-eighteen males into the police was taken by the Afghan government. Until then it was not uncommon to find policemen as young as twelve to fourteen years, at least in the south and it would seem that it remained common even after that so that in January 2011 the UN had to 'express concern' over underage recruitment again and the tendency of the police to sexually abuse the young boys. The MoI issued new regulations to fight underage recruitment.[62]

The causes of the low level of discipline were many. The poor quality of recruits could well have been one. From late 2009 onwards efforts started being made to strengthen the screening of recruits, in order to keep out children, drug users and Taliban infiltrators, by using iris scans, fingerprinting, drug tests, medical examinations including age assessments and the requesting of reference letters, but the impact of such measures was not obvious as of late 2010.[63]

Lack of equipment and poor supplies, in particular of fresh food, were certainly affecting morale negatively.[64] Moreover, living conditions in the police stations were very poor, with tens of policemen sharing one or two rooms for at least a month before getting a meagre two days off.[65] Even food allowances were inadequate, particularly in years of rising food prices.[66] The absence of a system of shifts also contributed to weakening morale and therefore discipline. As one NTM-A senior officer put it, 'the shifts system can give hope to those serving in the mud'.[67] More generally:

> The system lacked a uniform set of rewards and penalties. The Afghan security system paid low wages, a trivial pension, and poor care of the families of those who were killed or severely wounded. There was no incentive to run risks today in order to be rewarded later.[68]

A 2010 survey of a number of provinces found a variety of examples of police indiscipline:

> In one district, new recruits (under two years) had their guns removed before going off duty because they had been using them to rob people. There were many instances of police 'borrowing' goods from traders and not paying them back, along with reports of sexual assault and the misappropriation of aid by district CoPs.[69]

This type of misbehaviour of the police seems to be linked to poor pay, delays in paying salaries or to the fact that the salaries had been embezzled by somebody in the MoI.[70] In fact police commanding officers were often

INTERNAL ORGANISATION AND REORGANISATION

forced to operate and live in constant fear of their men mutinying or deserting. The situation was compounded by the non-existing logistics, which often left the policemen without winter clothes and poorly equipped, or completely reliant on American support.[71] At one point some units of mentors started paying the police units directly in order to bypass the MoI and avoid delays and reduce corruption.[72] From 2008 onwards a major effort has been made to improve the reliability of the system of payment in the police, using electronic payments. Until then, the system was entirely reliant on the commanding officers transferring the money to their subordinates, if the money was not embezzled before leaving the HQ of the MoI. Many commanding officers then took their own cut. It was calculated that on average the policemen would only get 60–70 per cent of the meagre salary.[73] MoI officials were even reported to have encouraged police officers in the field to lie to their men about the starting salary they were entitled to.[74]

Another factor feeding indiscipline was the insufficient number of capable and determined commanding officers. Even in the early years (2002–4) strong leadership could have a major impact on the police, because the system was built to respond to strong leadership: the expectation of the patrolmen was to be led.[75]

Drug addiction was clearly yet another major source of police indiscipline and misconduct. During 2010 the MoI started admitting that drug addiction was a serious problem among the patrolmen, but still had a tendency to underestimate the scale of the problem. Official figures indicated the existence of 1,800 addicts in the police, following the testing of 114,000 policemen.[76] After the launch of a drug rehabilitation programme, police commanders started claiming that the problem had been eliminated.[77]

Anecdotal evidence suggests that the level of addiction is much higher, with very high peaks in areas where opium derivatives or hashish are widely available. NTM-A data suggested an overall drug abuse rate in the police of 9 per cent in mid-2010. While opium abusers were not allowed into the police, users of lighter drugs were recruited despite testing positive, because 'it's so prevalent in society that we'd be kicking everybody out'.[78] Partial testing carried out in 2008–9 found that no less than 16 per cent and up to 95 per cent of recruits were testing positive to drugs.[79] Even a battalion of the elite ANCOP had to be sidelined from operations in Kandahar after a quarter of its members tested positive to drugs.[80] Another ANCOP unit in Nangarhar became non-operational due to abuse of marijuana.[81] Attempts to systematically test the police for drugs faced resistance among the policemen. Rosen writes of one of these tests being administered in Helmand: only fifty-three of eighty policemen showed up, some refused to take it and twenty tested positive.[82]

Over the years the MoI took some initiatives to improve discipline within the ranks. A claimed achievement in this regard was the distribution of ID cards and uniform badges to all police around the country but it faced greater difficulties in making sure that the police IDs were distributed only to those entitled to them.[83] By early 2010 a biometrics system was in place, keeping record of 90 per cent of the police, although there was still no follow-up and casualties often went unrecorded, as did desertions. The fact that the MoI did not have its own hospital system meant that it was unable to keep track anyway of those dying in the civilian, international or military hospitals.[84] In 2009 the MoI was still struggling to validate the eligibility of about 37 per cent of its force, mainly due to the lack of cooperation of three police zone commanders.[85] The fact that throughout 2011 terrorists could stage attacks even in Kabul using fake police IDs suggests that the system was still somewhat less than fully functional.

Other attempts to improve discipline followed. In particular, in 2010 a new code of conduct was approved and widely advertised within and without the police.[86] At the time of writing it was too early to say whether it was having any impact.

Cooperation with other government institutions

Another aspect of professionalism in which the police has been lacking since its early days is its ability and willingness to cooperate with other branches of the Afghan security apparatus. In particular, tension between ANA and ANP has been occurring frequently, sometimes resulting even in armed clashes or in arrests. Five police were arrested by ANA in Helmand in November 2006, for example.[87] Among other things, the ANA, which has been acquiring some air transport capability, regularly refused to evacuate ANP casualties. Such lack of cooperation pushed the MoI to demand its own autonomy capability in terms of helicopters and heavy weaponry.[88] The two organisations showed the tendency to pour scorn on each other, with the police accusing the army of leaving them to fight the Taliban alone and of being 'Western puppets', while the army accused the police of corruption, bad discipline, collaboration with the Taliban and inability to hold the ground cleared by the army.[89]

ISAF officers commented that:

there is no love lost between the ANP and the ANA [in Ghormach] and there have been cases where one refused to help the other while under attack.[90]

Another ISAF source reported an episode of tension between ANP and ANA in Helmand, where ANA soldiers did not want to fight and ANP officers shouted at them and insulted them.[91]

During 2009–10 cooperation between ANP and ANA showed signs of improvement, particularly where the command and control structure was stronger. In Kandahar, for example, the closer to the city, the greater the cooperation. Another factor determining the level of cooperation was the personality of the CoP, as well as of course of the ANA officers.[92] Efforts to develop institutional mechanisms to improve coordination with the ANA gradually developed, with the establishment of the Operation Coordination Center-Province (OCCP) and Operation Coordination Center-Region (OCCR).

INTERNAL ORGANISATION AND REORGANISATION

However, the ANP continued to complain that the ANA was extremely reluctant to come to the ANP's help when needed: only when pre-planned was cooperation successful.[93] They also complained that the ANA was better equipped than them, despite not really sharing the burden of fighting in a fair way: the lack of equipment to counter the IED threat was resented particularly bitterly.[94]

The police also regularly complained about the NDS not sharing information.[95] Distrust existed between police units and ISAF as well, in part because of a number of friendly fire incidents, but also because of disagreements over mentoring and training.[96]

Cooperation with the attorney general's office and with the judiciary was also poor, not least because of the inadequacies of the justice sector, with many districts not having any functioning judiciary at all.[97] There was no coordination, no cross reporting, no sharing of statistics among the various institutions supposed to be fighting crime: high office of oversight, NDS, audit department, counter corruption units in each ministry and of course MoI.[98] It was not even clear how to divide the caseload among CID, AUP and NDS.[99] The police, particularly in the early post-2001 years, often denied access to detention centres to court officials. The police and the legal professions were equally scornful of each other:

> Judges and prosecutors in Kabul complained that Kabul police arrest and release people without the involvement of the courts. The police contend that those they arrest end up back on the streets due to the misconduct and inefficiency of the courts. Judicial personnel suggested that the police act in this manner mainly because they do not know the parameters of their jobs and, therefore, the police are attempting to take on the combined duties of law enforcement officers, prosecutors, and judges.[100]

Investigative capabilities

The low level of professionalism of the police affects intelligence-led policing (CID) more than any other aspect of policing. One episode was reported, in which the police in charge of securing a murder scene allowed the brother of the victim to come and take the car of his brother, without any attempt to stop him. This is one of the reasons why officials in the attorney general's office do not trust police and cast them as a 'bunch of idiots'.[101] External observers believe that the office of the attorney general is actually the weakest link in the chain of the rule of law. Of 5,000 officials, 1,000 who should be in the provinces are in Kabul.[102]

It is clear that the CID was in an extremely poor condition in the early post-2001 years. In 2003 there was no budget for the CID at all.[103] A few years later the situation had changed somewhat. Despite the weakness of investigative capability, the CID had probably the greatest concentration of professional officers of the whole MoI, with the senior management being quite good, although quality declined rapidly down the ladder. In a district like Dawlatabad of Balkh province, for example, 50 per cent of the CID officers were illiterate in 2007.[104] On the whole, the ability to carry out investigative work remained very limited. The police would perhaps record complaints and confessions, but rarely venture into using forensic and criminalistic techniques, except to some extent in Kabul.[105]

Experiments were being carried out under EUPOL supervision from 2009 onwards in developing model police stations, starting from one in Kabul and then rolling the model out to the main cities, which would be able to implement professional policing and the rule of law.[106] In Kabul the increase in expertise was noticeable by 2009 as fingerprinting was then operational and the CID was building up its scientific investigations.[107] Progress notwithstanding, even in 2010 in Kabul the CID numbered just over 700 officers for Kabul's five million people, too little to achieve much. Even in this department (the best in the country) many were illiterate, even if the department head Yarmand was a professional with much experience.[108] In 2009 EUPOL helped in establishing the 'Serious Crime Scene Investigation Unit' within the CID and the FBI also contributed training.[109] However, the efforts to improve the quality of the staff were frustrated by the fact that many trainers formed by EUPOL were leaving the police just like officers from other departments. EUPOL was trying to work out how to retain them but without much success as of mid-2011.[110]

Reporting and record keeping

Record keeping and reporting from the bottom to the top might be boring features of modern bureaucracies, but have the purpose of limiting the room for arbitrary behaviour. In criminal investigation the development of a reporting system was slower than in counter-terrorism. The system was already re-established in principle at the beginning of Karzai's time. The Germans in the north in particular were trying to teach the Afghans filing and record keeping.[111]

In 2002–5, a series of visits to police stations by one of the authors around Afghanistan showed that orders and communications were being issued on plain paper and copies were not being kept, making it impossible to track the activities of the stations. Other surveys came to similar conclusions: 'Records of arrests and incidents, or other logs, are not being kept in any of the police stations that Amnesty International visited in Afghanistan'.[112]

In 2003–5, the police did not even have any paper or pens.[113] Paperwork and communications between police officers were very loose and disorganised in the early post-2001 days: a letter signed by Nangarhar CoP Hazrat Ali was on the letterhead of the Bank of Afghanistan and was addressed to 'All Security Guards and Policemen', advised that an individual was missing and instructed them to help 'find the person he suspects'. It featured no names, no addresses and no explicit order to investigate a possible murder.[114]

In the following years some improvement in reporting back to Kabul and in record keeping took place, sometimes facing serious resistance within the

INTERNAL ORGANISATION AND REORGANISATION

MoI. A former MoI official, Minister Atmar (2008–10) asked police stations to keep files, but earned little popularity for it.[115] By 2009 some police stations were keeping a rudimentary record of prisoners, but little effort had been made to create a proper administrative system as procedures hardly existed.[116]

In Kabul in particular, orders and criminal records were by 2010 being saved electronically. However, already in the districts of Kabul province the situation was different: there was no computerisation and paper records could still be easily manipulated and records were reportedly sold and stolen easily because they were not being kept online. It was particularly easy to free criminals for money in the first twenty-four hours after detention as the crime was not yet recorded and not reported to the office of the Attorney General, but even after that it was possible to buy one own's freedom, if only more expensively. The rudimentary filing system and the lack of qualified staff meant that it was difficult to keep track of old cases.[117] Reportedly when asked about files of specific cases, head of CID Yarmand could not produce them. Even important cases which had hit the headlines were not kept and manipulation of the files was frequent. One high-ranking MoI official stated to one of the authors his belief that files were mostly about showing that the MoI was improving to donors and mentors.[118]

The presence of educated officers and the inclinations of the CoP were, even in the case of filing, the decisive factors. The new, professional CoP of Herat could count on a number of educated officers to do paperwork and the use of official paper had by 2010 become standard in this province.[119] In the provinces of the south, by contrast, nothing was being written down at all.[120]

By 2010, each zone had a filing and investigation officer. The head of zone would receive a copy of each case from the provinces and then forward it to CID in Kabul. At district level very few qualified staff would be available in any province, except in the cities, and typically no record or file keeping would take place. In the event of a criminal case occurring, a file would be opened and taken to the provincial centre, where it would be recorded. The transfer of criminal files to the provincial centre in the areas seriously affected by the insurgency would have to occur through an escorted convoy, which might explain why the police was often disinclined to file cases. The district police as a rule had no capacity to investigate because in practice they were fully dedicated to paramilitary tasks.[121] A copy of each file opened in the police stations was in principle kept in the MoI, as well in the Attorney General's office.[122] Because of weak capacity, even when the police did open a file after an arrest or a crime, they would rarely search for any evidence, making filing and reporting an exercise of limited use.[123]

EUPOL recognised that reported crime was low because of a failure to report by the police.[124] A reason for the frequent failure to file was the desire not to alienate communities and strongmen, particularly those better connected with the government:

The police and chief prosecutor of a rural district of Kabul told the Tufts team that they had identified accused murderers and knew where they lived. However, armed men aligned to local commanders have prevented the officials from making the arrests. The police and chief prosecutors stated that they were very concerned for their own physical safety, as well as the safety of their families, and expressed frustration at their inability to enforce the law.[125]

Therefore, only a portion of crimes were recorded. Some police officers believed that this might be even worse than not recording all because it alienated the communities which were worst connected to the authorities.[126] Reportedly this was a particularly severe problem in the south, where the strongmen and the communities were the most closely connected to Kabul and were in a position to get sympathetic CoPs appointed.[127] In this regard little changed between 2002 and 2010.[128]

Even in the MoI HQ, record keeping was still weak in 2010, despite the delivery of new technology and capacity building by mentors and advisers. A particular weakness in the reporting system was the absence of a mechanism in the MoI to consolidate the data received. In 2010, the National Police Command Centre used a spreadsheet to capture what was going on, with no ability to analyse trends and compile statistics: the capacity was limited to basic quantitative assessments.[129] What the MoI could then issue were daily incident reports, detailed but of dubious quality. Sometime they missed incidents, but it is difficult to say whether this is due to deliberate misreporting or simply due to lack of awareness by the police.[130]

As of 2010 it was however still clear that most of the time the police stations did not formalise reports on most incidents. If reporting at all, they would most of the time limit themselves to radio reports.[131]

From a certain perspective, inefficient record keeping (as opposed to no record keeping at all) might even have made the Afghan citizenry worse off, as the MoI was not able to manage the paperwork produced. The system was very centralised and the middle ranks did not want to take any responsibility, so in the words of one adviser to the MoI, 'Everything floats up to minister and deputies, but there is a bottleneck there'.[132] In other words, setting up a more sophisticated system of policing is not necessarily 'progress' if a government is not able to man it properly. The tendency to race ahead towards more complex systems can be the result of the ambitions of local politicians, but often is also the result of the influence of foreign advisers and donors. In the case of Afghanistan, the only attempt made to assess the capabilities and background of the MoI officer corps was made in 2006–7 by UNAMA, which collated a database of police officers. It does not appear that much use was made of that.

Pay and retention

Of all the changes planned or discussed at the MoI, one which was easy to implement once a political decision was taken was pay rises. While the Afghan government was never opposed to pay rises (as long as donors funded them), among donors there were perplexities concerning the long-term sustainabil-

INTERNAL ORGANISATION AND REORGANISATION

ity of any pay rise. Eventually such perplexities were overcome as the need to motivate the police to fight the insurgency became paramount. Table 6 shows the salary levels of the police and compares them to inflation levels. Clearly salaries rose faster than inflation, even if they might not have always risen fast enough to allow the average patrolman to support his family. Moreover by 2010 the policemen serving in the worst insurgency-affected areas saw they pay entitlement rise to at least $260 per month.[133] In the villages, the 2010 salary level was enough to provide somewhat more than a basic livelihood to a family. In the cities that might not have been the case. It was estimated by some that for a family to live in Kabul with a lower middle class standard of living $600 were necessary.[134]

Table 6: Police salaries and inflation.

	2000	2003	2004	2008	2009	2010
Basic pay US$	–	16.0	70.0	100.0	120.0	176.0
Inflation index—consumer prices	100.0	100.0	113.2	191.6	168.5	172.4
Salary increases year/2000 (%)	–	–	437.5	625	750	1100
Salary increases year/ previous year (%)	–	–	–	142.9	120.0	146.7

Source: MoI data; World Bank inflation statistics.

The increase in police salaries had a clear impact on the ability of the MoI to recruit and retain personnel (see Table 7). The decision to raise salaries fast was prompted by a dramatic crisis in recruitment in September–October 2009, when recruitment levels fell well below the force reproduction level and forced the recruitment centres to work at 25 per cent capacity.[135] The fact that at the same time the leave system was overhauled and made more friendly to the patrolmen also helped.[136] Even before the crisis, in late spring or summer of 2009, some provinces were struggling to meet their quota of recruits: in the south only 160 a month were forthcoming, instead of 400.[137] The resulting series of pay rises from late 2009 onwards resulted in significantly improved recruitment and retention rates, contributing to bringing the attrition rate to a somewhat lower rate of 17 per cent by mid-2010, although it bounced back to 23 per cent in early 2011.[138] This was the level experienced before the crisis: until 2009 the annual attrition rate had been of at least 20–25 per cent, imposing on the police high turnover rates, with negative implications for the accumulation of knowledge and professionalism. Indeed at the end of 2009, 78 per cent of serving policemen had not received any training yet, because most of those who had been trained had left the force.[139]

73

The only temporary improvement resulting from the pay rise suggests that this is not a long-term solution to the ills of the MoI.

The importance of salary rises should not be overestimated, moreover. Another important factor contributing to a (temporary) lower attrition rate was the decision to increase the force level dramatically. The high number of fresh recruits on new contracts made the number of outgoing policemen look small statistically. The attrition rates were also brought down by reducing the tempo of operations: ANCOP in particular, after having been overexploited to fill gaps in the line during 2009 and early 2010, was given more space to recover. Its attrition rates had risen to above 70 per cent yearly in spring 2010 and were down to around 60 per cent in November of that year.[140]

Although the salary increases could be seen as a success story, there were a lot of problems associated with them. The declining overall attrition rates hid the fact that in the provinces worst affected by the insurgency the rates were much higher. In Helmand in 2008–9 the overall attrition rate was 57 per cent, of which 12 per cent were due to casualties and 45 per cent to desertion or dismissal, usually because of drug abuse.[141] Most importantly there is no evidence that higher salaries impacted on the level of corruption (see section 6.3). Perhaps worse of all, despite the strong salary increases as of 2010 the MoI was still unable to attract high quality, educated recruits. The problem was compounded by the expansion of the force level, which was at odds with the desire to improve the quality of the police and change the model of policing.[142]

Pay increases were in any case a major factor in the increase in the size of the police force from 2008 onwards. The exact police force level has always been quite a mystery, even if in 2009–10 the ability to account for serving policemen improved significantly. Table 7 shows the expansion of the personnel charts and the few estimates available of the actual manpower of the police.[143]

Table 7: ANP personnel charts and manning surveys.

Year	2005	2006	2007	2008	2009	2010	2011
Estimated numbers	–	–	39,500	–	–	85,000	–
Personnel charts	62,000	64,100	75,400	82,000	96,800	122,000	134,000

Sources of manning estimates: UNAMA (2007), EUPOL (2010).

Education

The fact that the police was starved of educated recruits was reflected in the decision of NTM-A to overhaul its literacy programme in order to at least in part make up for this deficiency. Taken in late 2009, the decision implied the investment of major resources in the promotion of literacy within the police.

The effort was inevitably reliant on the availability of Afghan trainers and was hampered by the low numbers present for duty, as well as by the unwillingness of NTM-A to lengthen the army basic training programme beyond the established eight weeks.[144] Most courses were adapted to incorporate literacy training, which had been hitherto an optional evening class. The evening classes, which had started already in 2006, had been initially hailed as a great achievement, but by 2009 were admitted to have essentially failed to improve the situation significantly.[145] The 313 hours over a six-week course of basic training by 2010 incorporated 48 hours dedicated to literacy, compared to 44 hours dedicated to marksmanship.[146] By December 2010 there were over 40,000 police enrolled in the literacy courses and over 6,000 had graduated from the third grade course, the highest level of literacy being taught.[147] The pass rate at the first and third grade tests was 90 per cent.[148] The main problem was that such a level of literacy was only sufficient for patrolmen. In principle the set standards were that NCOs were required to have completed ninth-grade education and a nine-month attendance at the Police Academy; officers were required to have twelfth grade education and three years at the Police Academy.[149] In the presence of a shortage of candidates those not meeting the requirements were upgraded to NCO and even officer.[150]

For a long time the MoI was in denial about the extent of the problem and tried sometimes to manipulate the statistics, for example by pretending that a higher percentage of police was literate than was actually the case. Official statistics showing a 30 per cent literacy level in 2007 seem at odds with other evidence, including the estimates of the chief of NTM-A himself, other NATO trainers and anecdotal evidence from the training camps.[151] Even Minister Mohammadi in March 2011 admitted that almost 90 per cent of the police recruits were illiterate.[152] A test administered to new recruits in November 2010 showed that only 174 out of 7,771 were literate (2.24 per cent). Sample testing of elite ANCOP staff, supposed to be all literate, showed that just 5 per cent qualified as literate.[153] A late 2010 estimate put 11 per cent of patrolmen and 35 per cent of NCOs as being literate.[154] The implications of a largely illiterate police force for the implementation of the rule of law are obvious, as they are for counter-insurgency. Moreover, it should be considered that the level of education of those who were educated was not necessarily very high. Even ANP officers were reportedly often unable to read maps. Belatedly the MoI, perhaps because it was under pressure from NTM-A, gradually developed its own strategy to attract and retain qualified officers, culminating in the decision of the Afghan government to devise rules which could prevent private security companies from poaching the best police officers and then, later in 2010, by announcing the disbandment of private security companies altogether.[155] Even if the disbandment might have had other motivations and was in any case only partially followed up, it probably favoured a greater retention rate within the police.

The task of raising the literacy levels in the police was complicated by language issues. Illiterate or barely literate policemen often were not bilingual and as MoI forms were written in Dari, many NCOs in the south had to learn a new language (Dari) in order to be able to fulfil their tasks.[156]

Competence and motivation

As mentioned already, the combination of CSTC-A/NTM-A's efforts and direct support for the MoI combined to represent a substantial financial effort even before the beginning of the escalation in 2008, particularly when looked at from the Afghan perspective. Assessing the impact of training, mentoring, re-equipping and expenditure is not easy, as not all sectors of MoI activity have been open to exploration. In some cases there were evident signs of improvement compared to the situation described above. Traffic police, for example, had improved by 2007 compared to the early post-Taliban days, when militiamen armed with machine guns were standing in the street trying to regulate traffic. The effort to control the traffic was visible, although not always well managed. The initial almost complete tolerance of unregistered cars without number plates was abandoned, so that it was no longer 80 per cent of cars which could travel around without plates, although powerful people still managed to get away with it.[157]

CSTC-A developed its own assessment system, known as Capability Milestones, which however was flawed in a number of ways. The first flaw was that it was a self-assessment, therefore giving CSTC-A staff all the incentives to embellish the results. The second flaw was that it attributed too much importance to the presence of equipment and to the level of assigned personnel, as opposed to more substantial measurements of the capability of the units.[158]

At least the CM system measured the creation of basic capabilities in the different units of the MoI. Initially it was applied to police units in the field, but from 2010 it was also applied to the departments of the central MoI. They were almost all assessed at very low capability levels (see Table 8). Something like 25 plans under the responsibility of the Deputy CoS MoI were launched in 2010, attempting to address the reform of all the main departments and directorates of the MoI. Their implementation struggled somewhat, even when measured by the CM assessment system. Five of the twenty-five units covered by the plans had by October 2010 moved from three (work done for Afghans) to two (work done by Afghans): anti-corruption, strategic planning, policy, ABP and operational planning. Four other plans were expected to advance to two but did not: information and communications technology, parliamentary affairs, procurement and intelligence.[159]

Even when the police could react to challenges, they were clumsy in their operations. Kandahar's residents, for example, reportedly complained that on the occasion of a terrorist attack on 12 February 2011 the police blocked the city bazaar entirely for eight hours, causing losses of millions of US$, in order to deal with just four attackers. Such an operation was greeted as a great success by the MoI, even if the fighting left sixty people killed or injured.[160] ISAF and the MoI often tried to portray the police as more effective and capable

INTERNAL ORGANISATION AND REORGANISATION

than it was, hiding the intervention of ISAF units to support it. This was in the case of the 2011 attack against the Intercontinental Hotel, when NATO officials praised the police for having contained and subdued the attackers, while intelligence officials noted that the police guarding the hotel failed to respond initially to the terrorists attacking the hotel and Afghan police officers acknowledged that without a NATO helicopter and New Zealand Special Forces they could not have coped with the terrorists.[161]

Table 8: CM ratings of MoI departments, beginning of 2010.

	Beg. 2010	End 2011
Public affairs	3	2A
Anti-corruption	3	2B
Legal affairs	3	3
Intelligence	3	3
Counter-narcotics	3	3
Strategic partnering	3	2B
Policy development		2A
Force management	3	3
Personnel management	3	2A
Logistics		3
Finance and budget	3	3
Facilities and installation	4	4
Surgeon medical	3	2B
Information, communications and technology	3	3
Training	3	3
Acquisition and procurement	3	3
Civil service		n/a
AUP		3
ABP	3	2B
Anti-crime	3	2B
ANCOP		3
APPF		4
ALP		4
Operational planning	3	2A
Force readiness	3	3
Public affairs	3	–
Inspector General	2	–

Source: ISAF.

Competence and motivation should not be confused. Even when competence was low, Afghanistan's police at times displayed surprising levels of motivation, at the individual level if not as a force. One MoI advisor noted how some policemen intercepted suicide bombers at their own risk, in some case getting killed in the effort.[162]

Table 9: CM assessment of MoI field units, by number of units.

April 2008				
	CM1	CM2	CM3	CM4
AUP	0	6	6	296
ABP	0	0	0	33
ANCOP	0	6	2	2
Counter-narcotics	0	0	10	3
Total	0	12	18	334
April 2010				
Total	15	38	52	25

Source: NTM-A.

By and large, however, it would be far-fetched to describe Afghanistan's police as a strongly motivated force. Mostly the police showed little motivation to fight the insurgents, at least in the perception of NATO personnel.[163] In fact even Minister Mohammadi stated in March 2011 that:

Undoubtedly, the police and the army do not have motivation. Motivation that we had during jihad, we defended [our country] and we had very strong motivation. Regrettably, they [police and army] do not have it.[164]

When the police showed motivation, it was rarely out of loyalty to the government; personal desires of revenge were a main source of motivation.[165] Col. Razzaq of the Border Police in Spin Boldak, famous for his lust for fighting the Taliban, had family members killed by the Taliban.[166] It was in fact quite common for people to join the police in the south in order to obtain protection against the Taliban.[167] Motivation was not favoured by the ever growing gap between the top ranks of the MoI and the rank and file, with the former ordering food from the Intercontinental Hotel and the patrolmen not being taken care of.[168]

Corruption

The corruption landscape

The fight against corruption represents another useful benchmark in the development of the MoI as an institution, because of the character of the corruption emergency and its increasingly pervasive spread within the MoI from

INTERNAL ORGANISATION AND REORGANISATION

2001 onwards. As Afghanistan became one of the most corrupt countries in the world, pressure from the Afghan public and foreign donors to do something about it started mounting. Apart from being widespread, corruption has been making the Afghan policing system dysfunctional, negatively affecting the morale of the police and the quality of the leadership. Many mentors believed that corruption was sabotaging all their efforts to develop the police. The misuse or diversion of personnel became common practice, further reducing the capacity of an already weak system.[169]

Evidence of the police's involvement in corruption is quite overwhelming. In fact even official statistics point in this direction. The number of cases opened against policemen increased over time quite dramatically. In 2002, 376 policemen were involved in 269 cases while in 2008 there were 2,676 such cases, involving 6,509 policemen. Of these, 323 policemen were being brought to the courts for cases of criminal conduct, including harassment and corruption.[170] During the first three months of 2009, 1,231 cases were filed involving 2,526 policemen. In total, until the first quarter of 1388 (2009–10), 18,276 police personnel were involved in 10,480 cases, according to the Attorney General's office, of which thirty were generals.[171] Having such a large proportion of the police force involved in cases of misconduct is remarkable, particularly since it is unlikely that the authorities might have been able to identify all the cases of misconduct occurring. A survey carried out by UNAMA in 2007 found a negative record for 38 per cent of the 2,464 police officers included in it.[172] Clearly the cases which were investigated were only a portion of what actually occurred although mentors and trainers were aware of the actual extent of the problem.[173] The fact that extortion and misconduct were still continuing on a large scale in 2010 is the best indication that only a minority of cases were being uncovered or followed up. Reports of complaints by drivers and passengers concerning the behaviour of police at check-posts on the highways remained very common.[174]

The corruption became so pervasive that in Dari-speaking provinces police posts are referred to as *sofreh*, a Dari word which refers to the tablecloth around which family members, led by the patriarch, eat their daily meals. This was to emphasise the role of these posts as a source of *peyda* (numerous types of informal income) and the role of the patron in securing them for his dependents/clients. Police posts, or *sofreh*, are ranked according to their *peyda*—opportunities for kidnapping for ransom and taxing brothels, bandits and other criminal networks. 'The more powerful your patron is, the more lucrative *sofreh* he can secure for you', stated a former militia commander who served as a police officer, 'and you are also expected to pay him more money for securing the job for you'.[175]

The behaviour of Afghanistan's police and the attitude of the population towards them has been the object of extensive opinion-gathering efforts. Integrity Watch, Asia Foundation, UNDP, ISAF and others have all tried their hands at it. The problems with surveys in countries characterised by an authoritarian political culture and even more so when such countries are at war is that they tend not to be reliable, first, because of the difficulty to access all parts

79

of the country and second, because when asked direct questions about state and government people tend to give positive answers regardless. This is well borne out by the surveying of public opinion in Helmand province, paid for by the British government. Even in districts where the government had no presence whatsoever the inhabitants commented favourably on government activities (including the police), with approval rates of around 70 per cent.[176]

Other polls typically showed countrywide approval rates of the police close to 80 per cent, although with significant variations between regions (typically the southern police doing worst). However, when asked more direct questions about the behaviour of the police, the interviewees reported with percentages as high as 60 per cent that they were aware of police corruption. In 2010 a survey showed some improvement in the perception of the police, with 24 per cent indicating a decrease in corruption and 8 per cent an increase, perhaps due to a reduction in the share of population directly affected by criminal acts, but also indicated by an increase in ethnic or tribal favouritism by the police. A quarter of the respondents indicated that they had seen police using narcotics and almost a fifth had seen police being involved in narco-trafficking. The same survey indicated that just 18 per cent of the respondents lived more than an hour away from a police station, which seems odd when the location of police stations relative to the population is considered (see Map 3).[177] The Integrity Watch survey indicated that 24 per cent of the households had no access to the police, whatever that meant. Fourteen per cent of the households surveyed reported that they faced police corruption in the past twelve months, mostly over moral crimes such as rape, adultery and use of alcohol and drugs, as well as traffic-related issues.[178] The UNODC survey instead showed a much higher percentage of respondents indicating that they had paid a bribe to police officers over the previous twelve months, 25 per cent, although the bribes were on average small in comparison to those paid to customs officers, officials, prosecutors and judges.[179]

Some police commanders themselves believed that much criminal activity was taking place with the complicity of the police. In February 2011 the Head of Kabul's CDI even went public accusing his subordinates of being complicit with thieves and threatened them with arrest every time that the police failed to prevent criminal acts from being carried out successfully when they had the capacity to do so.[180]

Box 1 contains a far-from-inclusive list of arrests of police officers made public by the authorities: it gives a sense of what type of acts of corruption were being committed. Box 2 reflects allegations made by a variety of more or less authoritative sources.

Box 1: Known episodes of policemen arrested for corruption.

In 2005 the CoP, Khan Mohammed, allegedly distributed some of the vehicles which were meant for the districts to his own friends and relatives and PRT had to replace the vehicles;[181]

INTERNAL ORGANISATION AND REORGANISATION

Three policemen were arrested for sexually assaulting a young girl in western Afghanistan in July 2005;[182]

In August 2006 police from Kabul had to replace highway police on the highway to Jalalabad (Sarobi) because of reports of extortion by the highway policemen;[183]

Two policemen were arrested in Kabul in November 2006 for extorting money from taxi drivers;[184]

The commander of the first brigade of the border forces was arrested in January 2007 on accusations of embezzlement;[185]

Seventy policemen were arrested in 2007 in the west for extorting money from drivers;[186]

The CoP of Wardak was sacked in 2007 under the accusation of pocketing the salaries of his patrolmen;[187]

'A number of policemen' arrested in Balkh in August 2007 for transporting illegal weapons;[188]

Ten counter-narcotics police officers were detained for embezzling salaries and expenses in November 2007;[189]

Ten policemen were arrested in Kandahar (Daman) in November 2007 as a result of a public complaints about robbing and illegal taxation;[190]

Three policemen were arrested in Kabul for involvement in robberies in January 2007;[191]

Twenty policemen were arrested on charges of kidnapping and extorting money in Farah in June 2007;[192]

Three policemen were sentenced in Kandahar for raping father and son in Dand in February 2008; the victims reported to Kandahar HQ and the policemen responsible were immediately arrested;[193]

200 policemen were sacked in March 2008 in Kandahar for extorting money from drivers;[194]

Thirty-five policemen were suspended in June 2008 for involvement in the kidnapping of drivers on the Herat–Kandahar highway;[195]

Seventy-nine policemen were suspended in Farah for extorting money on the highway in August 2008;[196]

Four policemen were arrested in Herat in November 2008 for burglaries and extortion;[197]

A police officer and five of his subordinates were jailed in November 2008 for selling a police vehicle;[198]

Fifty policemen were sacked in Herat in July 2010 for taking money from drivers on the highway, following complaints by the public;[199]

In January 2011 drivers using the Kandahar–Herat road complained about extortion by the police, at the rate of 200–300 Afghanis per checkpost;[200]

The commander of the border police in the western region went on trial in August 2010;[201]

The head of Administration Department Bayani was accused of stealing 350,000 Afs from Zabul police salaries, and was sentenced to five years in absentia;[202]

The CoP of Kunar province was accused of corruption, embezzlement and bribery (he was a law graduate);[203]

Gen Malham Nurzai, commander of police in western zone, was arrested and accused of cooperating with drug smugglers in June 2010;[204]

Gen Wasim, the head of the recruiting department of Interior Ministry, was detained in July 2010 for abuse of power;[205]

The acting police chief of Gereshk District of Helmand province was sentenced to sixteen years' imprisonment for abuse of power in 2010;[206]

The director of security in Sayed Abad District of Wardak province was sentenced to five years' imprisonment for providing facilities to drug traffickers in 2010;[207]

Six police officers were arrested between February and March 2001 and accused of smuggling narcotics in Nimruz province.[208]

Box 2: Typical allegations of police corruption and misbehaviour.

The people of Girishk district (Helmand) complained in February 2011 that the police posted at the highway road blocks were taking money from travellers and even accused them of one murder; over twenty policemen were then reported to the prosecutor;[209]

The District governor of Sangin said, 'The CoP is the real problem. He himself is a criminal and a murderer—he killed a fourteen-year-old boy. But I cannot control him'.[210]

A Sangin elder said, 'The police have beaten many people in this town. They have also taken money from them. There is nothing we can do to stop them…'[211]

British army officer said that the 'majority of ANP were actually a corrupt ragtag collection to tribal militiamen who owed their allegiance to their clan chiefs'.[212]

A British soldier in Maywand district said, 'Every village we went into, they complained to us'. The locals pleaded 'to stop the ANP coming here, saying "they beat us up and they steal our money"'.[213]

'There were policemen in Zabul, but like Afghan policemen everywhere in the region they were often feared and despised. Many lawmen were drugged-off predators, extorting 'taxes' at roadblocks, carrying off any young man or woman, some of them no more than children, who took their fancy'.[214]

British army officer: 'Intelligence and comments from the locals had definitely made me look on the ANP in a different light. In all areas in the Helmand province the ANP had ruled under their own iron fist and set of rules: often doing their own thing, causing a lot of upset in the towns'.[215]

> 'The ANP had a reputation among much of the local population for abusing the people they were supposed to protect. They were notorious for stealing, extortion and the molestation of juveniles'.[216]
>
> 'Residents of Pesta Mazar village of Sayad District in northern Sar-e Pol Province say they have moved to the centre of the district because of police misbehaviour. [...] [They] say a local police commander named Sayed Maruf has forced them to pay Ushr [10 per cent Islamic levy on production] and Zakat [one-fortieth of one's income]. [...]
>
> [Correspondent] The head of the provincial council of Sar-e Pol Province confirms claims by local residents of Pesta Mazar village and say that tens of local residents have so far complained about misbehaviour of a local police commander, but they have been threatened by local security officials and their voices have not been heard. [...]
>
> [Mohammad Aref Sharifi, captioned as the head of the provincial council of Sar-e Pol Province] Provincial security officials have failed to address the problems of local residents. In fact, instead of listening to their problems, they have imprisoned four local residents for four days now who had come to lodge a complaint and ask for justice.'[217]

Corruption in 2010 was so widespread that even foreign embassy staff were being asked for money in order to carry out investigations.[218] The Border Police were generally recognised as a hotbed of corruption. In Spin Boldak the Border Police was reported to be:

so involved in smuggling that the duties of several commanders who frequented the showroom [...] seemed to consist entirely of brokering goods. [...] Their days were spent sizing up cars, gossiping on the showroom's veranda over cups of chai, and sealing deals. Toward the end of each afternoon, a group of boys would arrive with various permission chits, fake registration documents, and receipts for the petrol taxes paid to Razik's force, and the boys and the commanders would round up a convoy of vehicles destined for Quetta.[219]

Even in cities, allegations of links between members of the police and criminal gangs were common and were unofficially acknowledged even by senior officials in the MoI.[220] They admitted off the record that policemen often facilitated in particular kidnappings, which for a period were happening even in full daylight in the centre of Kabul or Herat, both heavily policed areas.[221]

Bribes to release criminals and the embezzlement of prizes for patrolmen were also reportedly common occurrences.[222] In 2010 US Marines lawyers estimated that battalions sent forward sixty detainees for long-term imprisonment monthly, but after passing through four levels of Afghan police only 10 per cent were still getting to prison, the rest having been released, typically after payment of bribes.[223]

The limited supplies provided an incentive for petty corruption: in Herat the typical supply of fuel lasted only the first ten days of a month, forcing the police to tax the population in order to be able to continue patrols. The situation was compounded by the fact that much fuel was embezzled by police officers: in Herat in 2008 the Attorney General was investigating the CoP for the disappearance of 20,000 litres.[224]

One of the worst examples of corruption, spreading to the point where recovery was judged hopeless, was the Highway Police, which was disbanded in mid-2006 under pressure from the donors. The personnel were supposed to be redeployed in less profitable tasks but many refused, deserting with uniforms, weapons and equipment.[225] The check-posts system became a form of perversion, with or without Highway Police, as the number of posts multiplied, apparently with no other purpose than to tax drivers. On Highway 1 (Kandahar–Kabul) sixty-nine check posts existed in 2009.[226] In 2008 the going 'rates' charged to drivers ranged between 20–2,000 Afs, depending on the load and the location.[227] Gathering information on this type of corruption is relatively easy because a particular category of people is affected: truck drivers. For this reason is has been relatively easy to carry out a specific case study, which follows.

Case study: the ANP and illegal tolls

In order to gain insight into the extent to which the police engage in extortion and which factors could impact police accountability, a study of illegal police tolls along the ring road was conducted in Herat, Kabul and Mazar-e-Sharif during November 2010 and March 2011. The ring road starts at the Iranian border in the west of Herat, and passing through southern, eastern and northern provinces, connects the major provinces of the country. The interviews were conducted with eighteen truck and bus drivers who worked along the ring road. The accuracy of the information provided by truckers was cross-checked with another six interviews with police officials and traders who sent goods along the ring road.

The survey showed that the extent to which the police engage in extortion is inversely correlated with the scope of oversight over the police: the less effective the oversight of the police, the more extortion the police engage in. In other words, the oversight of the police increases the cost of extortion from the population and, thus, reduces its scope. For the sake of systematic study of the level of extortion and its relation to oversight, this section examines how much, in the form of illegal tolls, the police collect from truck and bus drivers who travel along the ring road. In general, two factors indicate the amount of illegal tolls: (1) the spatial distance from the provincial centres and districts where major government institutions are located; and (2) the likelihood of external oversight. The further away from the provincial centres the police are, the larger tolls they collect from truckers and the more abusive they are. Since the major government and police institutions—including the Provincial Police Headquarters and the Regional Police Headquarters—are based in provincial centres, as the distance from the provincial centres

INTERNAL ORGANISATION AND REORGANISATION

increases, the less likely are these two institutions to patrol the roads and oversee the police substations along the road. This allows the police substations in remote areas to extract more from truckers. The tendency of the police to collect tolls in distant places, however, is dramatically mitigated as the likelihood of external oversight, particularly by the ANA, increases.

Table 10 shows the frequency and amount of illegal tolls collected by the police along the ring road. As indicated in the table, the amount of illegal tolls collected along the road varies substantially. The first interval of the road starts from the Iranian border in the western province of Herat. The police in this province are overseen by the Provincial as well as Regional Police Headquarters. Both of these organisations send inspecting teams to the police stations and substations.[228] With this level of oversight, the police check points collect 20 Afs from truckers. It must be mentioned, however, that 20 Afs is collected only from truckers carrying legal goods and those who have not violated laws and regulations. If trucks carry smuggled goods—narcotics or legal goods which have not been taxed by the Customs—the police would charge much higher tolls. In addition, trucks are formally allowed to commute inside the city only from 9pm until 5am in order to reduce traffic congestion. If truckers commute during the prohibited hours, they would have to pay on average 150 Afs at each police substation.[229]

From Herat to Farahrud, which is a major town in Farah province, the police charge truckers 20 Afs only. Along this interval, there are twelve police substations which are part of the Shindand Police Headquarters (Shindand Garnaziyun) but under the jurisdiction of the Regional Police Headquarters based in Herat. The random visits by inspecting teams from the Regional Police Headquarters limits the freedom of these police substations to engage in more extortion from truckers. From Farahrud to Delaram, truckers pay very high tolls (80–150 Afs) and are often subject to predatory activities and abuses by the police. The police along this route are under the jurisdiction of Delaram Police Headquarters. They are monitored only by their own supervisors in the Delaram Police Headquarters and not by the Regional Police. Truckers suspect collusion among the police substations and their supervisors since frequent complaints by truckers to the Delaram Police Headquarters have not reduced the predatory activities of the police. The only time when the police in this area stop extorting from truckers is when the ANA patrols the road.[230]

An anecdote by a trucker depicts the importance of this external oversight:

When the National Army cars appear on the road, the police stop harassing truckers and demanding money. In many instances, I was stopped by the National Army patrols and asked whether the prior police substation had forced me to give them money. I told them that I was abused and forced to pay. Later I heard from other truckers that the police personnel in that substation were punished by the National Army and were disarmed. The police do fear the National Army and do not ask for money when they hear that the National Army patrols the road.[231]

Table 10: Illegal tolls collected by the police along the ring road and the level of oversight.

Area	Distance in kilometres	Frequency of illegal tolls collected in this interval	Amount collected at each checkpoint	Level of supervision and oversight	Collection of tolls from buses	Oversight organisation
Iranian border to Herat City	120	2	50 Afs	Medium	No	Border Police
Herat City	20	1	20 Afs	Medium	No	1. Herat Provincial Police 2. Regional Police
Herat City to Frahrud (Farah Province)	295	12	20 Afs	Medium	No	1. Shindand Police Headquarter (Graniziyun) 2. Western Regional Police.
Frahrud to Delaram (Nimruz Province)	110	17	80–150 Afs	Low	No	Delaram Police Headquarter (Garniziyun)
Delaram to Gereshk (Hilmand Province)	110	0	0	High	No	Afghan National Army
Gereshk to Kandahar	115	2 Within Gereshk town only	100 Afs	High	No	1. Afghan National Army 2. Provincial Police (within the towns)
Kandahar to Ghazni	405	2 Within Kandahar and Ghallat towns only	150 Afs	High	No	1. Afghan National Army 2. Provincial Police (within the towns)

INTERNAL ORGANISATION AND REORGANISATION

Route					
Ghazni to Kabul	120	4 within district centres only	100 Afs	High	No	1. Afghan National Army 2. Provincial Police (within the towns)
Kabul to Mazar-e-Sharif	440	0	0	Very high	No	1. Eastern and Northern Regional Police 2. Provincial Police Departments
Mazar-e-Sharif to Ghormach (Fryab Province)	455	20	0	High	No	1. Northern Regional Police 2. Provincial Police Departments
Gormach to Ghala Naw (Badghis Province)	170	12	500 Afs	Very low	Yes	Provincial Police Departments
Ghala Naw to Herat	155	5	50 Afs	Medium	No	Provincial Police Departments

Source: Interviews with truck drivers, merchants and police officers, Herat, Mazar-e-Sharif and Kabul: November 2010 and March 2011.

From Delaram to Gereshk, the road is under the control of the National Army. While along the other parts of the ring road police cars may establish temporary checkpoints and collect illegal tolls from truckers in addition to what is collected by stationary police substations, there are rarely such temporary checkpoints between Delaram and Gereshk. The control of the National Army over this part of the road means that truckers do not pay any tolls. The National Army neither collects tolls from truckers nor allows the police to establish temporary checkpoints and collect money from truckers.[232]

From Gereshk to Kabul, the road is controlled by the ANA with the exception of the segments which pass through district or provincial centres, which are controlled by the relevant district or provincial police. No illegal tolls are collected at the parts controlled by the army while, in the segments passing through towns and controlled by the police, tolls are collected from trucks.[233] The interesting case is the interval between Mazar-e-Sharif and Kabul, which is controlled by the police: nevertheless, no illegal tolls are collected. A key feature of this interval is the security of this segment of the road due to the low degree of insurgent activities. With the relative security of this interval, there is heavier traffic, and government officials and police officers who want to travel between Mazar-e-Sharif and Kabul often travel by car while those going to Kandahar or Herat have to fly. The heavy traffic and frequent commute of government officials and police officers along this section of road appear therefore to function as a strong check against the predatory acts of the police and prevent them from collecting illegal tolls.[234]

In contrast, the interval from Ghormach to Qala-i Naw is characterised by the lowest oversight, the largest illegal tolls, and the most predatory activities by the police. This segment of the ring road is unpaved and runs through mountains and rough terrain. Due to the difficulty of travel here, the police in this area receive their supplies every few months and are not subject to any regular oversight.[235] As a result, the police are able to collect the highest toll from truckers: 500 Afs. In addition, this is the only interval of the road on which the police collect tolls from buses which carry passengers. At other intervals, as the police do not want to deal with the protests of passengers (which is often a result of collecting illegal tolls, as discussed below), they do not stop buses. Along the Ghormach-Qala Naw interval, however, the remoteness of this region and absence of oversight allows the police to extort even from buses.[236]

In general, illegal tolls often involve some degree of coercion and bargaining between drivers and the police. Drivers want to avoid paying the illegal tolls. The police are, however, able to collect them by threatening that if the driver does not pay the toll, he will have to wait until the police searches the entire truck, which requires unloading the cargo.[237] In addition, many drivers reported the use of force by the police in order to collect the toll. For instance, many truck drivers reported that at police checkpoints between Farahrud and Delaram the police had beaten up and threatened to shoot truck drivers who refused to pay the illegal tolls.[238] With regard to tolls from buses

INTERNAL ORGANISATION AND REORGANISATION

along the Ghormach–Ghala Naw interval, the police stopped the buses and if the driver did not pay the toll, the police would not allow the bus to leave that checkpoint. As the passengers become impatient, they would insist that the driver pay the toll so that they did not have to wait on the road. Many drivers stated that they often try to refrain from paying these tolls or bargain with the police to pay smaller tolls, but in the end they would have to pay.[239]

The fear of the police for the ANA arises from the institutional and operational strength of the army. Historically, the army has been a stronger and more influential institution than the police in Afghanistan. In addition, the army is better equipped and has more firepower. On many occasions, upon drivers' complaints, army personnel have beaten up and disarmed the police who were accused of collecting illegal tolls.[240]

As the distance from the major towns increases, the police enjoy more freedom to engage in extortion. This freedom is, however, constrained when there is external oversight either by the ANA, other government officials or by the police units other than the immediate supervisors of the local police. In places with effective oversight, police extortion is limited while in remote places the police become more predatory.

Counter-narcotics

Collaboration with drug smugglers and direct involvement in the drug trade has probably been the most destabilising form of corruption since 2001, as well as one of the most difficult and dangerous to document. In fact the involvement of officials of the MoI in the drug trade might have helped the consolidation of what was a very fragmented sector of activity into an oligopoly dominated by a few major players, by collaborating with the wealthiest of them.

The trafficking networks that move opium from the north to the south also require the protection of provincial officials and CoPs in strategic provinces. In one important northern province, it is reported that the CoP has for the last number of years been appointed from Kandahar. An exasperated local law enforcement official reported that 'most of the "businessmen" who come from Kandahar stay with the CoP; at one point one of the biggest traffickers was living with the CoP.[241]

Sometimes, even clashes between police and army over the control of seized drugs were reported.[242] According to press reports, Afghan officials have admitted in the past that up to 80 per cent of police staff might be benefiting from involvement in the drug trade in some regions. Evidence exists, including in the form of taped conversations, that the border police is particularly deeply involved. Positions in sensitive places for drug smuggling have been for sale for some time, sometimes for hundreds of thousands of dollars even at the district level. The mentors talk of a 'feudal system of corruption' beginning at the top, where every member has to pay his superior and in turn request payments from his subordinates.[243]

The system appears to have been in decline during Atmar's tenure, but started recovering after his departure as vetting and anti-corruption efforts weakened.[244] The practice of selling posts and then creating 'pyramids of payments' was seen by many as the root of most corruption, although NTM-A believed that the extent to which posts are sold might have been overestimated.[245] On top of that, policemen had to pay unofficial fees for anything they needed: US$ 10 to the bank which transferred salaries, US$ 10 to the officer… Taxi drivers charged police officers more because of the risk involved in carrying them.[246]

The CoP of Badakhshan admitted in 2006 that 40–50 per cent of his policemen were involved in the drug trade and alleged that they were protected by powerful people within the MoI itself. The chief of counter-narcotics even resigned in protest at the lack of support from Kabul.[247] In Balkh in 2004 a major showdown took place between the CoP Khakrizwal and the governor, Atta Mohammed Noor, who accused each other of involvement in the drug trade.[248] In some cases in southern Afghanistan the police were even found to be growing opium poppies inside the compound of their station.[249] Colonel Razzaq of the border police in Spin Boldak was also often accused of involvement in the smuggling of narcotics.[250]

Police officers in the field often complained about the fact that arrested drug smugglers were being freed shortly after having been arrested, allegedly because of the corruption of judges. Often it was also alleged that Deputy Minister for Counter-Narcotics Daud (2005–10) was involved in the narco-traffic through one of his brothers. In 2005 a drug trafficker was caught by the police carrying a letter of protection by Daud, according to newspaper reports. He later tried to have him released from prison, before deciding to support the prosecution. The trafficker then managed to get transferred to a prison in Helmand, where he bought his freedom with a bribe. Shortly afterwards, Gen. Daud's bodyguards intervened to free another trafficker who had been stopped by the counter-narcotics police. An officer of the Counter-narcotics department accused Daud in 2005 of involvement in drug smuggling, before being arrested and then demoted. Daud appears however to have reduced his involvement in the drug trade after 2005, according to western officials.[251]

The chief of the border police in Nangarhar, Haji Zahir, was removed because of allegations of narcotics smuggling but refused to leave the job: a member of the powerful Arsala family, he was strongly supported politically and was reappointed to the border police.[252] Mutalleb Beg, CoP of Takhar in 2003, was sacked after his vehicle was found loaded with heroin in Salang but after intensive lobbying in Kabul, he was rewarded with the even more important post of CoP of Kunduz, where he soon faced new accusations of involvement in the smuggling of narcotics. In exchange he dropped his earlier support for Gen. Dostum's Junbesh party and switched his support to the central government.[253]

The few police officers who tried to fight the traffic found themselves isolated: the smugglers had easy access to the phone numbers of counter-narcotics officers, who were frequently threatened by phone.[254] In Takhar, one officer who had reported the provincial CoP to the MoI in 2006 for using police vehicles to move heroin along the main highway was then arrested and accused of having himself smuggled heroin; the officer was sentenced to seven years, while the CoP was not even prosecuted.[255]

Under international pressure, the counter-narcotics police had to implement eradication in very insecure areas at times: in 2007–8 100 members of the counter-narcotics department have been killed.[256] DEA officials believed that the counter-narcotics police was making some progress, such as:

the National Interdiction Unit's ability to conduct smaller ground-based interdiction operations on its own, the Sensitive Investigative Unit's ability to conduct simple counternarcotics investigations, and the execution of 180 wiretaps by the Technical Investigation Unit between October 2008 and June 2009, [...] this would not have been possible two years ago.[257]

In reality, it is difficult to assess the activities of the counter-narcotics police because it is never a matter of the police as a bloc fighting or collaborating with a single network of smugglers. Multiple, rival networks exist as well as a multitude of individual farmers and individual smugglers. A police officer might well be connected to a network and fight against another one. Typically, small smugglers without connections to the authorities are the ones who risk being apprehended. Therefore, even a corrupt counter-narcotics police officer might be happy to send his patrolmen against a particular smuggler, as he could in fact be weakening the competition. The farmers resist eradication of their fields, even if the remaining 90 per cent or so of the poppy-growing fields remain untouched. However, western officials who were involved with the counter-narcotics police gained the impression that the top positions within the force were held by individuals who were not corrupt. Although it proved impossible to staff the counter-narcotics police exclusively with professionals, as some western embassies would have liked, by 2007–8 serious efforts to clean up the force were being enacted: all in all it was much less corrupt than the ABP.[258] The attrition rate was lower, an indicator of better officering and better training.[259] The ABP, however, potentially was to play a much greater role in fighting the traffic: if it did not it was because of the spread of corruption within it. The ABP leadership at the zone level was often quite shameless in its efforts to protect corrupt individuals within the force and even when battalion commanders were removed on evidence of corruption, the tendency was to reassign them to other tasks. Even in the top levels of the MoI there was repeated resistance to removing officers accused by ISAF of corruption and even of cooperation with the insurgents.[260]

Ghost police

The inability of the MoI in the early years to get a precise picture of its staffing levels and to exercise supervision encouraged officers to abuse their position and inflate the ranks of their units with non-existing policemen, in order to cash salaries and allowances. The system of salary payment until the changes sponsored by the LOFTA fund (see above) involved the CoP collecting cash from the Ministry of Finance (MoF) representative and then paying his men. The MoF representative (mustufi) was supposed to supervise the CoP, but allegedly many mustufis were involved in the corruption.[261] Partial evidence collected in the provinces suggests that the number of police actually present for duty in the districts might have been as low as half or a third or even a tenth of the payroll in the most neglected ones but the provincial centres were usually better staffed.[262]

According to the head of the security department of police of Kandahar, the situation was worse in the districts closer to the border and far from the PRT and the Coalition, that is in the absence of any scrutiny or supervision.[263]

The following is a typical snapshot of ghost policing from Herat in December 2004:

>Officers: 33 of 784 missing;
>NCOs: 27 of 215 missing;
>Patrolmen: 129 of 1,638 missing;
>Administration: 11 of 21 missing;
>Servants: 61 of 137 missing.[264]

In some extreme cases, such as Kalafghan of Takhar in 2003, only three policemen were present for duty on the day of inspection, a rate of 5 per cent. In some provinces it was common for the few police who did go to work to turn up at work late in the morning and leave before evening. Some proactive professional officers from an earlier time (2003–4) tried to bring some order to the system by inspecting the districts. Some district CoPs were sacked for misappropriation of funds and some improvement occurred as the CoPs started keeping a higher number of active officers.[265]

The simple transfer of the responsibility for paying the police from the MoI to the MoF in 2003 and the related checks carried out by the MoF led to a fall of 20,000 in the payroll, from 72,000 to 52,000.[266] However, corrupt networks within the MoI rapidly adapted to the increased MoF supervision and found other ways to divert money. The problem of ghost policing was only temporarily reduced (see also Table 7).

The real turning point was, however, the introduction from 2008 of a system of electronic tracking and transfer of payments within the MoI. Although the system quickly reached almost 80 per cent of the police force, it remained dependent on LOFTA (UNDP) assistance for its functioning, particularly as far as it pertained to functions such as the verification and adjustment of transactions and financial data correspondence between MoI/MoF/commercial banks. Receiving reports from some of the most difficult provinces such as Khost, Zabul, Ghazni, Paktia, Faryab, Uruzgan, Kandahar, Daikundi and Nuristan proved difficult and the MoI had to insist heavily that the CoPs reported regularly. As a result, the problem was gradually reduced. Problems in reconciling data between databases, however, persisted. The MoI was not always fully cooperative, for example as it transferred trained LOFTA staff to other tasks without consultation. UNDP believed that officials in MoI perceived the new system as eroding their powerbase.[267] The rest (20 per cent) of the money was paid through mixed commission travelling to the districts.[268]

While it seemed clear that the new system of management and transfer of payment was reducing the problem of ghost police in the ranks, donor sources believed that the actual number of police was still falling significantly short of the theoretical payroll: perhaps by 30,000–40,000 out of a total of 122,000, compared to 36,000 out of a total of 96,000 in autumn 2009. Some local attempts to assess the actual strength of police units showed absence rates of 20–25 per cent.[269] NTM-A sources also agreed that the issue of ghost police, although reduced, was still a significant problem. Indeed Minister Mohammadi started a tour of provincial inspections just after his appointment (2010), also in order to verify if the police were actually getting paid.[270] A major problem in eliminating the ghost police was that because of the high attrition rate, it was difficult to ensure that the CoPs effectively reported attrition as quickly as they should, rather than pocket the salaries of the absentees.[271]

There were also allegations of corruption among the bank officials who cooperated with MoI officers in skewing the salaries.[272] In general, the fact that financial management was fully computerised by 2010 allowed the MoF to have a better idea of what was being spent and how.[273] Salaries aside, at the provincial level the MoI remained autonomous in how it spent money, except that it had to deal with a single MoF officer, without the ability to track expenditure.[274] Moreover, the internal financial system of the MoI was still the same old one of the 1980s, with no standard financial procedure and little transparency, which left a lot of room for misuse. The bureaucratic character of the system, with many signatures needed for even the most basic procurement, was also very cumbersome. The MoI lacked the appropriate civilian expertise to run a sophisticated financial management system, nor was the leadership keen to bring in such expertise, even as of 2011. Persistent mentoring at least enabled Afghan officials by 2011 to prepare the MoI budget on their own, in contrast to what was happening five years earlier, when the budget was entirely the work of foreign advisers.[275]

Fighting corruption

The rising number of policemen investigated for misbehaviour (see section 6.3.1) suggests that some effort to deal with corruption must have been underway, particularly by 2009–10. The issue in fact was on the agenda of MoI reform for a long time. The MoI decided around 2004 to create a professional standards unit in charge of fighting corruption and misbehaviour. During 2005, twenty-eight police officers were trained to staff internal affairs units in the five provincial zones, but then the training programme stopped and province-level units were not created.[276] It is not even clear that the zone-level units were effectively created.[277] Even when punishment was inflicted, typically it was confined to bad duties or transfer to a 'bad' province.[278] In fact investigation of police misbehaviour occurred rarely as most of the time it was a matter of checking with the accused for some explanation.[279]

The MoI internal affairs department (Inspector General's Office) was first strengthened in 2008, when sections were established in each of the six regional commands. Their functionality seems to have been limited, however. For example, a police officer serving at that time in Wardak reported cases of corruption and abuse by the police to internal affairs, but the delegation which collected the information did not take any action.[280] In fact a substantial number of investigations resulted from internal affairs' efforts, but they mostly targeted low-ranking policemen rather than senior officials.[281]

In part to address such limitations and under instruction from Minister Atmar (2008–10), the office established in 2010 a commission to inspect the provinces, particularly focusing on logistics. Moreover, the anti-corruption unit was developed into six teams connected with Interpol to travel to the provinces. Composed of a single investigator and five administrative members each and equipped with some special equipment by the British, the teams started work in mid-2010. In practice, however, deploying them to the provinces was difficult and it did not happen too frequently. This was not just because of the security situation, but also because the Inspector General Raghib was less than keen to see them go.[282] In addition, each zone then had a department in charge of inspecting the provinces, typically staffed by one head and eleven to twelve officers. Finally, at year's end, Kabul despatched officers to the provinces to assess their work. The departments of counter-terrorism, counter-narcotics and a few more had their inspecting department.[283] The major crime task force was also supposed to assist the Inspector General.[284]

Some of the MoI reformists dismissed such supervisory structures as more of a propaganda exercise than anything else.[285] What is certain is that internal affairs in 2010 still did not have any written procedures for their inspections and audits and never received formal training. They only got on-the-job training from older inspectors.[286] Somewhat surprisingly, the Inspector General's office was one of the very few not mentored by NTM-A as of the end of 2010. The serving Inspector, Raghib, previously legal adviser to MoI, had already been the subject of unproven allegations of corruption and few western advisers were impressed by him, perhaps because he shut the doors of his office to them. However, he is known to have become personally very wealthy.[287] Indeed, during Raghib's tenure, reporting abuses and corruption within the police dropped to almost nil.[288] Before Raghib's arrival there was at least a growing trend of police officers being prosecuted, even if still a small minority of those were reported cases of misbehaviour: fifty-six in 2008–9, 148 in 2009–10 and 270 in 2010–11. Not many of the cases brought to prosecution made it to the Office of the Attorney General: only two out of twenty-four senior officers (Lt. Col. and above) in 2010.[289] Still, one could at least say that things were moving in the right direction.

INTERNAL ORGANISATION AND REORGANISATION

In the absence of a functioning internal affairs department, those policemen who tried to resist the spread of corruption found themselves in a very difficult situation. Police officers who believed their police station was being affected by the corruption or were unsuccessfully trying to report episodes of corruption had to appeal to UNAMA (until 2006 or so) or ISAF (from 2006) onwards for help. One CoP in 2003 even stated his belief that communications sent to the Minister were being intercepted by dishonest MoI officials.[290] As in the specific case of counter-narcotics discussed in section 6.3.3, those police officers who tried to resist more actively the system of corruption placed themselves in extreme danger and often had to rely on the protection of their ISAF mentors.[291] At the very least they risked being transferred to a bad district, according to a police officer interviewed by a Tufts team in 2003:

The reason I am in this district is that I made a mistake in [rural district of Kandahar] when I caught six trucks full of iron being smuggled into Pakistan and I sent them back to the provincial centre to the police. The assistant of the governor and the head of customs were very unhappy with this. Shortly thereafter, I was removed from [first district]...and sent here.[292]

The new trainees from the Police Academy were from the beginning being distributed piecemeal to various police stations around the country, without having the chance to create a critical mass of new professional officers anywhere. Many of them were, as a result, absorbed into the predominant patterns of corruption:

One senior foreign police trainer noted that, while individual police could be properly trained, the entire policing system was so corrupt that putting a new officer into the system was like 'throwing people into a cesspool and expecting them to stay clean'.[293]

In part the occasional waves of anti-misconduct crackdowns were driven by public complaints.

- In March 2005 already a reshuffle of Kandahar police had been reportedly driven by a popular demonstration against the deteriorating law-and-order situation.[294]
- In January 2007 the newly appointed CoP of Kandahar launched an investigation about wrongdoings by Kandahar police, following reports by the public of police abuse and misbehaviour.[295]
- At the end of 2007 people from Logar accused the police of taking bribes from the smugglers of illegally mined precious stones.[296]
- In March 2008 shopkeepers in Herat went on strike against the inefficiency of the police and its alleged cooperation with criminal gangs. The Minister of Interior had to pay a visit to Herat to assess the situation.[297]

On the whole, however, although the Afghan public was very happy to denounce police corruption as one of the greatest evils affecting the country, efforts to do anything about it were rare. The story of the 119 emergency number is illustrative of the plight: the system was very centralised, with all calls coming to the operation room in Kabul. The decision to intervene in the event of a reported emergency had to go through a complicated bureaucratic process, which meant that it would take hours for police on the ground to be mobilised. Of the 1,200 calls received every day, 90–95 per cent were sexual harassment and threats against the female call takers. Despite a campaign to advertise the new service, often even the police themselves were not aware of its existence or of how the service worked. Although the 119 service had been conceived initially by EUPOL as a corruption hotline and then turned by the Americans into a general police emergency number, very few of the calls were about denouncing corruption, despite explicit invitation to do so in the public campaign.[298] Still the 119 line was by 2011 one of the main sources of information about police corruption for internal affairs to rely on.[299]

Both Minister Atmar and Minister Mohammadi made strong statements concerning their plans to fight corruption as they were appointed. Atmar stated his desire to stop the sale of positions within the MoI within six months of his taking office.[300] He might have reduced the extent to which the practice dominated appointments (see section 6.3.1), but he certainly did not succeed in eliminating it. He had several generals arrested, but they were released soon afterwards. He created the crime task force, which created controversy first and then fell idle after his departure.[301] Mohammadi also committed himself to fight corruption and implement merit-based appointments. In the early days of his tenure he offered to transfer staff of the anti-corruption unit if they admitted to any wrong-doing, rather than sacking them. At the time of writing it was still too early to assess his actions, but clearly the impact has not been overwhelming (see also below).[302]

On the whole, the strategies of police building deployed under international pressure after 2001 in the field of MoI organisation and internal management all failed to achieve their aims. The time scale was relatively modest (ten years at the time of writing this book), but not too short when the level of financial and human resources committed is considered. It is difficult to avoid the sense that there has been a lack of political will to turn the MoI into a more functional apparatus.

7

RECRUITMENT AND RETENTION

Even relatively accurate information with regard to the level of recruitment and attrition in the police is not available for the period before 2007 (recruitment) or 2009 (attrition): data for 2007–8 is not available in monthly breakdowns. The data gathered in Figures 7 and 8 show strong fluctuations for the more recent period. Fluctuations were mostly seasonal in character, with more recruits joining during the warm months. Probably the potential policemen knew that police stations were poorly heated and supplied. Similarly, attrition was in large part seasonal: the ABP was worst affected because its forces were deployed mostly in inhospitable areas, cold and difficult to supply adequately.

Another important factor affecting attrition was the pace of operations. ANCOP in particular was sometimes over-burdened with difficult and long deployments, leading to a very high level of desertions. The last but perhaps most important factor worth pointing out is political developments. In Figure 7 the Presidential elections crisis is highlighted, although the incomplete set of data prevents a precise picture from emerging. Anecdotal evidence, however, suggests that recruitment reached very low levels coinciding with the Presidential elections, which ended with a high level of tension among factions due to the high level of rigging and the controversial outcome. This suggests that political shocks might greatly affect recruitment into the police in the future, as well as retention.

The scarcity of professionals

The post-2001 MoI suffered from chronic shortages of professional officers, in part due to the lack of any training of police officers in 1992–2001, in part due to the dispersal of many police officers who were judged politically unreliable by the succession of regimes in 1978–2001. Moreover, many of the

Figure 7: Recruitment into the Afghan National Police March 2007–March 2011.

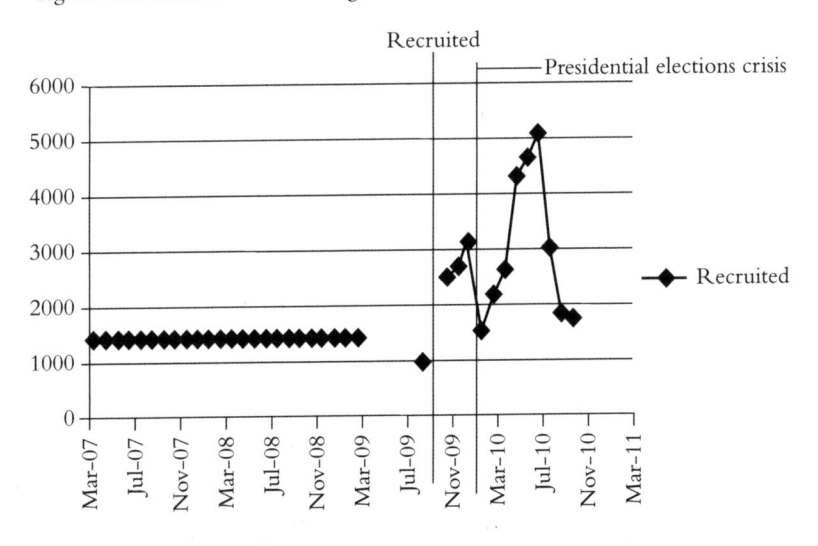

Figure 8: Attrition rates in the Afghan National Police October 2009–December 2010.

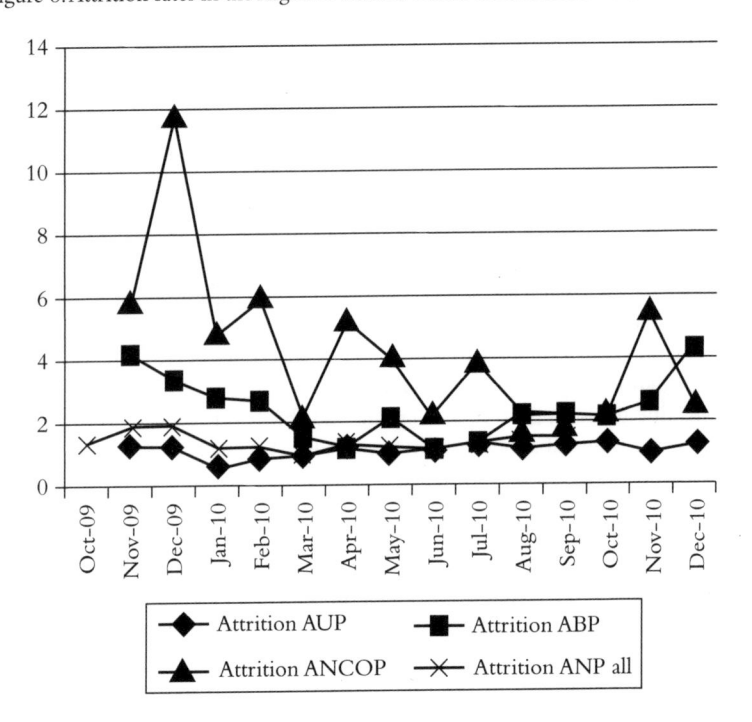

people trained in the Soviet Union only received specialist training and were not qualified for high level jobs.[1] This shortage was compounded by a lack of political will to mobilise available professional skills.

In 2002–5 the MoI was largely staffed by former members of the anti-Taliban militias. The MoI was used as a patronage resource, with political allies and cronies being rewarded by the concessions of high ranks in the police hierarchy.[2] As a result, in the provinces few professionals existed within the police ranks. In Takhar in early 2004, out of 560 police officers, only twelve were professional, the others all coming from the various anti-Taliban militias.[3] In Kunduz again in 2004, only 10 per cent of the 400 officers were professionals and none of the patrolmen (see also sections 9.1.3 and 9.1.4).[4]

During 2002–4 the changes at the district level could hardly be described as an attempt to improve the professionalism of the officers. Let us take the example of Koshki Rahbat-i Sangi in Herat. The first CoP was educated to twelfth class but in June 2003 he was replaced by an illiterate one, who stayed in his job for a year before being replaced by one with a few years of studying in a madrasa.[5] Officers could be replaced in the provinces by the leading strongmen without the approval of Kabul, which could only withhold registration if unhappy.[6]

Those police officers who were appointed in positions of responsibility felt sabotaged because they were not allowed to choose their subordinates.[7] One example was that of the CoP of Badakhshan, Kentooz (2008). A competent officer with a reputation for honesty, he was surrounded by corrupt CoPs and border police officers. He had no authority to remove them as the real power lay in the hands of Karzai's 'viceroy' in the province, Zalmay Mujaddidi.[8] In general, the morale and esprit de corps of professional police officers was very negatively affected by the appointment of illiterate and untrained individuals in senior positions.[9]

Under international pressure, the MoI had at least to show some effort to professionalise the officer corps. In 2006 a professional officer trained in the 1970s had estimated the figure at 60 per cent.[10] According the MoI chief of staff in 2007, of 7,500 officers in the MoI 70 per cent were professionals, trained in the academy.[11] By 2010 former deputy Minister Hadi Khalid estimated the percentage of professional officers at 80 per cent in 2008.[12] There is reason to doubt the validity of these figures because the definition of 'professional officer' was probably being used rather loosely in such measurements, including anybody who had served in the police for a few years or individuals with professional military training (as opposed to police training). Many of those serving as officers in 2006–7 had served as 'police' in the 1990s, under the Rabbani government. They did not have any professional training and had been sent from the various militias to take control of the police.[13] The short training courses provided by Dyncorp also enabled the non-professionals to claim that they too were trained now.

By 2011 the rapid expansion of the personnel charts and the failure to increase recruitment among educated Afghans led to the decision to tap the pool of former civil war militiamen once again. They were invited to join through a system of examinations, meant to determine their skills and suitability for the police.[14]

The hostility of the non-professional, political appointees towards professional police officers and the desire to confine them to non-key positions was just one aspect of the story. Professional police officers also displayed little interest in joining and deploying to the more dangerous and remote places. According to MoI Chief of Staff Nuristani in 2008, no professional was willing to go to the southern districts, forcing the MoI to recruit somebody locally 'who has his own men'.[15] Foreign diplomats shared the same views: professional and capable people did not want to go south and wanted to stay in Kabul or opt for the north.[16] Even those who might not have minded serving among Pashtuns (being Pashtun themselves) were often put off by the hostility of fellow non-professional police officers and local strongmen.[17]

As a result, in 2010 there was a shortage of 500 officers in the south and a surplus of 700 in the north. Khost province alone in 2008 lacked 100 lieutenants.[18] The MoI announced in 2010 new rules according to which officers would have to serve everywhere, but the impact remained to be seen as of mid-2011.[19] In reality even in the north the situation was not rosy: illiteracy remained a big problem here too and according to official statistics, over 72 per cent of the policemen were illiterate in early 2011.[20] Such was the quality of recruitment. The problem was compounded by the tight rules on literacy levels with regard in the system of promotion from the ranks, so that promising patrolmen or NCOs could not be promoted to officer over time if lacking the requisite educational background.[21]

Charismatic officers and patrons

As has been pointed out below (see section 8.1.2), throughout the 2001–11 period the functioning of the MoI units in the field remained dependent on the presence of charismatic leaders, particularly in the case of the mostly illiterate uniformed police units. The insufficient availability of such leaders was seen by mentors as a major factor negatively affecting the police.[22] The system therefore remained very much based on the charisma and abilities of a narrow pool of individuals, both professional officers (as discussed in section 7.1) and non-professional 'leaders of men'.

Referring back to the discussion of different types of corruption in the introduction, it is possible to identify two different types of corrupt officers: the 'roving bandits' who allowed the police to decay to a level of complete inactivity even in terms of territorial and population control, and the ones who at least tried to keep the system functional, if for no other reason than to protect their illegal activities. One such example was Mutalleb Beg in Takhar and then Kunduz, whose involvement in the narcotics trade is well documented, but who at the same time imposed some discipline and order on the police. His predecessor Ghulam in Kunduz, by contrast, had shown no interest whatsoever in keeping the police functional.[23]

RECRUITMENT AND RETENTION

Another such example was Akram Khakrizwal, CoP in Kandahar, Balkh and Kabul. He was a trained police officer and quite effective at managing his force, even if he was growing poppies on his private land in Kandahar and was closely linked to one of the three main militias of Kandahar, Mullah Naqibullah's. Yet another case is Daud, who might have been motivated by 'empire building' when he pushed for the development of counter-narcotics police during his tenure as vice-minister for counter-narcotics, but nonetheless brought his department to a level of capacity higher than most others. Similarly in his new job of Chief of the Northern Zone, Daud played a key role in mobilising the police against the Taliban, until his assassination in May 2011 (see section 6.3.3 above). Khalil Andarabi, who was compromised with the deeply corrupt highway police in 2006, reinvented himself as an effective and charismatic CoP in Faryab province in 2007–10.[24] Similarly, Maulana Sayydkhel, despite being considered by the UN as being involved in various criminal activities, had a degree of support among the people of Parwan and Baghlan where he served, because he was able to deliver some basic security. Clearly, however, his authority derived from his status as strongman and not from his police rank.[25]

In some cases, the police achieved a higher-than-usual level of effectiveness because of being managed by local power-brokers, who were not themselves police but had some formal control (usually in the capacity of provincial governors) as well as large financial, political and military resources to commit. The case of Ismail Khan was discussed in detail in a Chapter 5 case study, while the case of Atta Mohammed Noor, governor of Balkh from 2004 onwards, is discussed in section 7.3 below.

The implications of these two cases will be discussed in the Conclusion, but here it is worth asking the question of whether a fuller reliance on charismatic leaders would not have been a wiser choice after 2001, at least for a number of years. With the support of the central government and therefore a sense of self-confidence and ownership, could a crop of stationary bandits have perhaps established a more functional police system around Afghanistan? The answer is that while this might have worked, two main counter-indications immediately emerge. The first one is that the consolidation of regional power centres could have undermined the legitimacy of the central government and was deeply unacceptable to many of the key players in Kabul, including President Karzai.

The other main limitation of the reliance on charismatic leaders, was that the system did not have the capacity to identify, select and promote new talent from the ranks, forcing the Minister to rely on a small and shrinking pool of capable and loyal people (according to his own assessment) to make appointments. The number of charismatic figures in fact tended to decline due to Taliban targeting. There was a campaign of targeted assassinations against senior MoI officers, such as Sayyedkhel (CoP Kunduz), Khan Mohammad (CoP Kandahar), Daoud (Commander northern region) and Noori (CoP Takhar) just in the first few months of 2011. Some survived similar attempts, such as Sayyedkhel's successor Qatra.[26]

Provincial dynamics: Balkh's most durable stationary bandit

Atta Mohammed Noor became governor of Balkh province in 2004, having been one of the leaders of the armed opposition to the Taliban in northern Afghanistan and then one of the key militia leaders in 2001–4. Initially Atta had to contend with Kabul's authorities in his desire to establish full control over the police of Balkh, which had until 2004 and beyond been staffed by militiamen from Atta's own group (Jamiat-i Islami) and the other main players in Balkh, Junbesh-i Milli and Hizb-i Wahdat, but commanded by a Kabul appointee from November 2003 onwards: Khakrizwal. Although the two men came from the same political faction (Jamiat-i Islami), Khakrizwal had been sent there to assert central control from Kabul. In the ensuing power struggle, the two came close to an armed conflict in 2005 and vehemently accused each other of involvement in narco-traffic. Eventually Atta managed to get Khakrizwal removed in April 2005, but only to have him replaced by another CoP from the same group of Alokozais from Kandahar, Khan Mohammed. However, Khan Mohammed did not try to challenge Atta, who was able to bring more of his people into the police and bring it de facto under his full control.

Two of Atta's former bodyguards became respectively Chief of Traffic and Chief of Intelligence. As one close associate put it, 'Atta is good because all the thieves of Mazar are under his control'. He incorporated policemen linked to other factions active in Balkh and based among Uzbeks and Hazaras in his system, allowing them to retain control of the police station but under his orders.

Then Atta proceeded to impose new rules on the police, at this point mostly staffed by militiamen and gangsters. He guaranteed them a fixed revenue on top of their salaries, but in exchange he imposed a system of regulated taxation, akin to state taxation except that it was carried out covertly. Atta could count on the cooperation of the business community, who saw this as a better alternative to the unregulated extortion practised by gangs and police until then. The system allowed Atta to maintain order in the street: few crimes were taking place, because criminals were given the choice to join Atta's system or were crushed relentlessly if they refused. From time to time Atta had to face episodes of indiscipline among the police, with officers protesting at the ceiling imposed on their extortion activities and engagement in unregulated criminal activities. The police continued to arrest people for the purpose of extortion. Men caught accompanying women were detained and forced to pay for their freedom even when they could prove that the women were their relatives. From 2007–8 kidnappings were also becoming more common, suggesting that the monopoly over crime was breaking down. In some cases Atta was forced to send a rogue police officer into exile because of the intervention of other agencies, like the NDS. Atta responded with determination to indiscipline and a few rogue officers were forced to flee or were murdered.[27]

RECRUITMENT AND RETENTION

Façades of reform

Efforts to bring some kind of meritocratic appointment process to the MoI started in Jalali's time. Minister Jalali established a High Police Commission to decide on appointments and a selection board was later established (2005), composed of three Afghan civilians, one general, one INL (DoS) staff and one UN official. The board would check the background of individual candidates to top and second tier positions, test and interview them. The board was de facto ruled over by President Karzai, who decided for political reasons to inject his own candidates to top leadership positions.[28] External pressure to improve the meritocratic character of police appointments led again in 2008 to the establishment of a special advisory board for police appointments, staffed by respected individuals who were to vet the MoI appointments after collecting information about their background and reputation. In total about 9–14 cases were referred to the board, but it then stopped and the board was never convened again, rapidly being forgotten even by the foreign donors who had been insistent on its establishment.[29] In practice, the signature of the Minister and of the first deputy minister for security was deemed sufficient for all appointments.[30]

In 2006, under pressure from the donor countries, the central government established again a vetting procedure for senior appointments in the police, within the framework of pay and rank reform. The selection process required senior officers to pass a written examination and human rights vetting by the UN and the US DoS. This effort to mobilise more professional officers from civil society (officers trained in the 1970s and 1980s and then dismissed during the various changes of regime) essentially failed, despite being touted as the 'great pay and rank reform' (see sections 9.2 and 9.5). A common view among police professionals in Afghanistan is that pay and rank reform contributed to:

deprofessionalising the police by reforming professionals out of the system. The pay and rank reform process should have accommodated the police academy graduates into the police force.... In order to reduce numbers of generals we should put a freeze on promotions, and also let some work in lower positions but without a demotion. But we should not demote the professionals. The result is that we are losing some of the best people through 'reform'. The end result of the reform effort is that we are taking away rather than building capacity in the police.[31]

In Ghor province, all the few professional police officers who served there were sacked during the reform and replaced by individuals involved in drug trafficking.[32] The examination was set up as very basic and all non-professional police were able to pass, often with better marks than the professional ones.[33]

Even when non-professional officers failed to pass the examination, rescue options were available. Famously, Karzai in June 2006 re-appointed eighty-six generals who had failed the examination, many of whom were linked to illegal activities or had a chequered past. Among them was the current head of

103

Border Police, Noorzai, allegedly connected to Karzai's half-brother Ahmad Wali. The President disregarded the recommendations by the Selection Committee and appointed, to top senior positions within the police, fourteen individuals who failed the examination and faced allegations of human rights abuses, drug trafficking, murder, torture and corruption. It took six months of intense pressure by the UN, donor countries and the human rights organisations before the President removed these officials from their posts within the police, but most of them were then appointed to top positions outside the police—as governors or mayors.[34] UNAMA was up in arms against the decision, forcing the President to pretend that he would reconsider and eventually subject the eighty-six generals to a kind of probation for one year.[35]

Apart from the larger, internationally-sponsored efforts, newly appointed police officers in positions of responsibility routinely claimed to be overhauling their police department and to be crushing corruption. Sometimes foreign mentors agreed with these claims, but external and aftermath assessments rarely endorsed them.

- Matiullah Qati, CoP Kandahar in 2008, claimed to be cracking down on corruption, Canadian mentors agreed that he was 'a breath of fresh air'. He was killed by a CIA militia in a rift later, but it seems clear that his reforms were not having too much impact;[36]
- Amanullah Guzar, CoP Kabul in 2006, announced the start of night patrolling in the streets of the capital but few of Kabul's inhabitants noticed any difference. Guzar, on the other hand, was accused of extortion and other illegal activities;[37]
- Ali Shah Paktiawal, chief of the Criminal Department in Kabul, boasted of his successes in fighting crime in Kabul and prided himself for showing up at every police scene in the capital, but was found to be unprofessional and violent in his approach. He was sacked in February 2009, possibly because of foreign pressure.[38]

When Atmar took over in October 2008, he too launched a high-profile effort to crack down on corruption and sacked 320 generals and 200 other officials at the MoI, including twelve of fourteen CoPs District in the capital.[39] However, few would have argued that by the time Atmar left that the police had got less corrupt. Bismillah Mohammadi also carried out his own extensive reshuffle in 2010, beginning just after his appointment as Minister. After managing to get a retirement law approved by Karzai (it was before not possible to force police officers into retirement) he reassigned forty-one generals, including three deputy ministers, and also retired fifty-eight generals, of whom twenty-six were from active service and thirty-two from the reserve, for age limits. The enabling of the retirement system allowed room to be made for younger and more energetic officers, in NTM-A's view.[40] The introduction of a system of compulsory rotation after three years has also been seen as an important innovation by foreign advisers.[41] At the time of writing it was too early to judge the impact of his actions, but as shown in 6.3, anti-corruption might not have been the main driver of Mohammadi's actions.

RECRUITMENT AND RETENTION

Anti-corruption measures that were relatively easy to implement, such as the regular rotation of police officers, turned out to be very contentious even before Mohammadi's tenure. In 2008 there was a proposal by deputy Minister Hadi Khalid to rotate officers between the capital and the provinces, but Minister Zarar rejected it. Hadi Khalid tried to incentivise officers to serve in 'bad places' for six months by promising them a good transfer afterwards, but was not able to deliver because of Zarar's opposition.[42]

Purges, clean-ups and patronage

Virtually every Minister of Interior made major changes at the top of the MoI, shuffling senior staff between jobs or placing them in the reserve when determined not to have them in his team. In turn, heads of department and CoPs regularly made major changes among their staff on taking charge. It is considered acceptable for a new boss to surround himself with subordinates whom he is comfortable with. In some cases, the changes have been massive. When Gen. Daud was appointed Chief of the Northern Zone, he replaced almost all the district CoPs of Badakhshan, a province whose strongmen always resisted him when he was Commander of Army Corps in 2002–5, with loyalists from his own province of Takhar.[43] When Minister Mohammadi took over in 2010, he engaged in one of the most massive shifts of personnel recorded by the MoI yet. He removed eighty generals and 2,000 officers between June 2010 and February 2011, appointing as many replacements. Some of them were removed on various allegations, but mostly out of the Minister's policy of appointments.[44] Hundreds more were replaced in the subsequent months. This instability in the staffing of the MoI has been much criticised, because it greatly disrupts the operations and the planning of the MoI.[45] The removal of people meant that others were being appointed or promoted. Since, as discussed above, meritocracy did not play much of a role in the MoI, it should be expected that patronage in various shapes and forms dominated appointments.

The combination of features of patrimonial and legal-rational administrations described above arguably led to the establishment of a hybrid system which could be described as 'prebendalised', an extreme form of clientelism characterised by the allocation of resources in a way that favours the mobilisation of political and ethnic identities.[46] In the following sections the extent to which prebendalism took hold in Afghanistan is tested in detail.

Ethnicity

Accusations of ethnic favouritism have been frequent after 2002. Under Jalali, new appointments largely targeted the north-west and rarely the south or the east. This gave the opportunity to those opposing reform to campaign claiming an ethnic agenda.[47] In late 2010 accusations flourished against Minister Mohammadi, as already mentioned.[48] As we have seen, on the whole it cannot be said that Tajiks gained much ground under Mohammadi, even if in specific sectors that might have been the case. While Gen. Patang, the general Commander of Education Department appointed by Mohammadi, was widely respected as capable and competent, in the Police Academy many Pashtun officers were being eased out.[49] In the context of competition among rival networks, it is easy to overstate the importance of developments affecting a particular department or section.

There was certainly awareness of the ethnic issue in NTM-A and in the MoI, at least by 2011. A statement by NTM-A read:

As of 15 January 2011, Minister Mohammadi proposed moving fifteen senior officers. These senior officers included at least two Sadat and one Hazara individual, making up at least 20 per cent of the proposed changes. These personnel changes would significantly increase Uzbek, Sadat, Hazara, and other minority ethnicities within the senior MOI leadership.[50]

This section features a study of appointments under different ministers, measuring ethnic patterns. The position of CoP was selected at the provincial level because of the high number of appointments involved, the homogeneity of the positions, and the importance of the position within the Afghan police system. Tables 9 and 10 show how in 2002 Tajiks and Uzbeks were strongly over-represented, while Pashtuns were under-represented, clearly a result of the distribution of the spoils following the fall on the Taliban regime and the triumph of the anti-Taliban coalition led by the United Front. However, in subsequent years there was a gradual rebalancing of the ethnic composition of the CoPs. By early 2011, Pashtuns were actually moderately over-represented, while the representation of Tajiks was in line with their composition of the population. Hazaras and Uzbeks were both strongly under-represented. Although NTM-A has been claiming an ethnically balanced policy of appointments in 2010–11 (under Minister Mohammadi), the data provided to support the case does not demonstrate much, because of very large categories such as 'others' and 'unknown', which lend themselves to easy manipulation (see Table 11). Moreover, not all leadership positions have the same value.

The most significant aspect of the data shown in Tables 11 and 12 is the steady trend towards a strengthening of Pashtun representation, at the expense of all other ethnic groups. Such a trend continued under the tenures of different ministers, despite the accusations against some of them (Moqbel Zarar and Mohammadi) of favouritism towards Tajiks. Indeed under Zarar there was a lull in the growth of the Pashtun share, while Tajiks recovered ground quite strongly, but at the expense of the smaller ethnic groups. What has therefore been driving appointments at the senior level? In order to find the answer it is worth looking at the ethnic background of MoI staff as provided by NTM-A (Table 14). As can be seen, as of 2010 within the officer corps Tajiks were still greatly over-represented, mostly at the expense of Hazaras, Uzbeks and smaller minorities, and to a lesser extent of Pashtuns. Among the patrol-

RECRUITMENT AND RETENTION

men, by contrast, the different ethnic groups were represented in a more balanced way, even if Tajiks were still over-represented. This is not surprising as patrolmen were being recruited locally and therefore had to represent the composition of the local population more closely. The sharp difference between the senior leadership of the MoI and the officer corps as a whole suggest that political scrutiny by the government and particularly the presidency, as well as from external donors and partners, influenced appointments and forced successive ministers to be more balanced as far as top appointments were concerned. This influence did not have a similar impact below the senior level, where scrutiny from outside the MoI was inevitably more difficult to exercise. The role of the presidency is highlighted by the fact that Pashtuns, protected by the President and his circle, did well under different ministers, whereas Hazaras and Uzbeks suffered because they lacked powerful political patrons and the support of donors and international partners for a greater ethnic balance.

Table 11: Provincial CoPs in charge, by ethnicity (actuals)

	I 2002	II 2005	II 2008	I 2010	I 2011
Pashtun	10	15	15	17	19
Tajik	11	10	14	11	9
Hazara	3	3	2	1	1
Uzbeks	5	3	3	3	1
Others	3	3	0	1	3
Unknown	0	0	0	0	1

Source: interviews with former MoI officials, MPs, officials of international organisations.

Table 12: Provincial CoPs in charge, by ethnicity (%)

	I 2002	II 2005	II 2008	I 2010	I 2011	Composition of population
Pashtun	31.3	44.1	44.1	50.0	55.9	48
Tajik	34.4	29.4	41.2	32.4	26.5	26
Hazara	9.4	8.8	5.9	2.9	2.9	12
Uzbeks	15.6	8.8	8.8	8.8	2.9	8
Others	9.4	8.8	0.0	2.9	8.8	6
Unknown	0.0	0.0	0.0	2.9	2.9	

The CoPs' data might not be entirely representative of trends within the MoI. At the higher levels of the central MoI, in 2006 a former high-level official of the Ministry estimated that of thirty-six top officials, twenty-two were

Pashtuns, ten Tajiks, two Hazara, one Uzbek and one Nuristani.[51] This data attributes a much greater role to Pashtuns than in the case of the CoPs, but as hinted earlier these thirty-six top positions are in fact very dishomogeneous in terms of power and influence.

In general it can be argued that ethnicity is a factor that has played a role in appointments at the MoI, but not a particularly prominent one as it has been mitigated by political pressure towards rebalancing.

Table 13: Retirements and appointments of police leadership personnel under Minister Mohammadi, Afghan year 2010–11 (%).

	Retirements	Appointments
Pashtuns	34	41
Tajiks	29	31
Hazaras	3	0
Others	5	9
Unknown	29	19

Source: NTM-A, 2011.

Table 14: Afghan National Police by ethnicity according to NTM-A, 2010.

	Pushtun	Tajik	Hazara	Uzbek	Other
Officer	42%	47%	4%	3%	3%
NCO	32%	55%	6%	4%	4%
Patrolmen	47%	36%	4%	6%	7%
Total	43%	42%	4%	5%	6%
MOI Goal based on National Proportion	44%	25%	10%	8%	13%

Others included: Turkmen, Baloch, Nooristani, Bayat, Sadat, Pashayee, Arab, and Alevi.

Political affiliation

There is of course no official data about the political affiliation of MoI staff. Collecting data in this regard is tricky, but in most cases the political background of the CoPs is well known and not the matter of much controversy. As Tables 15 and 16 show, the predominance of Jamiat in 2002 was overwhelming as no other political group could count on anything even remotely resembling its influence. However, after 2002 the appointees linked to Jamiat sharply declined as a percentage, even if they remained by far the largest group. The decline was only interrupted in 2011, as Minister Mohammadi brought back many Jamiatis of the various networks in which the party is divided (see Chapter 3). President Karzai is known to have expressed unhappiness about the re-Jamiatisation of the MoI, but among foreign advisers and diplomats opinion was divided: some were critical, but others accepted that Mohammadi needed people he could trust for an aggressive counter-insurgency.[52] A competition for influence could in fact be noticed even within the ABP, where Mohammadi was trying to promote individuals linked to him or at least hostile to the Head of ABP, Yunis Noorzai, a close ally of Karzai.[53]

The partial decline of Jamiat, moreover, was not to the benefit of any other political group, but to that of non-politically affiliated officers, whose percentage grew from a very low level in 2002 to a majority in 2010, at the end of the tenure of Minister Atmar. Even under Mohammadi, his successor, non-politically aligned officers accounted for over 40 per cent of the CoPs. Most of these non-aligned officers served in fact under the pro-Soviet regimes of 1978–92 (in the police, army or security services) and were mostly card-carrying members of the pro-Soviet HDK. However, there is no indication that they maintained a connection with the successor parties to the HDK (there were several of them in Afghanistan after 2001) or that they were organised in factions or even networks. In fact, bitter rivalries divided those among them who had belonged to different factions of the HDK in the 1980s, and those who took different paths after 1992: some took the road of exile or went into hiding, while others collaborated with the Rabbani regime while a few even worked for the Taliban regime.[54]

The data suggests that pressure on Jamiat to give more room to professional elements within the police had some impact. It is worth noting that Jamiat counts on the loyalty not just of Tajik CoPs, but also a number of CoPs from other ethnic backgrounds, particularly Pashtuns. Comparatively speaking, the 'de-Tajikisation' of the MoI proved easier than its 'de-Jamiatisation'. It is worth adding that while the data in the tables had to be broken down to factional level for the sake of simplicity, important intra-factional dynamics also occur. In Jamiat, for example, different factions are loyal to Vice-President Fahim, to the historical leader of the party Rabbani or to President Karzai himself. So when Gen. Daud, linked to Fahim's faction, took over command of the Northern Zone and set off to purge the police of Badakhshan, he was in fact targeting loyalists of Rabbani and of pro-Karzai Jamiati Zalmay Mujaddadi.[55]

The other parties were never in a position to impose their own nominees regardless of their qualifications, except in 2002 when a CoP position was agreed at the provincial level by the main local factions and strongmen. After that, it became increasingly necessary to propose candidates with credible qualifications as senior police officers. By 2005 Junbesh-i Milli had for example a single CoP at the provincial level, a professional officer with a Parchami background. Although the Minister and the President agreed in 2006 to appoint an Uzbek linked to Junbesh-i Milli as one of the MoI deputies, finding a suitable candidate proved difficult.[56] Only in 2009 was Siddiq Noor, an Uzbek, appointed as deputy of communications.[57] By 2011 the few

Uzbeks in positions of responsibility within the MoI structure only had the loosest connection to Junbesh, which was by then trying to operate as an ethnic lobby, bringing Uzbeks into government even if they were not so close to Junbesh.

Table 15: Provincial CoPs in charge by political affiliation (actuals).

	I 2002	II 2005	II 2007	I 2010	I 2011
Jamiat	16	12	11	10	13
Wahdat	2	3	2	–	–
Junbesh	3	1	–	2	2
Karzai	1	2	–	1	1
Ittehad	2	–	–	–	–
Hizb	2	3	2	–	–
None	3	10	14	18	14
Others	3	3	5	3	3
Unknown	–	–	–	–	1
Total	32	34	34	34	34

Sources: interviews with former MoI officials, MPs, officials of international organisations.

Table 16: Provincial CoP in charge by political affiliation (%).

	I 2002	II 2005	II 2007	I 2010	I 2011
Jamiat	50.0	35.3	32.4	29.4	38.2
Wahdat	6.3	8.8	5.9	0.0	0.0
Junbesh	9.4	2.9	0.0	5.9	5.9
Karzai	3.1	5.9	0.0	2.9	2.9
Ittehad	6.3	0.0	0.0	0.0	0.0
Hizb	6.3	8.8	5.9	0.0	0.0
None	9.4	29.4	41.2	52.9	41.2
Others	9.4	8.8	14.7	8.8	8.8
Unknown	0.0	0.0	0.0	0.0	2.9

Professionalism

In section 7.5.2 it was hinted that the growing number of non-politically affiliated CoPs reflected the professionalisation of the police. In this section this claim is substantiated (Tables 15 and 16). In 2002, professional police only accounted for about 6 per cent of the provincial CoPs, with another almost 16 per cent accounted for by former military members. Former militiamen (combatants of the anti-Taliban factions) accounted for close to 80 per cent of the CoPs but only a small minority of them was educated to high school level or higher. In the subsequent period the growth in the percentage of professional police was steady until 2008. After that it initially stagnated and then started declining again.

The proportion of former military officers in CoP positions fluctuated in numbers under the different ministers, although grew very strongly overall. Jalali and even more so Atmar appointed many of them, while Zarar and Mohammadi reduced their numbers. The general trend towards militarisation of the police, a result of the intensifying insurgency, was obviously the main factor favouring the former members of the military. The deputy minister for security affairs had always been a former military man, but after 2003 the militarisation of the police became generalised.[58] The shortage of professional police officers willing to serve in the most difficult areas was another factor. Mohammadi showed some interest in civilian policing in the early days of his tenure, but then quickly reverted to promoting militarisation, encouraged by his American advisers and by his own military background.[59]

The number of former militiamen declined in parallel to the rise of professional police and military and touched the bottom at well under 20 per cent at the end of minister Atmar's tenure, but started recovering markedly under Minister Mohammadi. Because most former militiamen in the police were Jamiatis, the considerations made above in section 7.5.2 apply here too. However, it is worth adding that the return of the former militiamen was also caused by the demands of war fighting, which had been driving the growing role of the former military in previous years. As the former military did not always perform that well in counter-insurgency, there was a rational for bringing back former militiamen. The advantage of the latter in the a context of a widening counter-insurgency effort consisted in a stronger commitment to fighting the Taliban (for reasons of factional allegiance and sometimes even personal ones) and in an easier relationship with the ANP rank and file, who often were politically and culturally closer to the former militia commander than to the professional police and military officers, particularly in the rural areas. An additional advantage is that often the former militia commanders were connected to the legal and illegal militias opposed to the Taliban, emerging around Afghanistan in reaction to the spread of the insurgency.

Official data on the professionalism of the police is not reliable, because it mixes people coming from the Police Academy with those with a military background and those who just underwent short training courses or who had accumulated 'years of experience' in the police.[60] The data collected for this study shows that as late as 2006, fourteen provincial CoPs were illiterate or virtually so.[61] Even in the central MoI, finding high-level officials who were illiterate was not uncommon. In 2008, the head of the special unit for the protection of historical sites could not even write his own name: still somehow he had managed to pass the test of the reform process in 2006.[62] In fact there was a major purge of professional officers in Kabul during Zarar's years.

At least ten senior officers were removed from the MoI in Kabul and replaced by cronies of the Minister and political allies, mostly junior officers suddenly promoted to generals. Among them were:

- Haidar Bassir, an NCO who became deputy minister;
- Amin Sharif, another NCO promoted to head of ANCOP;
- Azam, a typist, became head of general operations;
- Ahmad Zia, a low-rank officer, became general head of office;
- Esmatullah Ahmadzai, a low-rank officer, became head of administration.[63]

While the appointment of illiterate or semi-illiterate individuals in top positions at the MoI clearly could only contribute to make the Ministry dysfunctional and inefficient, it would be wrong to assume that professionalism was always an asset or at least that it guaranteed a strong performance and honesty. Current and former senior officials at the MoI acknowledged that quite a few professional officers were very corrupt and that some non-professional officers were not only honest but also quite effective, particularly when serving in the provinces. An often-cited example was that of Shahjahan Nuri, who was killed in 2011 when CoP of Takhar. Trained as a mullah, Nuri acted proactively against the cultivation of the poppies and collected many weapons from illegal armed groups.[64]

Table 17: Provincial CoPs in charge by professional background (actuals).

	I 2002	II 2005	II 2008	I 2010	I 2011
Professional	2	10	13	13	10
Ex-military	5	7	5	13	10
Ex-militiaman	22	16	14	5	11
Militiaman—educated	3	1	0	1	0
Other—educated	0	0	2	0	0
Other—no education	0	0	0	1	1
Unknown	0	0	0	1	2
Total	32	34	34	34	34

Sources: interviews with former MoI officials, MPs, officials of international organisations.

Lobbying

Lobbying by groups, political parties, factions and powerful individuals certainly affected to a great extent appointments within the MoI. The appointment of the CoP of Zabul in 2007 was the result of lobbying by the Taraki tribe. Counter-lobbying by Hizb-i Islami led to his removal in 2008.[65] When Shah Jahan Nuri, mentioned above, eased his relationship with Jamiat, he lost his job and it took a while before he was reappointed. Political parties also

RECRUITMENT AND RETENTION

used MPs to put pressure on affiliates who were distancing themselves from the party.[66]

President Karzai himself is known to lobby in favour of individuals connected to him, or to somebody close to him. He always has a few protégés within the Ministry, although most of the time it is his brother Ahmad Wali Karzai or others linked to the family who benefit from favourable appointments. One noteworthy case was that of the Chief of Border Police Noorzai, who owed his long period of leadership of the controversial ABP to his connection with the President.[67] Karzai's lobbying had a particularly noticeable impact at the time of Disarmament, Demobilisation and Reintegration (DDR) of the militias assembled under the control of the Ministry of Defence in 2003–5. Several important militia commanders were resisting DDR and demanding to be transferred to the police in order to maintain their support for the central government. Minister Jalali resisted such an option, but President Karzai won the day and several commanders with their men became part of the police. Among the best known of them were Hazrat Ali, one of Nangarhar's strongmen, Khan Mohammed, one of the strongmen of Kandahar and Khalil Andarabi, one of the commanders of Baghlan.[68]

Table 18: Provincial CoPs in charge by professional background (%).

	I 2002	II 2005	II 2008	I 2010	I 2011
Professional	6.3	29.4	38.2	38.2	29.4
Ex-military	15.6	20.6	14.7	38.2	29.4
Ex-militiaman	68.8	47.1	41.2	14.7	32.4
Militiaman–educated	9.4	2.9	0.0	2.9	0.0
Other—educated	0.0	0.0	5.9	0.0	0.0
Other—no education	0.0	0.0	0.0	2.9	2.9
Unknown	0.0	0.0	0.0	2.9	5.9

Criminal networking and corruption

At least in specific periods of the history of the MoI, criminal and trafficking networks influenced to a great extent appointments within the organisation. In 2006–8 UN sources commented that appointments along the route used by the narcotics smugglers to Iran seemed to facilitate the traffickers: all the police appointees had a record of suspected involvement in the narco-traffic. The criminal networks could easily exploit the possibility of purchasing positions within the MoI, as discussed in section 6.3.3. It is difficult to say whether the appointment of police officers linked to the criminal gangs was merely the result of a mercenary attitude within the MoI, or whether some form of complicity was present. Arguably, once the number of police officers compromised by criminal networks started reaching a critical mass, they should have been able to draw in more and more of their likes, but this is of course difficult to demonstrate. Police officers who had been sacked for corruption before 2006 were often re-hired in 2007–8.[69]

The case of the Highway Police is particularly illustrative of the degree to which the MoI could be affected by the takeover of criminalised networks. The original plan conceived by Minister Jalali was to establish a Highway Police which would be under central control and act as a kind of mobile force but in reality it was recruited locally and was completely taken over by former militiamen. It quickly became so corrupt that it had to be disbanded in 2006.[70]

The recruitment policies of the MoI after 2001 once again convey a sense of the lack of a consistent political will to turn the MoI into an efficient machine. The main strategy being deployed (on and off) was one of professionalisation, but too many non-professionals were left in the system for this to achieve much. One cannot really speak of bureaucratisation of the recruitment process, which meant that the attitude of the various figures who succeeded each other at the top of the ministry was the determining factor in regulating the speed of professionalisation. Periods of acceleration were followed by periods of regression or stagnation (see Chapter 9).

8

THE ULTIMATE TEST OF FUNCTIONALITY

THE PARAMILITARY DIMENSION

As discussed in Chapter 1, the ability of a government to control its own territory and population or at least to secure itself against the threat of armed opposition are important benchmarks of its functionality. While, as argued in the Introduction, not all governments are ready to make the effort required to achieve effective control over the country and therefore qualify as 'modern states' in the Weberian sense, we can safely assume that all governments do want to survive the challenge of insurgencies and revolts. In the case of Afghanistan, these tasks are largely pertinent to the paramilitary dimension of policing, which we examine here in detail.

Commanding and controlling the police

The early days

The confused structure of the MoI in the early days of the post-Taliban era was not conducive to effective command and control, even when the concern was in principle at least one of self-preservation for the Kabul regime. As found by Amnesty International Researchers in 2003:

At the time of research, at least five senior ranking officials held positions apparently with responsibility for policing. General Assefi was appointed as General Commander of the National Police in September 2002. Despite his title, he appears to have the least control over the police. When interviewed by Amnesty International, he admitted that he does not have authority over the police, who are loyal to local commanders rather than to central government. General Hellal, a former air force pilot, is Deputy Minister for Internal Security. He told Amnesty International that provincial commanders report to him regularly. General Salangi is the head of Kabul police, has a ten thousand strong force and holds much actual power. He has a military background. General Naseri, Special Adviser to the Minister of the Interior, also appeared to have some responsibility for policing. General Jurat, the 'Head of Security and Public Controls' also holds a powerful role in Kabul, controlling his own force of approximately 4,000 police. They patrol Kabul twenty-four hours a day, and control checkpoints at the airport and at the gates of the city. His police force operates separately from the Kabul police force that is under the command of General Salangi. General Jurat told Amnesty International that he reports directly to the Minister of Interior.[1]

In some cases the command and control structure was so weak that it was even difficult to be sure who was the CoP in charge at a given moment. In one case in Kandahar in 2003, the Americans had to demand that Khan Mohammed, who was claiming the post of CoP, produced a letter of appointment or be forcefully removed.[2] Often the CoP did not know exactly how many men were effectively under their command.[3] Equipment and facilities were also in short supply:

There is a widespread lack of communications and transport equipment, preventing the police from being able to effectively tackle crime and disorder. Many police districts have only the use of the police commander's private car.[4]

The initial Turkish imprint of centralisation, plus the heritage of the Soviet model of rigid discipline and decision making, plus predominant attitudes towards authority and political realities all contributed to make MoI decision making extremely complicated.[5] The extreme centralisation (in principle) of the command and control structure meant that units had no capacity to make decisions and on top of this, they had no analytical capacity. That would not have been as bad a problem if the MoI HQ itself had not been constrained by its own limited capacity: it was not able to micromanage its units in the field. It had little or no capacity for strategic thinking and limited analytical power.[6] To all this we should add the high level of political interference, disrupting the chain of command.[7] The commander of the Border Police in Eastern Afghanistan (Gen. Aminollah Amarkhel) complained in February 2011 about the involvement of 'senior government officials' in drug smuggling and other illegal activities and of their interference with the activities of the police.[8] Shifts were not organised in a bureaucratic way, but based on personal connections.[9]

Impact of improvement efforts

Gradually after 2001 the improvement in technological resources strengthened the role of provincial HQs, at least enabling all senior police officers to work as a team if they wanted to. The problem was the lack of capacity and political will.[10] By 2006 the technical ability to exercise command and control had already improved significantly, but it was common for the police in the provinces to resist orders from Kabul.[11]

THE ULTIMATE TEST OF FUNCTIONALITY

During the second phase of MoI reform, which started in 2006, some more small but important steps were taken to ensure that the centre had some control over the force. The quality and updating of MoI personnel databases (non-existent in 2002) at least allowed the MoI to plan some improvements in its administration.[12] In 2006 a new National Police Command Centre was opened, with advanced communications facilities that enabled the MoI to communicate with its provincial units, ANA command and control centre, and ANA units in the regions. Although the technical capacity of the national command centre was greatly improved, the large international presence there and in the regional centres meant that its ability to function autonomously in an integrated way remained questionable.[13,14] A secure system of communication was established, featuring videoconferencing capabilities as well at the zone level. Reports from the districts were delivered via mobile phone messages, while radio communication with the provincial HQ was a standard feature of police stations by 2005.[15]

For all these technological improvements, by November 2010 bypassing the chain of command was still a frequent occurrence when officers had political connections.[16] The UN rapporteur wrote that he received reports of a number of cases in which police did attempt to carry out investigations, but senior government officials interfered with or prevented the investigations.[17] One example of disobedience of a direct order by a police officer on the ground occurred during the 2010 elections. During a demonstration by defeated candidates from Baghlan province, the ANP was ordered not to let them in. The ANP commander, who was a relative of one of the candidates, decided instead to let them in without even searching them.[18]

Even a popular Minister like Mohammadi struggled to assert himself vis-à-vis the CoPs. In February 2011 the Uruzgan CoP refused to process payments for the ALP programme, which he opposed, and the MoI could do nothing more then send a few finance specialists from Kabul to get the salaries processed.[19] Deputy Minister Wahdat had to issue ciphers to provincial HQs explicitly directing them to pay ALP wages.[20] The head of ALP, Khan Mohammed, had to be removed within a year after being accused of bringing too many of his cronies into the force.[21] The ALP's indiscipline was such that the AUP was often afraid of it, particularly in those districts were the ALP expanded more rapidly, coming to number as many as five times more 'policemen' than the AUP. In Baghlan at least the ALP was able to behave without restrictions and did not allow the AUP into the villages.[22]

The limitations of the MoI command and control capacity were recognised by western advisers. NTM-A described the MoI system as 'not joined up'.[23] The command and control of the ANP was described even by official NATO sources as 'at best fragile' and 'generally reliant on key commanders'.[24]

The inability of the MoI to plan coherently resulted among other things in uncertainty about the latest version of the Tashkil, whose status even as late as 2010 remained undefined for months, confusing the CoPs in the provinces.[25] Even in 2010 the MoI had huge problems in simply disseminating information from the top to the bottom and CoPs were often unaware of recent decisions and developments.[26] When messages from the top were communicated to the units on the ground, implementation still varied according to local context. Sometimes orders were implemented: in Herat for example the directive to prosecute bad police drivers resulted in police driving getting better.[27] More often they were not.

Some good managers reportedly existed in the system and under an effective CoP performance could improve and there was some willingness to get the police's act together.[28] Indeed, anecdotal evidence on the ground seemed to indicate that where there were improvements, it was not so much down to any increased ability of the MoI to provide direction, but to the appointment of an effective and committed CoP at the provincial level. Opinions about the qualities of individual CoPs vary, so it is not easy to clearly identify such charismatic and capable individuals. Some believe that Mohammad Hussein Andiwal in Helmand province (2007–8) was one of them as he reportedly did a lot to change local perceptions of the police and improve its public standing.[29] The situation had been very different before his appointment, with the population of some districts even asking not to be allocated any police because of their bad behaviour.[30] In Helmand the police did 'good work' on voter registration in 2009. In some other areas such as parts of the north-west and of the north-east of Afghanistan police were in the vanguard in 2009–11, with army support.[31] The more proactive CoPs would travel to the districts, inspect their men and assess their needs, even if in several provinces such activities were made difficult or risky because of the insurgency.[32]

If the presence of a proactive and charismatic CoP at the top of the provincial structure was still in 2010 the decisive factor in the performance of the police, command and control at the tactical level was still precarious or non-existent. Logistics and planning were always weak even in the best provinces.[33] Moreover, until a critical mass of professional officers was created, a single professional CoP at the provincial level could only go so far, often being unable to impose some discipline even on his CoPs in the city districts, if he was not particularly charismatic or determined.[34]

At the central level, specific departments showed signs of growing maturity by 2010: decisions about big operations were processed relatively quickly, although political interference and lack of communication were an obstacle. In the case of the 2010 Nangarhar counter-narcotics raid which involved Russian agents, the ministry had cleared it following the procedure, and it was President Karzai who protested.[35] The biggest problem the MoI still faced was organising and coordinating rapid responses. The MoI of 2010 could implement a plan, but not react quickly to contingencies. For example, when the afore mentioned riots occurred in October 2010 in Kabul between Hazaras and Kuchis, the police could not cope and the Minister had to deploy on the ground to manage the situation.[36]

THE ULTIMATE TEST OF FUNCTIONALITY

Persistent patrimonialism

An important consequence of the weak institutionalisation of command and control within the MoI structure was that a minister had to rely on appointing loyal or personally committed provincial and zone CoPs. Map 3 shows the picture in April 2011. The bulk of the provincial CoPs were either professionals or personally/factionally linked to the Minister of Interior (Bismillah Mohammadi): the few who were not had been appointed under his predecessor. Minister Mohammadi's decision to send key members of his faction to the frontlines of the north to repel the advance of the Taliban paid off in terms of instilling some greater activism in the police. Maulana Sayyid Khel, at the centre of many allegations of corruption during his tenure as CoP in various provinces, oversaw the counter-offensive against the Taliban in Kunduz in late 2010 to early 2011, before being assassinated by a suicide bomber in March 2011.[37] Gen. Daud, transferred from being deputy for counter-narcotics to being Head of the Northern Zone, also played an important role in energising the police against the insurgents.[38]

The concern for the situation in the north was said to be driven by a fear of incipient civil war and by the desire to consolidate the control of the region by Jamiat. This was also reflected in Mohammadi's effort to push the formation of ALP in the north as hard as possible, even faster than the Amer-

Map 3: Professional and political background of provincial CoPs, April 2011.

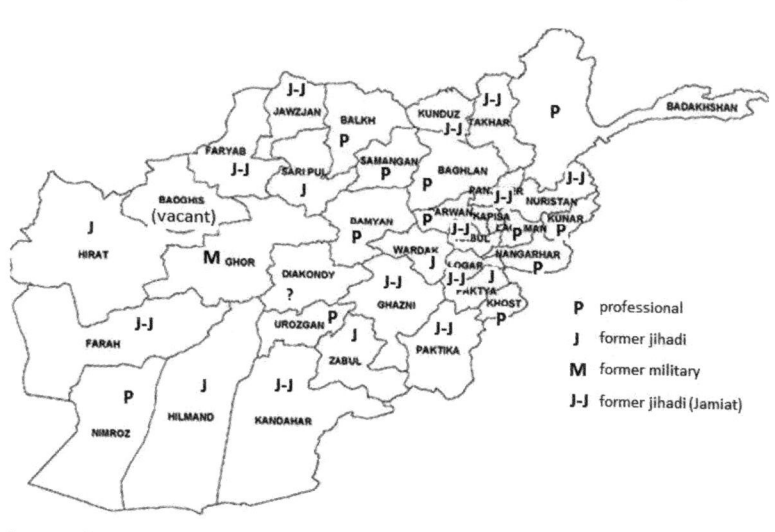

P professional
J former jihadi
M former military
J-J former jihadi (Jamiat)

Sources: interviews with MoI and UN officials, as well as with security and political analysis based in Afghanistan, 2009–11.

icans themselves were able to: many unofficial 'ALP-to-be' militias started forming in the north in 2010, encouraged by Mohammadi.[39]

The same problem was faced by provincial CoPs with their subordinates. In Herat, for example, for the first few years after the removal of Ismail Khan, for political reasons the district police chiefs had to be given a lot of leeway in the process of recruitment. Whenever the MoI appointed a new police chief—whether at the province or district level—he was allowed to bring with him his own team of bodyguards and secretarial staff, sometimes as many as twenty individuals. In addition, the police chiefs could recruit new patrolmen and officers independently and had a significant role in deciding who would work for them. They often brought in their loyalists and colluded with each other in order to collect more bribes from the population.[40] The practice was certainly not limited to Herat.

The establishment in 2010 of the Recruitment Command (see section 6.1) was an important development in terms of police staffing. The MoI established few recruitment centres across the four provinces constituting the Western zone—Herat, Badghis, Farah and Ghor—under the control of the Regional Police Headquarters. The recruits, after receiving training, were to be assigned by the Regional Police Headquarters to police units in any of the four western provinces, depending on where they were needed.[41] As a result, the recruitment process has become formal and regulated, and the influence of police chiefs over the recruitment process has declined. The police chiefs could hardly make recruitment on their own or bring their personal bodyguards and secretariats to their new posts. Many police officers viewed this development as a positive step towards reducing corruption and improving police accountability.[42] However, it is also easy to imagine how CoPs might feel that in the presence of a weak system of command and control their room for manoeuvre was reduced by the new rules. Corruption might have been reduced (though not eliminated, see 6.3), but like the Minister himself the CoPs might feel that unless they were allowed to bring in people they trust, their task would get even more complicated.

Collaboration with the enemy

The worst cases of misconduct, at least from a state's perspective, include collaboration with the insurgents. A police force where collaboration with the enemies of the state is frequent can be without question described as deeply dysfunctional. In Afghanistan, cases of police selling weapons and ammunition on the black market or even directly to the insurgents were common: one episode of police handing over weapons to the Taliban was even filmed and shown on the BBC.[43] Perhaps the most serious episode of alleged collaboration of policemen with the insurgents was the April 2008 attack on President Karzai, who was presiding over a military parade in Kabul.[44] There were also indications that the attack on the Kabul Serena Hotel in January 2008 was facilitated by MoI employees.[45] In June 2010 Brig. Gen. Sayed Aziz Wardak was arrested and accused among other things of having collaborated with the insurgents.[46] One of the top officials in the MoI was even sacked in 2011 under the accusation of having sent information to the Taliban.[47]

The majority of demonstrated cases of Taliban infiltration were at relatively low levels of the MoI hierarchy.[48] However, below the known cases of collaboration, much more is likely to have been going on and there are indications of that. Mentors and ISAF believe that several operations were compromised because of Taliban infiltration of the police: in Helmand in 2009 the police were being kept out of planning in order to avoid forewarning the Taliban.[49] Often eyewitnesses have reported instances of police collaboration with the Taliban, or at least passive tolerance of their activities.[50] There were also reports of police helping the Taliban carry out attacks against US units.[51] Proactive police officers sometimes allege that they are isolated in their struggle with the insurgents and are singled out for attacks while surrounding district police stations are quiet.[52]

According to UN sources, many CoPs in the districts of the south and south-east had contacts with the Taliban and developed agreements with them.[53] Often such deals appear to have been the result of the police's fear of not being in a position to fight with local insurgents. In an area of Kunar opposed to Bajaur in 2010, the police and the Taliban were mainly from the same tribes. Reportedly, because in a fight there would be casualties on both sides and revenge afterwards, the police tried to avoid fighting as much as possible.[54] In Arghandab in Kandahar in 2008–9 police reportedly made a deal with the Taliban because of the weak ISAF presence.[55] In August 2008 there were reports of the Marjah police having opened negotiations with the Taliban.[56] Diplomatic sources highlighted that even in the north, deal-making between the police and Taliban might be a problem, as for example in the case of Almar's border police.[57] Evidence of collaboration between Laghman's police and the Taliban was reported in 2010.[58]

At the MoI, high-ranking officers admit that in some areas there might be informal ceasefires with the armed opposition.[59] Another high-ranking officer stated that the MoI knew about these deals, but also that hard evidence was hard to come by.[60] According to the Chief of Staff of the MoI, officers were sometimes removed for cooperating with the enemy.[61] In 2006 a police officer in Kandahar alleged that the CoP of five districts of Kandahar city had contacts with the Taliban. One of them was in fact the cousin of a Taliban commander, but was protected by a high-rank MoI official on the basis of their shared Alokozai background.[62] A source within the MoI even believed that an important provincial CoP had links to the Taliban, but was protected by one of the southern strongmen.[63]

Various other forms of collaboration (apart from ceasefires) of the police with the Taliban were alleged. In Helmand the British often suspected the police of passing on information on British troops to the Taliban.[64]

The ANP found all sorts of ways to pass information […] They'd click on their radios, or find an excuse to wander outside the gates just as a patrol was ready to leave, where it was an easy thing for them to signal one of the [enemy spotters] waiting outside.[65]

We were suspicious that some of [the police] were in contact with the Taliban and were passing on information about our movements and what we were up to.[66]

[Major] Birchall noted that the Afghan police's usual night routine when within 100 or so meters of the enemy was to 'get stoned and to go to sleep maintaining a single sentry (looking in the wrong direction)' [...] He estimated that 70 per cent of the police[...] were in cahoots with the Taliban—'the ANP is a treacherous organisation at best and downright sympathetic to the Taliban at worst.'[67]

The Danes also suspected the police of collusion with the Taliban.[68] Repeated episodes of ANP units opening fire on ISAF units were also reported.[69] Even if the number of individuals involved in the worst incidents (murder of foreign troops) was small, it appears that sometimes investigations highlighted widespread complicity. After the killing of five British soldiers in Nad-i Ali in November 2009, a 'wholesale clear' of the district's police force was carried out, leaving in place only thirty of the 150 policemen.[70] In Nawa in 2010 the police split between supporters and opponents of the district CoP, accused of having links to the Taliban. Four of the 100 policemen in the district, known to oppose the CoP, were murdered in unclear circumstances in a matter of days. Eventually the CoP was forced to leave by the district council and the governor.[71]

In some cases the police seemed to be cooperating with the Taliban on a commercial basis. Wardak police, for example, lost 160 weapons to the Taliban in alleged clashes during 2005–6 and the suspicion was that they sold them for cash.[72]

Although there are no overall figures, defections from the police appear to have been relatively frequent events (see Box 3). In December 2010 the MoI spokesman reported that desertions from the police were on the rise, particularly when units were deployed to the areas most affected by the insurgency.[73] Trainees from the Police Academy in Kabul openly stated their fear of being deployed in areas affected by the insurgency.[74]

The overall picture is one of loyalty of the police to the central government being often suspect, despite what in principle should be very strong odds in favour of the government and ISAF, compared to what the Taliban have to offer. This does not augur well for any situation where the odds were perceived to be shifting away from the government.

Box 3: Police defections.

In March 2006 forty policemen defected in Ghazni with weapons and equipment, following delays in paying their salaries;[75]

In June 2006, police in Sangin were down to just seven men, who refused to wear uniforms or conduct joint patrols. The brother of the deputy CoP was a Talib commander, suspected of passing information to the Taliban; they all defected or joined the Taliban;[76]

THE ULTIMATE TEST OF FUNCTIONALITY

> Twelve policemen reportedly defected to the Taliban in Zabul in August 2006;[77]
> Desertions were reported again in Ghazni in September 2006;[78]
> Five policemen were killed in Nimruz in July 2007 by fellow policemen, allegedly linked to the Taliban;[79]
> An officer and three patrolmen were killed by fellow policemen who then defected to the Taliban, Helmand (Musa Qala), September 2007;[80]
> Sixteen border policemen defected to the Taliban in September 2008 on the border with Iran;[81]
> Five policemen were killed in Helmand (Nad-i Ali) in November 2008 by a group of colleagues, who then defected to the Taliban;[82]
> Twelve policemen defected to the Taliban in Farah (Bala Boluk) in December 2008; forty more policemen were arrested on charges of alleged links to the Taliban;[83]
> Seven border policemen defected to the Taliban in Baghdis province in January 2010;[84]
> Twenty-five policemen reportedly joined the Taliban in Jalrez (Wardak) in February 2010;[85]
> In February 2010 a group of policemen joined the Taliban in Chak district of Wardak province;[86]
> A senior policeman was arrested in February 2010 for planting and storing roadside bombs in Kapisa province;[87]
> A police officer killed five fellow policemen in Ajristan district of Ghazni in June 2010 and was alleged to have links to the Taliban;[88]
> In November 2010 up to twenty policemen defected to the Taliban in Khogyani district of Ghazni;[89]
> In June 2011 two policemen defected to the Taliban in Jowzjan, Derzab district.[90]

Alternative models?

Much of the difficulty in setting up a functional chain of command and control at the MoI might have been self-inflicted. The model adopted, styled after the European bureaucratised version of a police force, is very demanding in terms of human resources. An adviser noted that although the police usually had no written orders or records and relied on an oral system, they had formidable memories and could handle their tasks. This could be considered a basic form of professionalism in its own way.[91] Similarly, the Canadian mentors in Kandahar by 2010 were recognising the fact that rather than not planning at all, the ANP 'plan[ned] differently'. They were becoming more lenient with the Afghan command in their appointments, recognising that the Afghans did have an understanding of who was suitable for a job.[92] It is difficult to say whether a more decentralised system would work in Afghanistan, but in the absence of a realistic plan to attract better skilled human resources towards the MoI, alternatives would be worth considering.

If we were to assume that a balanced version of the western-Turkish model adopted by the MoI was not feasible in the post-2001 context, perhaps it would have been better to look for alternative models rather than develop a wholly unbalanced one. The so-called Anglo-Saxon model of policing relies more on local accountability, making several levels of bureaucratic supervision less necessary.[93] The problem in Afghanistan is that there are no local institutions to be accountable to, except for provincial councils with a reputation for being elected in rigged elections.

While in some cases the police might have been able to strike a good relationship with local communities (being drawn from them) or with local authorities, on the basis of shared professionalism or more likely of a shared political background, seeing this pattern repeated throughout Afghanistan seemed an unlikely development in the country in 2011. The main problem is the fragmentation of the country into often rival communities, even within a single district. Strong police connections to a particular community would often exist to the detriment of relations with other communities. The 2005 and 2010 parliaments were both quite keen on exercising oversight over the MoI,[94] but had little support from other institutions of the Afghan state and limited legitimacy of their own, particularly in the case of the 2010 parliament, given the extensive rigging which took place during its election.

There are of course several more models of policing being used around the world, from where Afghanistan could draw inspiration to develop its own model.[95] Perhaps having access to a wider range of models of policing could facilitate Afghanistan's search for a suitable system.[96] The section about the Herat case study discusses the option of a patrimonial, but decentralised police system, such as existed in feudal Europe, for example. The MoI of 2011, however, did not have the capacity or incentive to develop its own model of a police force and the result was a bureaucratic-centralised model of policing twisted and corrupted by the lack of adequate human capital and local political will to make it function.

Control of territory and population

The early days

In 2001–2, territorial and population control were in fact franchised out to factional and strongmen's armed forces, over which the MoI had little control even when they formally belonged to the police. At the provincial level and below, the involvement of the centre was very modest and the decisive factors were the CoP and the governor, as well as local powerbrokers. Even the weapons were initially owned by the CoP or by the policemen themselves as there was no form of registration.[97] By 2010 the centre was still directly managing only the payment of salaries.[98] The governor no longer had the authority to order the police to arrest somebody, nor had he access to the police files; until the 1970s it was even possible for the governor to get people arrested without a written order.[99] The police law of September 2005 was in part the source of the problem: its unclear language regarding 'leadership of the MoI from Kabul' and 'guidance of governors' ended up causing major disagreements between the MoI and the governors. Governors reportedly were issuing orders and trying to influence the hiring, promotion and assignment of police in the provinces. The governors were sometimes also accused of utilising police human and financial resources for personal and political gains. The governors, on the other hand, argued that without being able to show control over the police, they did not have sufficient power to govern the provinces.[100]

Lasting disagreement over who was ultimately in charge of the provincial police, the governor or the provincial CoP, had a negative impact on the potential of the police to collaborate with communities. This remained a point of contention also in recent years between the MoI and the IDLG.[101]

The Tufts team in 2003 found that:

a government head of a rural district in Nangarhar complained that his police chief was not following official directives from local officials; rather, he was arresting and releasing people upon the orders of the chief of the police in Jalalabad, to whom he had greater loyalty.[102]

They also found that:

In [a rural district of Kandahar], the head of the police [name withheld], was traveling to the main road and asking for 20,000 Afs per car for passing on the road. If they would not give the money, then he would take their car. He had power because the rest of the police supported him. Since he was from [rural district] people in the district would cover for him, because he had tribal and friendship support. The regular people were very unhappy and tired of this situation and they would complain to me since I was the district authority there at the time. But I could not stop him because he was powerful and well supported by his tribe. The same pattern was also occurring when I was the district authority in [another rural district], with a person … who was stealing cars and robbing houses. When I caught him, he admitted in front of the shura that he stole the cars and robbed the houses. I sent him to the provincial centre to the police. The governor [now the former governor] became involved in his case. After one month the suspect was released and promoted as a commander. Now he has guards and cars and power. Instead of being punished, he was promoted, in part, because he is of the same tribe as the head of the military division of Kandahar.[103]

Persistent weakness

Gradually, as a system of command and control started retaking shape, the picture got more complicated. However, in many cases the CoPs still maintained relations with the local strongmen and factions and avoided policing them. Under Sayyed Khel's authority, the Baghlan police as a whole showed little willingness to challenge a range of armed groups which were becoming increasingly violent during 2008.[104] Another example was the murder of six people by Member of Parliament Mullah Terakhel in Kabul in August 2010: no action was taken.[105]

The degree of support the strongmen could get from their associates appointed as police varied, as did the behaviour of the latter. In some cases they could prove difficult to restrain even for the strongmen. In Herat, for example, an associate of Ismail Khan was appointed head of the intelligence department when Ismail was governor. His rogue behaviour (house searches without warrant, arrests of people opposed to Ismail Khan, 'virginity' checks on young women) forced Ismail Khan to transfer him to CoP of Injil district.[106]

As before the war, in the tribal areas the communities were left to deal with crime and disputes through their own mechanisms. In section 9.6.5 we will discuss the relevance of this to the rule of law. Here we are looking at the same issue from the perspective of territorial and population control. Official statistics dramatically under-represented the actual level of crime. A 2007 comparison of a UNAMA survey of official crime statistics and UNDSS data on crime showed that the latter was increasing, while the former was decreasing, concluding that what was really happening was a loss of outreach and probably of trust towards the police among the population. It was estimated in 2008 that crime statistics only reflected about half of all crimes.[107]

According to the Khost CoP, he was receiving rarely more than a single case a month from the districts.[108] In reality, the murder rate in Khost was very high, fuelled by tribal feuds. In three districts of Khost, for example, ten murders occurred during the first half of 2008–9, a rather high murder rate considering the population of over 300,000.[109] In Chak (Wardak), in 2008–10 not a single arrest was made nor a crime reported to the police, as the insurgency and the predominant insecurity was deterring the population from going to the police.[110] UN sources mentioned forty honour killings in 2007–8 in eastern Afghanistan alone, probably wildly underestimating the number of cases because of the tendency not to report them. Typically these were cases of women killed because of adultery accusations, or for disobeying their families. The UN rapporteur himself:

> spoke with a family member of a boy and girl (cousins) who allegedly had sexual relations outside of marriage. They were invited to a 'dinner' by their uncles and, when sleeping, were shot and killed. The boy's body was sent to his father. The girl's was buried without any funeral prayers. No family members complained to the police. The police knew about the deaths, but did not investigate, claiming that they could not do so without a complaint from the family.[111]

Although as we will see below (section 9.6.5) the authorities often referred cases to community councils, in general liaising with community elders was not very common. In Jalali's time (2003–5) the CoPs were instructed regularly once a month to talk to the elders (not just the ones they may have been connected to), but the practice was abandoned after he left the MoI.[112] One of the main advantages (from the state's perspective) of empowering customary justice institutions was therefore lost: establishing a relationship with the elders and getting the pulse of the situation. Reliance on customary justice also meant that the state had little control over what was going on in much of its territory. This might not have been too much of a problem as long as the matter was common criminality, but in the case of political criminality the matter was very different.

Because of not patrolling or having outposts away from the district centres and the highways, the police were often not even able to act as a territorial 'early warning' system, able to detect negative developments and perhaps to do something about them. The burden of 'early warning' fell as a result entirely on the shoulders of the NDS, itself not particularly able in much of Afghanistan's territory, not least because it was being re-established from scratch in 2001. Moreover, while the NDS could carry out information gathering, without the police there could be no enforcement. In practice, therefore, any infiltration by insurgents in areas where the police did not operate would either go undetected, unless the communities themselves wanted to report it, or even if detected could not be prevented. This seems to be one of the reasons why in 2002–5 the Taliban were able to gradually remobilise and even infiltrate Afghan territory without much hindrance.[113]

Map 4: Police check-posts in Kabul, August 2008.

Source: Survey carried out by Niamatullah Ibrahimi, Crisis States Research Centre.

In Kabul and the other cities the strength of the police's control over territory and the population improved markedly between 2002 and 2010, particularly in some key areas such as airports, and by 2006 computerised immigration and passport controls were in place.[114] The repeated terrorist attacks in Kabul every year after 2001 (including in the heavily policed central districts of Shahr-e Naw and Wazir Akbar Khan), however, cast some doubt about the solidity of this territorial and population control, as do the repeated cases of riots in large cities getting out of control (see Box 4 and section 9.6.4): Kabul 2006 and 2010, Herat 2004, Jalalabad 2005, etc. In general, the interaction of the police with the population was very weak or non-existent. Even talking to shop owners to gather information was a rare occurrence in most of the country.[115] Map 4 offers a snapshot of the police presence around Kabul city on one day in August 2008.

Wasteful use of human resources

Poor management of human resources and the low skill level of most officers and NCOs meant that many patrolmen had to be allocated to static guard duties, an inefficient way of meeting threats. The long shifts (sometimes as long as six months in a wooden hut in a street of Kabul) also had demoralising effects on the police, lowering their level of alertness. The demands on the police in terms of providing security to all state institutions were typically overwhelming: university and schools, banks, sub-national administration offices, provincial councils.[116] Indeed, as pointed out by analysts and mentors on the ground, the ANP remained in 2009–10 still largely engaged in static security check-point and guarding functions. Guard duties were moreover implemented inefficiently, wasting personnel. In part this role was driven by the demand of donors, who wanted their and associated compounds guarded—this led to the establishment of 6,733 'out of Tashkil' positions (i.e. not in the personnel charts) to guard infrastructure and a 2009 request for 5,920 more.[117]

The presence of a variety of private security forces, either commercial ones or paid for by ISAF and Enduring Freedom, was supposed to relieve the police of this burden at least in part, but in other ways it complicated the security environment and the tasks of the police. Often violent incidents occurred between police and private armed forces, the most notorious of which was in June 2009, when Kandahar CoP Qati was killed by a CIA-recruited militia.[118] The MoI failed to supervise and control effectively the rapidly expanding world of private security companies.[119] In February 2011 the MoI started organising itself in order to exercise oversight of private security companies at the Zone level.[120]

Reduction of coverage faced with the insurgency

This was so much more the case as the insurgency gradually gained strength from 2003 onwards. In many districts, the CoPs started opting to stay out of trouble as much as possible and avoiding sending their men on patrol beyond the immediate vicinities of the district centre. In most cases, even if patrols were taking place the CoP would avoid accompanying the patrolmen, contributing to a climate of low trust towards the officers and to undisciplined behaviour by the police. Much depended on the attitude of the provincial CoPs: those who insisted on following the rules managed sometimes to enforce a greater degree of compliance.[121]

However, in terms of asserting control over the territory and the population, professional qualifications were clearly not enough. The Americans, for example, viewed Khost's CoP Ayub as a 'useless bureaucrat who rarely left his office'. Even his more proactive replacement, respected professional Qayum, only visited four of twelve districts in two and a half months, because of insecurity (the Chiefs are required to visit each district every six months for supervision purposes).[122] Where the insurgency was active, even the highest rated police units failed to secure control. In Baghlan Jadid, the commanding officer of the local CM1-rated police unit acknowledged that 30–50 per cent of the district was under Taliban control.[123]

The appearance of a variety of pro-government militias from 2009 onwards was meant, as discussed in section 6.2.1, to enhance territorial and population control. As of late 2010 these militias were still too unevenly distributed and too few to have a major impact (see Map 5). What was clear, however, was

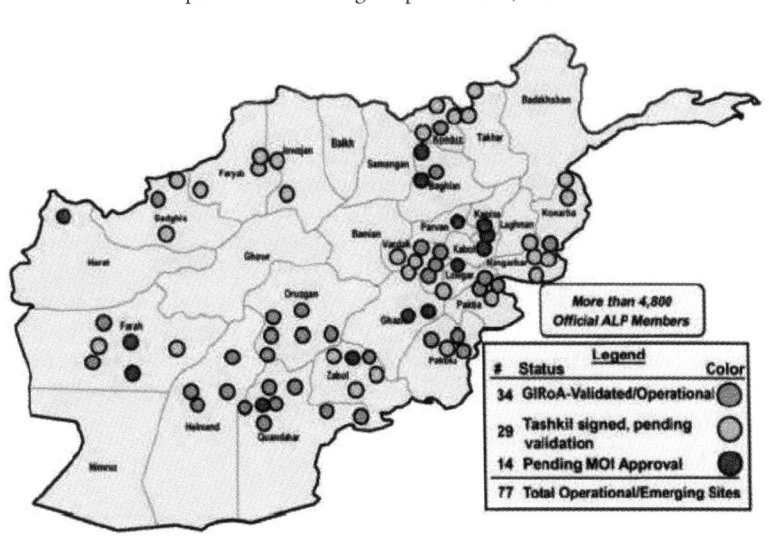

Map 5: Location of Afghan police units, late 2010.

Source: Cordesman 2011.

that the police was having trouble controlling the militias themselves even if these were supposed to be under the responsibility of the MoI. In other words, while the militias might plausibly have contributed to weaken the insurgency, it does not seem at all that they contributed to strengthen the central government. Several reports have already emerged concerning the difficult relationship between VSO and ALP and the AUP.[124]

Reporting

In terms of reporting, counter-terrorism had priority from 2002 onwards, compared to CID. Using interception-proof mobile phones, reports about incidents in the provinces started being sent to the MoI and were filed there. Reporting was improved in 2009–10 with the introduction of the Afghan Police Incident Reporting System (APIRS):

[a] standardized reporting system in which incidents are consolidated in a national database and automatically analyzed. The program generates a multitude of reports: logistics, intelligence, readiness, casualty and operations. [...] Presently, there is no consistent reporting database in place. Reports are hand written and then saved as text documents. This often results in unreliable information, inhibiting operations and intelligence collection efforts. "Sometimes in a situation we don't even know how many personnel we have available," said Colonel Nematullah Haidary, Operations General Director of the ANP. [...] The driving forces behind its use in Afghanistan are the police mentors of CSTC-A.[125]

By 2009 at least the ABP had a reporting system of some kind in place between the HQ and the brigades. Paperwork was done and records kept in three copies. When the Head of ABP Gen Noorzai requested information from the bottom, he would normally receive a response. Paperwork was still mostly travelling by road, but there was an ability to communicate in code as well.[126]

If the technology and the technique of reporting undoubtedly improved, the willingness of the field units to report correctly remained in doubt. In the words of a MoI adviser, 'nobody wants bad news and there is a lot of misreporting up the chain of command'.[127] Information rarely travelled upwards.[128] Statistical data was transferred to Kabul slowly, typically a year late. Moreover, statistics were not reliable. As a result, the MoI did not really know in detail what was going on. Even in the department of education the provinces tended not to report upwards as the MoI was not seen as a 'mother organisation'. In practice, there was more information at the provincial level than at the centre.[129]

Logistics

From 2002 onwards MoI units in the provinces grew increasingly dependent on the support of the US armed forces and other ISAF contingents. This dependency continued growing until 2010 as the Americans were deploying to new regions and taking under their patronage more and more police units. Even where the Americans were not deployed, they offered logistical support to the police. They also supplied the police with large numbers of vehicles, mostly Ford Ranger pick-ups, and then with the necessary fuel to operate them. Even the comparatively plentiful American support was not enough to completely enable the police to operate at full capacity. In particular, supplies of fuel were kept at just 6 litres a day, which were insufficient for regular patrolling in rugged terrain. The Americans also failed to supply the police with weapons of suitable characteristics and quality for the counter-insurgency tasks they were taking on.[130]

Still, there is no question that American support enabled the MoI to dramatically enhance its capabilities. It also created a chronic dependency that NTM-A started addressing only in 2010. Arguably the MoI logistics system only existed in theory. Aware of the complete inability of the MoI to provide any logistical support, the police units were unlikely to develop much confidence in the ministerial leadership and morale was negatively affected. Deliveries were dependent on the support of the ISAF mentors, to the point that the police became fearful of losing their mentoring team, because of the impact that such a loss would have had on logistics.[131]

The other side of reliance on plentiful American support was the neglect of any opportunity to establish a more efficient system for managing resources. No workshops were created in the provinces for maintaining vehicles,[132] which, as a result of the impracticality of sending them to Kabul for repair and maintenance, were often overused until repair become uneconomical. In January 2011 NTM-A identified almost 630 MoI vehicles which were already beyond repair, despite having been delivered in 2005–10.[133] This lack of maintainance applied to all the equipment the MoI was receiving.[134]

Apart from the weakness of the logistical apparatus, which could not always be offset by direct American support, corruption also contributed to prevent the police in the field from being adequately supplied.[135] Equipment was often sold on the black market and fuel was siphoned off.[136]

Only in 2010 did the MoI start acquiring at least an embryonic logistical capacity driven by Minister Mohammadi's concern with improving the effectiveness of the counter-insurgency.[137] In 2009 ISAF was still distributing winter clothes for the police, but in 2010 Timur Shah, head of logistics, were able to control the distribution through the new system created by NTM-A,[138] even if the first year of Afghan winter gear distribution was quite messy, with different field units competing to appropriate it.[139] By 2010 the police was able to manage the Parliamentary elections, the Peace Jirga and the Kabul Conference relatively competently by improved searches and guard duties, ability to deploy where needed and the processing of logistical requirements. The distribution, however, was organised by ISAF logistics and contractors.[140]

ANCOP received particular attention from NTM-A in terms of enabling MoI logistical assistance. The MoI transport battalion was developed in terms of capacity, even if it still accounted for a small fraction of all supplies being delivered. Efforts were also made in book-keeping training.[141] In March 2011 the MoI logistics team acquired the flexibility to manage logistics requests which were not standard, as opposed to simply rejecting them.[142] The basic type of logistical system which was being developed is shown in Figure 9.

Whether the NTM-A plan to expand MoI capabilities could succeed as long as the easier path of relying on the mentors was available is however open to question. Timur Shah himself was reported to have asked ISAF to stop pushing orders, which disrupted MoI accountability by bypassing the Afghan national property books.[143]

Reforming the logistical system of the MoI through the injection of new personnel appeared particularly problematic. The supply link to the contractors was essential to keep the MoI going in the middle of a war. The risk implicit in bringing new people in was that they could be sabotaged by older people, relying on networking between officials and suppliers. One MoI official estimated that one to two years were necessary for new staff to establish themselves within the logistical structure.[144] This aspect once again highlights that reform carries some costs and potential gains have to be offset against potential or even certain losses.

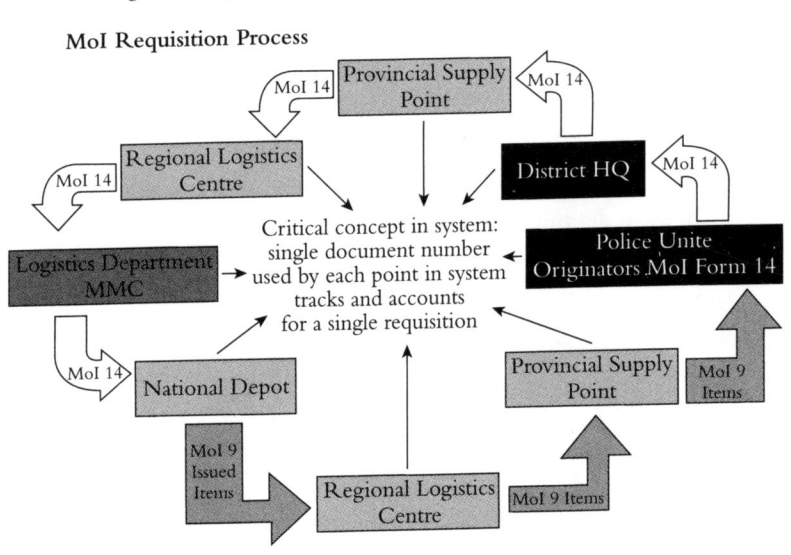

Figure 9: Logistical system in development by NTM-A, 2010.

MoI Requisition Process

Source: Cordesman.

THE ULTIMATE TEST OF FUNCTIONALITY

The Afghan government did not even try very hard to strengthen the paramilitary dimension of policing, until the threat of the insurgency became very direct with the infiltration of northern Afghanistan and Kabul itself by the armed opposition. Arguably the government identified the strongmen and their retinues of armed men as its primary constituency and did not want to challenge them with the rapid consolidation of a force capable of managing small-scale violence more effectively. In facing the threat of the insurgency, the MoI achieved something more, but overall its performance was far from convincing and as of early 2012 it was still not clear whether Afghanistan's police had improved enough to contain the insurgency. Arguably the government's cosy relationship with selected strongmen undermined the effort to improve the functionality of the MoI once the insurgency started being perceived as a more vital threat by important factions of the ruling elite.

The strong presence of foreign troops in the country seems to have contributed to weaken the government's need for a strong and effective paramilitary force. The constituency of strongmen, on which the government relied for support, had a vested interest in opposing a functional paramilitary police, because their leverage vis-à-vis Kabul would have been rapidly eroded.

9

THE AMBIGUOUS IMPACT OF REFORM

The first wave of reforms and the difficulties of re-centralisation
Nature of the reforms

When the police was under the full control of President Karzai's rivals, allies of Jami'ati Islami (combining the Panjshiri, Parwani and other networks) in 2001–2, the President strongly argued for the professionalisation of the police and ending the control of the militia factions over the MoI and the police, probably seeing it an opportunity to weaken Jamiati control.[1] As a result, change started occurring under the tenure of Jalali (2003–5). His deputy Hilal liaised and negotiated with the factions, allowing them to retain much say in terms of appointments, but also reclaiming back some influence for the centre, although not everybody agrees on whether Hilal worked to the benefit of Jalali or the strongmen.[2]

Jalali himself was a convinced reformer and during his time at the MoI there was an effort to assess the performance of individuals before making appointments. However, he was not a very assertive man and only in a handful of cases did he resort to strong-arm tactics to impose some of the appointments which he was trying to decide on merit.[3] Jalali succeeded in ridding the MoI of Din Mohammad Jurat, a powerful Panjshiri in charge of the Department for National Public Security, which was supposed to intervene in the event of major disturbances.[4] He also intervened forcefully in Gardez, Herat and Faryab in the course of three years of tenure, using his Quick Reaction Force. The force, initially called Stand-by Police, was his creation: a central reserve of police, recruited independently of the provincial fiefdoms (although provincial detachments also existed, see above). At the peak of its strength this force counted on 4,000–5,000 men, not enough to compel the rest of the police to abide to Jalali's decisions. The Quick Reaction Force was not given any special training, nor was specially selected, it was simply slightly better equipped and, most importantly, recruited directly by the MoI through a single office based in Kabul.[5]

In general the militias which had in many cases been controlling the highways were forced to give up their check-posts to the police, initially with positive effects.[6] Jalali also deployed 300 police from the centre to increase his influence in the troublesome province of Balkh in the north, but the impact was only short term.[7] Jalali's appointments were mostly Pashtuns and Khalqis which gave space to the Jamiati networks to claim that a process of Pashtunisation was going on.[8]

However, even under Jalali in most cases the police maintained relations with the strongmen and rarely dared confronting them. The fact that in 2004–5 about 20,000 militiamen were transferred from the Ministry of Defence to the police (in order to avoid DDR) certainly did not help in weakening the link with the strongmen.[9]

After a period of good cooperation with Karzai, Jalali rapidly found himself isolated as the President refused to sign his decisions and appointments aimed at reducing the power of the strongmen.[10] Using his power over appointments, Karzai frequently interfered in Jalali's decisions and blocked his attempts to dismiss corrupt provincial police chiefs and officials within the MoI. Jalali eventually resigned in protest at the end of 2005. Jalali's resignation is believed to have been prompted by President Karzai's refusal to act on a list of 100 corrupt officials compiled by Jalali.[11]

The centralisation effort vis-à-vis the strongmen

In general this period was one of modest re-assertion of the MoI faced with local strongmen, but President Karzai offered Jalali only lukewarm support and decreasingly so as the heads of the various anti-Taliban factions approached him to lobby in favour of their associated strongmen in the provinces. One typical example is that of Samad, a rogue strongman in the Qataqala area of Faryab, who ruled over forty villages. Police never dared to confront him despite a long list of complaints by locals, until ISAF gave its support to remove him from power.[12] In Kandahar in 2006, the security officer was stating openly that he was a tribal appointee and would respond only to his tribal chiefs.[13]

The removal of even the most obviously corrupt police officers was always problematic. When the CoP of Takhar, Mutalleb Beg, was removed in late 2003 because of evidence of his involvement in drug smuggling, he started a double strategy of lobbying Kabul for his reappointment and distributing weapons to his militiamen, threatening to destabilise the province. Shortly thereafter he was appointed CoP in neighbouring Kunduz.[14] Even around Kabul the police were often impotent vis-à-vis the strongmen and their associates.[15] As late as 2010 it was still considered acceptable that Sayyaf would demand to have his own people appointed in his stronghold of Paghman. For example, In Kabul city itself, Dostum could demand the appointment of a trusted CoP in district 10 of Kabul (where he has a house) and Vice-president Khalili in districts 3, 6, 5 where Hazaras are mostly concentrated.[16] In the south, where political protection from Kabul was strongest, powerful strongmen actually enhanced their position within the police over the years. Colonel Razzaq of the Border Police is the best example of this process. Despite having ignited an Achakzai-Noorzai tribal war due to the arbitrary behaviour of his men, which eventually benefited the Taliban, his position in Spin Boldak was at the end of 2010 as solid as ever, and in 2011 he was appointed CoP in Kandahar.[17]

The persistent role of the strongmen gave rise to two different sets of problems. The first and most obvious one was that the centre was dependent on the goodwill of the strongmen and at least a degree of loyalty on their side. The second was that even for the strongmen themselves it was not easy to control the police when it was staffed by their own men. The most successful strongman of the north, Atta Mohammed Noor, governor of Balkh, felt once obliged to complain in public about the bad behaviour of his own police.[18]

The process of re-centralisation, initiated by Jalali, was not only limited by its own slow progress, but also by flaws in the way the police force was being put together. The replacement of militias by the police in parts of the country, mentioned above, was initially welcomed by the population. Soon, however, drivers were being robbed and beaten by the police who had replaced the strongmen's militias, sometimes behaving even worse than them.[19]

Even before the creation of ANCOP, ANP mobile battalions deployed from Kabul were often treated with hostility by the local police.[20] The mobile battalions numbered 6,000 in November 2003, but were poorly equipped and not very mobile at all, lacking vehicles and most of their members were untrained.[21]

Provincial dynamics: Faryab province, 2004[22]

Local political conflicts made any effort of centralisation particularly difficult to implement. Faryab province is a case in point. Conflict between Pashtuns and Uzbeks characterised Faryab since the early 1980s and peaked in 1997– 2001, when the Taliban ruthlessly crushed those who had resisted them and the Uzbeks retaliated by targeting the Pashtun community once the Taliban regime had fallen. When in April 2004 Governor Enyatollah was forced to flee, many of the Pashtuns serving in the administration and police did the same, as well as some allies of Hashim Habibi. Some have since returned, but not all. Governor Enyatollah had been appointing what appears to many locals a disproportionate number of Pashtuns in positions of power. These included among others the mayor of Maimana, the provincial CoP and the CoP of Maimana.

Following the departure of Hashim Habibi, Faryab's police experienced a deep crisis when many soldiers and officers who had been appointed by

Habibi quit. Others who did not leave voluntarily were replaced by the commanders loyal to Junbesh, so that quite a major turnover took place, before stabilisation occurred under Junbesh's control. Several officers who had served in the position in 2002–3, before being removed by Hashim Habibi, were reappointed. The MoI tried to resist the attempt to impose a new de facto decentralisation of the police and the majority of those appointed or reappointed were not confirmed by Kabul.

In Faryab's case at least, professionalisation and centralisation did not march together. By the end of 2004 there were few professionals in Faryab's police. Out of 211 officers, only thirteen were professionally trained, often employed in administration, intelligence and as deputies. However, almost all the officers and troops underwent short training courses in Mazar-i Sharif during 2004, which qualified them for the financial treatment reserved to national police, that is, about four times as much as what they used to earn previously. The police department could also draw on the skills of a significant number of police officers who, despite having not been trained at the Police Academy, spent many years in the police force and could therefore be said to be quite experienced.

Several of the few professionals were, however, mainly at the top of the police organisation. This included the chief of Faryab police himself, a professional from Paktia, who had been appointed just four months earlier. At the district level, in November 2004 only two of the district chiefs were illiterate former jihadi commanders, all the remaining ones could be said to be well qualified for the job, with the partial exception of one who had only military training. This represented a marked improvement on 2003, when former jihadi and militia commanders accounted for two-thirds of the chiefs. Interestingly, 2003 had seen a dramatic worsening of the professionalism of police in Faryab compared to 2002, as shown by Table 19:

Table 19: Faryab's district CoPs by professional background, 2002–4.

	Professional police training	Professional military training	Jihadi commander	Experienced policemen	Other	Vacant
2004	3	1	2	3	–	–
2003	1	6		1	1	–
2002	3	1	4	–	–	1

Although this type of information is difficult to gather, evidence was found that factional control over the police force by November 2004 was not very strong. Although, on the whole, the policeforce was still avoiding confronting the major commanders, biographical information about the provincial CoP and the district chiefs suggests that the majority of them were not connected to Junbesh or to other military-political factions. However, patrolmen serving in Maimana seemed to come mainly from Qaysar district, home to the last commander of 200th Division Fataullah, a militia leader. Under Habibi, their predecessors had come from his native Belcheragh district.

In sum, in order to increase central control the MoI even adopted strategies such as bringing in non-professionals who had little title to their appointment, earning therefore their loyalty. Local strongmen sometimes brought in professionals, excluded from the MoI appointments, in order to legitimise themselves and to keep away other appointees who may be disloyal to them.

Provincial dynamics: Kandahar province, 2005[23]

In dealing with the resistance to centralisation in the provinces, the MoI had limited tools at its disposal. In Kandahar too, as in Faryab, the MoI withheld recognition (and higher salaries) for police officers appointed by the local CoP without MoI approval: 276 officers were registered as of February 2005, which is an improvement from the 137 of 2003, but still left an estimated 400 more who were not. Among the rank and file, 1,471 were registered, while the number of those not registered was unknown even to police HQ in Kandahar.

Another tool was preventing police officers and patrolmen from attending the quick training courses set up by Dyncorp. The CoP in turn used that tool to favour allies and discriminate against rivals. In no district of Kandahar by mid-2005 had the majority of the policemen gone through the training and there were huge variations between districts, depending on their relationship with the CoP, Khan Mohammed. In Arghandab (Khan Mohammad's home district) a total of twelve officers and policemen had, for example, attended the training course by the end of February 2005, while in Gul Agha's influenced Dand only two had. Missing the courses deprived the men of a pay rise which would have more than quadrupled their salaries. The average policeman in Kandahar still earns 800 Afs (US$16) and lives away from his family, being housed together with tens of colleagues in the same police station. Governor Gul Agha Shirai stepped in and started paying top-ups and salaries to police during 2002–3, but then stopped once the custom were taken over by the Ministry of Finance.

In contrast to Faryab, the politically well-connected province of Kandahar had little incentive to bring in professionals to legitimise its autonomy. The level of corruption and ineffectiveness of Kandahar's police was at least in part a reflection of the low professional level of its leadership, although corruption was also ripe when Mohammad Akram Khakrizwal, a professional officer, was in charge. The CoP in 2005, Khan Mohammed, was the former commander of 2nd Army Corps, who was transferred to the police in the autumn of 2004, following the decision to disband the Corps within the framework of the DDR programme. He did not have any previous experience in the police and as far as education was concerned he was barely able to read and write.

The district CoPs fared hardly any better. Not a single one of them was a professional policeman and only two had education to the twelfth grade. The others were either illiterate or had been educated for just a few years or still had only been to Islamic schools. They all used to be jihadi commanders, or at least described themselves as such, although a few were simply tribal elders, in some cases residing in Pakistan until relatively recently. The smaller or worse-connected tribes were not represented at all among the CoPs: seven of them were Popolzai, four Alikozai and three Barakzai.

In terms of imposing some more meritocracy in appointments, pressure applied by the local PRT appears to have been more effective than the MoI's efforts. In March 2005, for example, two of the chiefs (districts of Khakrez and Ghorak) were suspended because they failed to 'meet expectations'. The MoI however managed to impose a policy of rotation of the district CoPs, to ensure that a district was not garrisoned by police who were originally from that same district, but also to prevent the CoPs from developing roots in any particular place.

The composition of each police unit varied considerably, being in some cases a mix of individuals from different districts and in others a homogenous group originating from the same village, likely formed around the armed retinue of some commander, then appointed CoP. This was the case of the Daman CoP, for example.[24] Most police were from Kandahar province, except in Kandahar city, where many were from the surrounding provinces, including the large majority of the officers.[25] In the districts, the officers were mostly from the surrounding districts.[26]

Reform, counter-reform and external scrutiny

The Trojan horse which was not

The tenure of Jalali's successor Moqbel Zarar could be characterised as one of a reform effort which boomeranged back as a counter-reform. In Jalali's own words, 'reform was reversed—institutions used to advance factional interests and legitimise their activities'.[27] Under Zarar's tenure, international pressure to reform the MoI increased dramatically because at this stage UNAMA was still having a significant influence in the shaping of the strategy of reform. Zarar himself had been chosen because of his close association with one of the main networks of strongmen in the fraying anti-Taliban coalition. The Parwani network, often referred to as 'Parwani mafia' by UN officials and foreign diplomats, had been a powerful player in the MoI since Qanuni and the Panjshiri had drawn them in (2001–2), but the idea was to mollify it towards change by allowing it to ride the tiger of reform and playing it against other powerful networks in the MoI, in particular the Panjshiri network which had risen to power under Qanuni.

At this point (2005–6) neither the Americans nor the Europeans had strong views on how to proceed to reform the MoI: the Americans were primarily interested in getting the MoI to contribute more effectively to the emerging counter-insurgency effort, while the Europeans were in principle still com-

THE AMBIGUOUS IMPACT OF REFORM

mitted to institution-building, but were starting to lose hope in the possibility to put it in practice in the Afghan context.[28]

Zarar was therefore conceived as a Trojan horse of reform by UNAMA but unfortunately neither UNAMA nor another international player managed to exercise sufficient supervision over the reform process and in particular over the introduction of a more meritocratic process of appointments. Those who worked with Zarar described him as 'not a very decisive man', uncomfortable in his seat of Minister of Interior and timid too, rarely putting forward an idea of his own.[29] On the plus side Zarar was seen as a team player and a patient man, ready to listen.[30] Reportedly it took him a year to familiarise himself with MoI rules and regulations. Some of his advisers liked him because of his reliance on them and his tendency to agree to whatever they advised him to do.[31]

International pressure did achieve some results. By 2007 the MoI had moved towards a more equitable distribution of power at the centre, compared to the complete dominance of Tajiks affiliated with Jamiat of the early days. 'Out of 30 of the newly appointed top generals, thirteen are Pashtun, fourteen Tajik, two Hazara and one Uzbek'.[32] However, it was still the case that over half of the top leadership of the MoI was from Parwan, Kapisa and Panjshir.[33] The fact that virtually all the Tajiks at the top of the MoI were from the Jamiati networks described above complicated the equation, as trying to reduce the influence of the networks would attract accusation of ethnic discrimination.[34] Moreover, the selection of non-Tajiks was rarely based on merit, but more often on their readiness to cooperate with the Jamiati networks, or on the purchase of positions for cash (see Chapter 3).

The lone reformer at the top

The appointment of Hanif Atmar as MoI in 2008 was initially greeted with relief by donors and reformists within the MoI as he was perceived to be a committed reformer, even if Atmar himself had made clear that he did not want the job and that he only accepted under pressure from the President. Despite being supported initially by the UN and the British, Atmar believed that the bulk of the police had to be a paramilitary force.[35] His reform plans, aiming to curb corruption and promote meritocracy, faced strong resistance from the networks now well-embedded in the MoI structure, even before they started being implemented. Soon after his appointment, MoI officials were visiting the leaders of the jihadi parties, asking them to lobby for his removal and even professional generals were involved.[36] His efforts to sack corrupt and untrusted officers failed due to political vetoes.[37] He was not on speaking terms with his own deputy for counter-narcotics Daud, but was never able to sack him.[38]

Although he was seen as receptive to advice and as having real leadership qualities,[39] by 2009 even his erstwhile British supporters were admitting that Atmar was not succeeding in implementing intelligence-led policing and the rule of law. Indeed his idea of generating a complete policy change seemed very ambitious from the start, given the lack of political support from the president. Professional policemen had initially tepidly supported Atmar, but they also soon lost faith in him. Atmar's main achievements were not insignificant, but modest: he pushed FDD faster, pushed for Afghan trainers for the ANP, against CSTC-A's advice, and for an expanded role for policewomen.[40] Atmar also tried to create a more institutionalised system of appointments, refusing to make choices himself, tasking deputies to put together lists of candidates. He was aware of the controversial character of any appointment he could make and would typically follow the recommendations of his deputies. Still Atmar, like Jalali before him, could not avoid accusations of promoting Pashtuns like himself within the MoI: the best candidates for promotion were Pashtuns who had served under Gulabzoi.[41] Atmar also kick-started several reforms, which only began coming to fruition under his successor. Minister Atmar introduced a new department for policy and planning, headed by a deputy minister to highlight its importance, however the department never acquired the crucial role that Atmar had meant for it.[42]

Isolated at the top, Atmar had to work out how to establish some control over the MoI. He was widely seen as avoiding contact with his officers, communicating by telephone and avoiding visiting the police stations.[43] He was much criticised for his importing of staff into well-paid positions from other ministries which he had run earlier, in order to create his own network within the MoI. They were appointed as department heads or as heads of detective department in various provinces, despite their lack of police background and they were seen as spies of Atmar, reporting on their colleagues. Another criticism was that he hired many advisers, who could not be seen doing useful work at the MoI. Many of the Afghan advisers and mentors he brought to the MoI were also seen as mainly devoted to reporting on the staff of the Ministry.[44]

Already in 2009 Karzai wanted to sack Atmar, under pressure from the lobbies and the networks, but reportedly asked for six months in order to find a suitable excuse vis-à-vis the international community.[45] Some sources mention a direct clash with the president in early 2010, on matters of corruption and criminal activity of members of the presidential family.[46] The opportunity to get rid of Atmar arose in 2010, following a terrorist attack at the Peace Jirga presided over by Karzai: even if the attack had not been particularly successful compared to previous incidents, Atmar had to resign.

Trends initiated under Jalali and continued under his successors were still facing strong resistance in 2008–10. This is the case for centralisation, for example. The deployment of non-local police, particularly if from a different ethnicity, resulted in a number of problems. Educated officers displayed an ability to cooperate with colleagues of different ethnic backgrounds, but such ability decreased the more one moved towards the bottom of the hierarchy. Hazara police in Kandahar province acquitted themselves very well professionally, not least because of the young generation of Hazaras being better educated than their compatriots of other ethnic backgrounds and therefore easier to train, but were not able to maintain a good relationship with the local population in the Pashtun-populated Zhari district. The population did not trust them because they could not speak Pashto so their professionalism was therefore not appreciated.[47]

The 2010 deployment to Marjah of the most professional of Afghan police branches, ANCOP, was in part a failure because of the strong predominance of Tajiks within the ranks of the battalion deployed there.[48] The dislike for ANCOP by local AUP units was often reciprocated:

'The police in this district are police during the day and Taliban at night', commented the commander from the elite Afghan National Civil Order Police, the best-equipped and trained police force in the country, who was about to bring his men to replace Arghandab's cops during their two month classroom training phase. He didn't have high expectations for the training program, saying, 'The donkey is the same but the clothes are changed'.[49]

However, in general the deployment of police from the centre was not welcomed in the provinces. Although more disciplined, they were also inclined to treat the southerners in particular as suspects in a rather indiscriminate way, although American mentors were instead inclined to attribute the critique to the jealousy of the local police.[50]

The deployment of out-of-area CoPs also created problems. If they were sometimes appreciated because of their impartiality, they were also sometimes criticised because they were unaware of local developments. Some areas were so hostile to out-of-area CoPs that no HQ would dare appoint one: one case was that of Dand's CoP in 2010. The most typical example is Arghandab district of Kandahar, the more so as the local Alokozai were fed up with their loss of influence and jobs in Kandahar's police after 2005. This kind of patrimonial leadership was very difficult to change: in Arghandab even after the CoP was badly injured in an IED attack it was not possible to remove him: in April ISAF was thinking of finding a deputy to handle the police station without alienating the Chief.[51]

Thermidor: from reform to technical improvements

His successor Bismillah Mohammadi, a Panjshiri, inevitably started bringing back members of the Panjshiri network to the position of pre-eminence as it had been under Qanuni. His appointment had been motivated by several factors, including Karzai's desire to remove him from his very influential position of Chief of Staff of the Ministry of Defence and the need to accommodate the Panjshiris somehow, as they were essential to the smooth functioning of the armed forces. Another consideration was that, as with Zarar, perhaps only somebody well connected with the dominant networks in the MoI could hope to make the MoI work to some extent. Contrary to Zarar, however, Bismillah had a reputation as a proactive and dynamic leader, a fact which raised hopes of a better performance.[52]

Bismillah was clearly given much greater authority than Atmar to decide directly over the lobbying of various networks and factions. For example, Gen. Dostum and his group, Junbesh-i Milli, were pushing to have one of their men replace Deputy Minister Mangal, who was accused of corruption. Bismillah opted to ignore their requests and even removed a number of Junbesh sympathisers from the intelligence section, reducing Junbesh's influence within the MoI to almost nil. The Hazara/Wahdat network had never been very strong but is even weaker now after the removal of Haidar Bassir, formerly deputy minister. Bassir allegedly complained about being asked to do things that were not within his job specifications, but there were also allegations of corruption.[53] His successor Wahdat had been commander of Hizb-i Wahdat's militia (34 Division) in 2002–4 and so was not unfamiliar with engagement with the factions, but as an old professional who worked under Gulabzoi he was seen as not as close to the faction.[54]

At the same time Bismillah avoided appointing exclusively Panjshiris and their closest allies, a sign that the old days of complete Panjshiri dominance at the MoI were gone forever. Out of fifteen appointees to key positions in the first wave of appointments, none was actually from Panjshir, although most of the six Tajiks were linked to the Panjshir network and in particular to Vice-president Fahim and four were from Parwan.[55] He also appointed five Pashtuns, two Uzbeks, one Hazara, one Turkmen and one Sadat.[56] Arguably, therefore, his policy of appointments resembled that of Zarar, retaining a solid core of Panjshiris and allies and distributing the rest of the jobs to elements perceived as non-hostile.[57] Like his predecessors, Bismillah was soon accused of ethnic favouritism towards Tajik officers, particularly by Pashtun officers who were feeling threatened.[58]

As of early 2011, there was little sign that Bismillah was willing to confront the southern networks. These had already been somewhat weakened in some cases by international pressure, which had allowed professional elements to float to the commanding heights of the MoI in a number of cases (for example Helmand). Indeed the gains of the professionals were mostly concentrated in the south, with some impact in the north at the expense of the smaller or weaker networks, like Dostum's. In some regions, the professional elements had already risen to leadership positions in previous years, because of the weakness of local factional networks: for example, in parts of the South-East. There were ambiguous signs concerning the fate of professionals in parts of the South. When Col. Razzaq was appointed CoP in Kandahar, he rapidly purged the provincial police of its professional element, which had been in control of the CDI, but also promoted others to positions of responsibility.[59]

The networks competed primarily over the control of the smuggling economy and of illegal taxation. However, political issues were never irrelevant. The progression of the insurgency and by 2009–10 its expansion to the half of the country north of the Hindukush started being seen as a real threat by several of these networks, including Mohammadi's, and he seemed intent on restoring some basic functionality to the MoI, which by 2008 had turned into

THE AMBIGUOUS IMPACT OF REFORM

an incoherent mess of rival gangs. Deep levels of distrust existed among the deputy ministers, who were all accusing each other of corruption and only in 2010 did the interaction among them seem to be improving.[60] The coordination across departments required the encouragement of senior leadership or did not happen.[61]

It is not clear to what extent Mohammadi was actually trying to fight corruption but he was saying the right things—and not just to foreigners, but to Afghans too. The replacement of a relatively proactive Inspector General with a passive one in 2010 does not show much of an intent of following up on statements. Foreign advisers were divided between those who believed Mohammadi did not want to challenge the economic interests formed around the MoI, as these were mostly run by political allies, and those who believed he was doing all he could.[62]

Mohammadi, on the other hand, signed off several new policy documents in the first few months of his tenure, enabling the internal development plan to mature quickly.[63] He also stated his intention to decentralise the MoI.[64]

The most immediate impact of Bismillah's actions was to improve the morale of the police, previously very low. In particular his trips to the provinces, where Atmar had never been, were welcomed by a police force which had felt neglected and abandoned. He stated that he found bad police leadership wherever he visited.[65] At the same time he was often criticised for spending too much time travelling to the provinces and too little managing the MoI: he even resisted Karzai's demands that he attend the Kabul Conference in July 2010.[66] His modest education (six years in a madrasa) was also seen by some professionals in the police as a major limitation.[67] He was not able to use a computer and under him the various organisational systems developed under Atmar went into decay for lack of management.[68]

In practice, decision making and action taking at the MoI was in late 2010 still being driven by personal interest, informal communication and networking, rather than by anything resembling an institutionalised process. The minister himself was receiving information through his personal connections within the structure of the MoI, based on what individual officials thought he should see: often this was not based on any concept of strategic direction or of long-term decision-making.[69] Single departments showed significant improvements in their performance when led by effective heads,[70] but on the whole the functioning of the MoI remained patchy in late 2010.[71]

The debate over paramilitary or civilian policing

Particularly among donors and the expatriate community, the debate over the reform of Afghanistan's police has been dominated by the discussion about the pros and cons of paramilitary and civilian policing, whereas among Afghans civilian policing has attracted little interest. Among the supporters of civilian policing, moreover, there have been different views concerning how centralised or decentralised it should be. Inevitably, the outcome of the debate has been largely determined by the financial weight of the different advisory missions. As the American military increasingly took over responsibility for funding the development of Afghanistan's police, their view that the main purpose of the police had to be in the counter-insurgency effort prevailed (see section 5.2.2).[72]

The argument in favour of a greater focus on civilian policing skills was also weakened by the predominant attitudes of the trainees coming out of the Police Academy. As of 2010, the newly trained police from the police Academy were still being deployed overwhelmingly in Kabul (74 per cent), with just 2 per cent going to the south.[73] By 2011, there was a shortage of 600 officers in the south. According to the Chief of Personnel in 2011, he was under pressure to deploy the trainees from the Academy in Kabul city, but he was trying to resist. By 2011 an effort to spread recruitment of Academy trainees to the south of the country was occurring, with a special delegation being sent there to advertise in high schools the fact that a positive discrimination worth twenty high school exam points was available to southerners who were willing to apply for the admission test to the Academy.[74] Whether even southerners trained in Kabul would want to deploy back to their home provinces was, however, far from clear.

Among the larger players, only the British and the Germans remained for different reasons strongly committed to civilian policing, but even there an understanding emerged that professional policing would be a long-term development and that a gendarmerie-type force was in the short term the priority. Their argument remained however that 'heart and mind' community policing was also functional to counter-insurgency, in winning the support of the population: mixing with the population would earn their trust and help gathering information.[75]

The FDD programme (see section 5.2) embodied the triumph of the supporters of para-militarism. It dedicated twenty-eight out of 263 hours of instruction to basic police skills, with the rest going to military training. After November 2008 even the very limited training on community and democratic policing, as well as domestic violence and women's rights was replaced by more military training. Despite the fact that the same training centres were used to train Ministry of Justice personnel, no overlapping of training with the police was established.[76]

As the FDD faded from the centre-stage of police reorganisation, paramilitary policing did not. The paramilitary bias of the training effort meant that the AUP (the bulk of the police force) as well as the ANCOP were in practice paramilitary forces, with little if any police training. Other dimensions of policing received much less attention, although they were not discarded altogether.

Within the MoI the biggest proponent ever of civilian policing was Minister Atmar (2008–10). His plan was to separate civilian police from gendarmerie, which also was to combine police and gendarmerie skills, over a period of five years, and ID, passport and traffic were meant to be civilianised.

THE AMBIGUOUS IMPACT OF REFORM

The AUP would gradually disappear, replaced by a new civilian police or in part transferred to ANCOP, ABP or APPF. The plan was eventually approved by the international partners of the MoI after some debate, but never implemented as Atmar left his job shortly after that.[77]

The failure of the debate to lead to coherently implemented decision making meant that the AUP was left in limbo between local policing/militia, paramilitary police and civilian police, being unable to benefit from any of the positive characteristics of any of them. As of 2011 the contribution of the AUP to the ongoing war was as doubtful as in 2002-3.

Gender issues

At least in the views of western observers, a key benchmark of police reform in Afghanistan was represented by the role played by women within the police. In the Afghan context, however, gender issues proved much more controversial. Afghanistan's police first admitted women in the 1960s and the first batch of six women graduated at the Police Academy graduated in 1969. They received specialist training in how to deal with children, crimes against children and teenage girls in particular.[78] The use of policewomen increased in the 1980s, because female emancipation was a key policy of the leftist regime. Some policewomen even made it to the senior ranks of the MoI. Needless to say, policewomen disappeared from the scene after the collapse of the regime in 1992 and stayed out of the picture until 2001.

In 2001-5 only a handful of policewomen served in the police, including several who had already served in senior positions in the 1980s. In 2004 about 100 or so women served in the MoI, but largely as NCOs and officers. The first group of seven graduated as NCOs from the police academy in 2004: characteristically they were all widows. In practice, those few women who did join the police ended up being under-utilised, particularly outside Kabul, in the conservative south, policewomen were not even able to talk to other women because the families were afraid that they could have a corrupting influence. Moving up the ranks and asserting their role within the police required a very determined character and a willingness to take risks. The highest ranking policewoman, Lt. Col. Kakar, was assassinated in Kandahar in September 2008.[79] Another female police officer was allegedly killed by her own son in March 2011.[80]

Already in 2003-4 the MoI was setting very ambitious targets for policewomen recruitment, such as 10 per cent of the whole police force by 2005. Little was done to implement these targets, which were essentially meant to show a degree of commitment to foreign donors.[81] External pressure to seriously recruit more policewomen started in 2005 from the German and the Swiss governments. A 2007 conference on policewomen highlighted the issue. Under Atmar the MoI itself decided that it was time to start delivering and increased pressure, issuing in 2009 a directive to hire 5,000 policewomen. Individuals who attended the meetings suggest that Atmar himself was much more supportive of female recruitment when speaking to foreign representatives than when speaking to MoI officials. The individual MoI units paid lip service to the plan but no attention was paid to the quality of recruitment or the job conditions, and not even job descriptions were prepared. Few commanding officers had any idea on how to use the new policewomen. The situation was compounded by the fact that families were not at all keen to send their women to join the police, because of predominant cultural attitudes. The fact that the police was perceived as corrupt and criminalised did not help either.[82] The fact that transportation was not provided made recruitment even more difficult, in a country where women are not supposed to hire a taxi alone. As a result the quality of recruitment left much to be desired: almost all the women recruited after the 2008 acceleration of the process were illiterate. Moreover, they were hired without being assigned a specific task and were not given specific training.[83]

By late 2010 there were 1,200 policewomen, of whom 900 were patrolwomen and NCOs.[84] They were mostly employed in menial jobs, or at most secretarial ones, although in the courses taught by the Italian Carabinieri (western Afghanistan) the female trainees were usually doing better than their male colleagues.[85] Herat was one of the few provinces where policewomen made their appearance outside the cities, but even here almost all the policewomen were deployed in the city, just a few districts too had one or two women.[86]

A purpose for the presence of policewomen in the force did exist, even if recruitment was not linked to it. The first Family Response Unit was established in 2006 in Kabul district 10, one of the most affluent of the city. The unit was completely staffed by women and the experiment was considered a success. The decision to expand the programme clashed with the shortage of policewomen and contributed to the decision to expand recruitment.[87] The population was by 2010 starting to become aware of the existence of the Family Response Units, but usually men did not allow their women to approach them. This turned out to be a particularly serious problem in Jalalabad.[88] This attitude was strengthened by the fact that such units were not always led by women. Eighty-six Family Response Units were in existence by 2010, but only seventy were staffed by women: sixteen were in Kabul alone. The remaining ones were led by men (in particular in Nangarhar and Herat), although the MoI said they were planning to replace the men with women.[89]

The untargeted recruitment process had led to just 200–400 educated policewomen working for the MoI in late 2010, which were not enough to staff the officer posts in the Family Response Units.[90] Beyond these units, the chances of women being appointed as officers were very modest. The police officers themselves were wary of promoting policewomen, because they would have had to place them in the job of a man without them being able to take over all the tasks, such as patrolling. As a result there was serious institutional resistance to hiring women, including among some senior officials.[91] Some police officers argued that it would be better to bring women into administrative work rather than trying and failing to get them into operations. The system and procedures adopted for the employment of women were based on the 1980s system, failing to recognise the much greater resistance to women's employment.[92]

Minister Mohammadi did not initially pay much attention to the Family Response Units which he inherited from Atmar, except for renaming them with a dari expression.[93] In March 2011, however, he announced a major recruitment campaign to reach a target of 5,000 policewomen, which was to include some improvements in the conditions of service.[94]

A separate aspect of the gender issue is the attitude of patrolmen and officers towards women. There is no doubt that compared to the picture in 2002, Afghanistan's police had experienced some evolution by 2010. In 2006 Tonita Murray noted that:

Women are going to police stations in Kabul and Mazar-e-Sharif to report acts of violence to the new police family violence units, and police are sometimes approached on the streets for help.[95]

Civil society organisations provided a lot of training to the police on how to treat people, including women.[96] More specific courses on domestic violence, abuse, and so on, were also held, but MoI was predominantly hostile and at least a three-star general opposed them.[97] These short courses might have helped improve the behaviour of the police, but only to a small extent: they were attended just once and lasted a mere three days. A media campaign in 2010 might have been more effective and reportedly resulted in more women approaching the police.[98]

The main factors in leading to the improved behaviour of the police towards policewomen appears, however, to have been the appointment of more professional officers into leading positions and direct orders from the MoI. Anecdotal evidence suggests that the former might have had a greater impact. Helmand police was in 2007–8 led by professional officers: in Lashkargah, surveys showed women being by 2008–9 the greatest supporters of the police. In part this was due to the fact that they had less interaction with the police and were not being asked to pay money, but it was also due to a greater sense of security, which enabled women to move around the city relatively freely. Women accounted for a disproportionate share of those 42 per cent of Helmandis who responded to surveys that the police was doing a good job.[99]

Vice versa, evidence suggests that orders issued by the MoI often had little impact. The MoI ordered that women running away from their family were not to be treated as criminals and arrested, but although in some areas the police started to help female victims it was still common in 2010 to arrest them in most provinces: the police would say that people would not understand this change. The MoI characteristically denied being aware of the lack of implementation because for them 'no problem ha[d] been reported'.[100]

In terms of the impact of reform on the functionality of the MoI, this short look at gender issues shows that reforms imposed from the outside have little impact of any kind and that in the absence of a capability of the MoI bureaucracy to monitor what the MoI organisations in the field are doing, pushing reform against the stream is probably only going to waste resources and energy.

Pay and rank reform

One clearly successful reform was the adoption of a more realistic pay and rank structure, as illustrated in Table 19. Until its implementation in 2005–6, the ranks of the MoI were top heavy, a result of the tendency to use appointments primarily for patronage purposes. There were too many generals, too many colonels, too many majors and too many captains, and too few lieutenants. The structure took a more pyramidal look after the pay and rank reform.

The reform allowed the MoI to pay higher salaries to a smaller limited number of police officers. It was initially resisted because it reduced the potential for distributing appointments as patronage, but pressure from the MoF and from donors proved decisive in forcing the reform through.[101] In other regards, however, it is not clear whether the reform meant much in terms of actual improvements, as the process of selecting the new appointees was itself very corrupt (see section 7 above).

It is also clear that the management of human resources within the MoI remained weak. Even by 2011 not all policemen had been registered by the MoI. Little investment had been done in human resources management and the system remained unable to promote merit-based appointments. In order

Table 19: MoI and ANP Officer Corps Structure before and after Rank Reform.

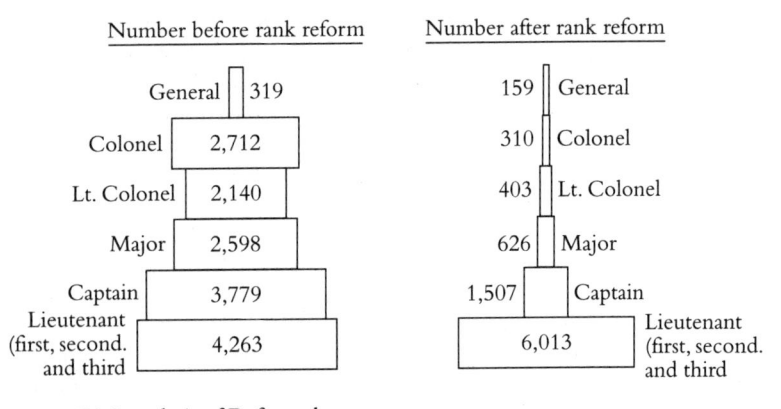

Number before rank reform		Number after rank reform	
General	319	159	General
Colonel	2,712	310	Colonel
Lt. Colonel	2,140	403	Lt. Colonel
Major	2,598	626	Major
Captain	3,779	1,507	Captain
Lieutenant (first, second, and third)	4,263	6,013	Lieutenant (first, second, and third)

Source: GAO analysis of Defense data.

to contain nepotism and the sale of positions, Atmar had to monitor personally appointments to the top 400–500 positions.[102]

Reforms such as gender issues locked into a never-ending struggle against opponents. Pay and rank reform, instead, looked like the right type of reform needed to weaken the opponents of MoI reform and create a wider base of support. Pay and rank reform faced strong opposition initially, but once implemented saw its enemies either co-opted (once they passed the tests one way or another) or expelled from the system. From this point of view it was largely a missed opportunity because there was much compromise, as hinted above and discussed in greater detail in 9.1 and 9.2. So much compromise occurred, that many of the potential gains of reform were lost.

The rule of law

The Afghan Leviathan and the rule of law

The tasks of the MoI's police departments are described in the Police Law as ensuring not just public order and security, but also the legal rights and freedoms of individuals. It is also tasked to regulate road traffic, responding to natural disasters and safeguarding borders.[103] The enforcement of the rule of law was therefore, from the beginning of the post-2001 phase of Afghan history, written into the duties of the MoI.

The Ministry, however, was ill-equipped to fulfil such a task. The long tradition of staffing the top positions of the MoI with militarily trained people led to an environment focused on the hardware of militarised policing, asking for better equipment all the time, but showing little interest in getting the software of policing up to scratch. Moreover, the almost exclusively rural recruitment of the police meant that they have little understanding of the cities and the needs of the urban population. The MoI has not been able to recruit in the cities, nor did the training provide rural recruits much in terms of supplying tools suitable for urban policing. The result was frequent friction and heavy handedness by the police.[104]

In January 2003, a decision was made by the US government to fund a US$ 26 million crash course in human rights and non-violent handling of crime.[105] A more substantial step was taken in April 2003, when a Human Rights department was created within the MoI with the aim of curbing abuses by the police and was closely linked to UNAMA and the AIHRC. The staffing level of the unit was increased from the original three to fifteen in MoI and two in each province and later it was stipulated that each checkpoint in Kabul should also have an officer trained to recognise and report human rights abuses.[106] None of this must have been very successful, as following a AIHRC workshop in 2006 police officers reportedly commented that they were surprised to see that citizens had all these rights.[107] By 2009, fifty officers were responsible for human rights reporting in Kabul's police, but the improvement by all accounts was very marginal.[108]

External oversight and accountability

External oversight, which could at least in part have offset the lack of internal MoI understanding of the issue, was another key weak spot. In 2003 Amnesty International assessed that:

> There is no consistent, nationwide mechanism in place for monitoring and evaluating the actions of the police or for independent investigation of reports of wrongdoing or human rights violations by officers in Afghanistan. Although in some provinces there are attempts by local governors and commanders to implement public complaints procedures, these are largely ineffective, if well-intentioned, gestures that fail to address key problems. In some cases there are concerns that any systems in place do not function effectively, and may only be instituted as an attempt to exert control over the public rather than take any effective action. In numerous cases of human rights violations by police documented by Amnesty International, not one had been investigated. Some police commanders told Amnesty International that they had disciplined their officers, but would not disclose the reason, nor whether any investigation that had taken place following an alleged incident. Disciplinary procedures mentioned included suspension, or several days' imprisonment. It was not clear who took the decision to discipline a police officer, or on what grounds, reflecting the potential for personal enmities or conflicting allegiances to inform any disciplinary action taken.[109]

The complaint procedures present in a few provincial capitals were limited to complaint boxes, which were occasionally checked by the authorities. Amnesty International also pointed out the absence of any independent oversight mechanism. The exception was the AIHRC, which however was overwhelmed by many other tasks as well and did not establish a dedicated department to deal with this task. The AIHRC in fact never assumed the role of an external form of accountability and oversight.[110]

The fact that the Afghan government never appeared very proactive in trying to establish any kind of accountability led foreign mentors and advisers to believe that communities had to be enabled to demand a better police force. A first step was the establishment in 2009 of detention councils (shuras), where local notables were asked to review arrests.[111]

Innovation and experimenting continued in 2010. A police accountability board was being set up in late 2010, but seemed to be making slow progress in November 2010.[112] Police shuras were launched in Helmand under British sponsorship and in the north under the Germans, but MoI did not seem interested in external oversight, nor did there seem to be much demand for it outside the MoI. Individual police officers in the provinces sometimes showed greater interest in forms of oversight which also helped enlist the cooperation of the communities. Receiving letters of appreciation from NGOs clearly affected the morale of the police positively. Perhaps more substantially, there was a declared increase in the number of IEDs reported by the communities, although no exact figure was provided and in the areas affected the insurgents were not very active. At the same time, however, the police also perceived that oversight might turn out to be a double-edged sword. The people, for example, began approaching the police to report all kind of trouble, beginning with the lack of electricity supply.[113]

Other related experiments include UNDP democratic policing in a few districts, mostly in the safer parts of the country, and some Canadian activities in Kandahar. Efforts to convince the MoI to set up an office coordinating all these disparate activities were generating little enthusiasm in the MoI as of November 2010.[114] As a result, by 2010 the MoI was still characterised by weak oversight and the lack of periodic review of established procedures and transparent decision making.[115]

The foreigners' influence

Even when steps to bring elements of the rule of law to Afghanistan were effectively taken, their actual suitability to the environment was doubtful. Such steps were virtually always taken under external pressure. The impact of foreign advisers was weakened by the existence of a clash between common law countries and Roman law countries, with the latter relying on the judiciary as the main actor in investigating crimes and the former giving investigative powers to the police.[116]

After 2001 the criminal procedure code of 1965 amended in 1974 was applied in conjunction with the law on investigation of crime of 1978, the law on the Attorney General's office of 1991 and the law on organisation and jurisdiction of courts of 1991. In 2004 the new Constitution gave primary authority for criminal investigation to the Attorney General's office, which however lacked investigative capacity at that time, and the police mandate was limited to the discovery and detection of crimes. This was at odds with existing laws and practice, but in line with the previous constitutions. Already the constitution of 1964, art. 103, said that investigation was the job of the Attorney General: the constitution of 1976 was along the same lines.[117]

The real change derived from the adoption of an Italian-sponsored Interim Criminal Procedure Code (ICPC) in 2004, which was flawed in many ways. Prosecutor ratification of police acts and judicial police were Italian transplants which nobody in the Afghan police and justice system really liked. The first post-2001 Attorney General Abdul Mahmood Qaqiq and other prosecutors as well accused Italians of forcing him to accept the ICPC under threat of withholding of aid. The vast majority of Afghan professionals opposed the ICPC as a replacement of the then existing criminal procedure code of 1974, which the ICPC did not take into any account. Other flaws of the ICPC were that it was not sufficiently detailed to comprehensively regulate the field and that it left a lot of room to individual interpretation of which laws were replaced by it.[118]

The ICPC granted the investigative prosecutor the power to confirm, nullify or modify police actions and decisions during the detection phase within the first twenty-four hours of arrest. Its articles 36 and 6 limited detention of a suspect for investigation to only thirty days before indictment was to be filed. These two aspects of the ICPC were particularly controversial because they prevented any complex or compound investigation and ignored the realities of slow or non-existent transportation during winter.[119] Further confusion was added by the Police Law (1384 or 2005–6) which contradicted the ICPC in many cases. The Police Law added to the powers of the police vis-à-vis the prosecutors and the courts, broadening existing police powers to stop, detain and search individuals, vehicles and residences. The ICPC was simply ignored. The Police Law also gave police seventy-two hours to investigate a crime, whereas the ICPC gave twenty-four hours. It used to be ten days before the new laws were introduced, which many experts see as more realistic given the Afghan environment. The result was a decline in the quality of investigative work, with almost universal complaints by the police.[120]

The police, on the other hand, often disregarded the law, simply avoiding reporting arrests and detaining suspects as long as it liked. Sometimes private prisons were used to make bypassing the law easier.

External influence, exercised in such a chaotic way, had a mostly pernicious influence in other fields as well. The much touted Afghan National Police Strategy (ANPS) was a kind of externally influenced policy document, which flew high over a much murkier and down-to-earth Afghan and MoI reality, hardly affecting it. For example, it does not even discuss guarding duties, which occupied most of the police most of the time.[121]

Efforts to introduce Afghanistan's police to the 'rule of law' have taken place from time to time, but on a small scale. For example in early 2010 NTM-A organised a course held by three Afghan attorneys.[122] The low-scale character of such efforts is likely to be one of the causes of the very limited progress in terms of the rule of law.

Different ministers showed different degrees of interest in fostering the rule of law and/or responding to western pressure in this regard. After peaking in Atmar's time (2008–10), concern for the rule of law declined afterwards. In 2010 Minister Mohammadi issued an order, authorising the police to shoot suspects who were trying to escape. The order proved very controversial among human and civil rights advocates, even if the police maintained that the order allowed them to greatly curb the number of serious crimes in Kabul city (down 17 per cent in the last quarter of 2010 compared to the third quarter).[123]

Abusive and arbitrary behaviour

The weakness or absence of the rule of law translated into extensive abusive and arbitrary behaviour. Among the NATO troops who fight alongside Afghanistan's police, the belief is widespread that the arbitrary behaviour of the police is one of the key factors driving recruitment into the Taliban: their views were based among other things on the interrogation of prisoners.[124]

Given where Afghanistan was coming from, it is perhaps not surprising that in 2002 the police showed little concern over its own abusive practices. In 2002, tools of torture were commonly found in the police stations and nobody seemed ashamed of it.[125] Torture by the police was a common occurrence in 2003 onwards too, as reported by Amnesty International.[126] The Afghan press continued to report instances of torture by the police and even death in custody following physical abuse.[127]

Given the growing awareness of the role of police abuse in driving recruitment into the insurgency, it not as easy to understand why several years later the situation had changed relatively little. Discussing the behaviour of Afghan police in 2006, Canadian military personnel described them as 'thugs' who 'kept order in the streets by hitting people and who had a reputation for mistreating prisoners'.[128] During the 2010 offensive in Kandahar (Hamkari) the border police reportedly committed abuses against civilians.[129]

Torture

ISAF troops serving in the south often heard allegations of torture by the police in the villages.[130] Journalist Graeme Smith interviewed many detainees who showed him signs of torture.[131] In the first half of 2009 a report by the AIHRC found that just 17.4 per cent of Afghan policemen were aware of the fact that torture is illegal in the country. An even smaller number was aware of the rights of the accused according to the Afghan constitution. Almost all detainees interviewed by the AIHRC believed they had been tortured by the police or other law enforcement institutions and over 65 per cent of the detainees claimed that it had been the police who tortured them. The most common reason for turning to torture was obtaining confessions, itself a consequence of the weak investigative capability. Although Afghan citizens were in principle able to fill a petition form and complain about having been abused by the police, the police interviewees themselves acknowledged that in most cases such forms are not followed up.[132]

Illegal detention

Similarly, in 2003, Amnesty International found that illegal detention was widespread. Lack of facilities and means of transport was cited as one cause of illegal detention being so common, as this made carrying out investigation within the allowed seventy-two hours very difficult.[133] People could be detained and spend long periods in prison without trial even for minor offences. In 2003:

police in a rural district of Nangarhar were unlawfully holding more than a dozen people for minor offences. The Tufts team requested to visit the jail, but the deputy police chief arranged to have the prisoners removed from their cells and hidden in another part of the building before the Tufts team arrived. In another instance, police removed prisoners—covered in blood and unable to walk—from a metal shipping container in an attempt to relocate the detainees before they were seen by the Tufts team.[134]

Somewhat more surprisingly, in the second half of 2009, UNAMA had to report that illegal detention was still widespread, particularly in northern Afghanistan where mentoring by ISAF was not prevalent. CoPs seemed to believe that the seventy-two hours custody limit was discretional.[135] As demonstrated in the case of the large-scale Kandahar prisoner escape of 2008, none of the 900 inmates had been fingerprinted or photographed.[136] Searches

---

Box 4: Example of abuses reported.

In August 2006 ANP officers in Uruzgan Province raided a local bazaar to seize contraband items, including poppies. Several storekeepers and shoppers reported being harassed and having their money and goods stolen. During a subsequent inspection of the ANP provincial headquarters' evidence locker, authorities found only small amounts of the contraband.[140]

In the autumn of 2006, residents of the village of Galouch claimed that ANP and ANA soldiers seeking a local commander entered villagers' homes, verbally abused them and stole personal items from the residents.[141]

Following a September 2007 bus crash in Ghazni, ANP officers allegedly looted valuables from victims and told victims that unless they paid the police they would not receive medical attention.[142]

In September 2007 in Ghazni Province police beat two prisoners in custody. The cases were referred to the MOI's human rights unit, and investigations continued at the year's end.[143]

In 2005, a Kabul Police Chief allegedly tortured and killed a civilian named Hossain.[144]

In December 2005, another detainee was beaten and subsequently died in police custody in Kabul. No tangible developments occurred in the prosecution of these cases, not least because official investigations were ineffective, and authorities did not file formal charges.[145]

There were continued allegations of rape and sexual abuse of individuals in government detention but investigations did not result in charges. The AIHRC reported that in 2005 local authorities granted one woman medical treatment after police provided her to men for sexual exploitation. In 2006 in Pol-e-Charkhi prison, the AIHRC also reported that two police officers and several prisoners raped a young male prisoner.[146]

In 2008, the Afghan Ministry of Women Affairs reported that the police 'frequently raped female detainees and prisoners'.[147]

THE AMBIGUOUS IMPACT OF REFORM

remained poorly organised and the habit of arresting all bystanders when in doubt was still common.[137]

Arrests were often being carried out on the basis of the slimmest evidence; Nir Rosen reported about a suspect being apprehended because of the ring tone of his mobile:

The day after the attempted raid on the mosque, Ahmadullah radioed Prowler's translator, Mansur. 'We found a Taliban. What should we do, kill him?' Mansur told Ahmadullah not to kill the prisoner but to bring him to the Americans. [...] [The police commander]'s evidence was the Taliban ringtone on his prisoner's cell phone. The policemen were angry with their commander and wanted the man released. Zahir, another translator, was outraged. 'This is why people hate the fucking police and support the Taliban', he said. One policeman told me that [the police commander] bragged he had killed many people in 'personal hostility' in Babaji, a village near Lashkar Gah. [The mentors] interrogated the prisoner. [...] Dyer asked him about the music on his cell phone. 'One of my friends put it there', Zeibullah said. [...] Zeibullah's cell phone also contained videos of a graduation from a religious school and battles. 'Everybody has them on their phones, even I have them', Zahir said. [The police commander] told the Americans that he knew Zeibullah's father, that he was a good man. 'But I don't know him', [the police commander] said, 'and his uncle is Taliban'. Mansur scoffed. [...] Another policeman, originally from Babaji, also insisted the prisoner was innocent. But Zeibullah was sent to the prison in Lashkar Gah. He might be released for money, Dyer told me. Or he might still be there.[138]

In 2010 arrests and house searches without warrant were still common, despite not being allowed by the constitution. Arrests of relatives were also common in order to force escapees to deliver themselves to the police. Cases of individuals being arrested because rivals paid the police to do so were also reported. Backdating documents in order not to show that people had been detained without authorisation for more than seventy-two hours was also common. It was also usual to arrest people without warrant in order to extort money for their release. Those being arrested often were not told why and were not informed of their rights.[139]

Arbitrary executions

During his fact-finding mission to Afghanistan in May 2008, the UN Special Rapporteur on extrajudicial, summary or arbitrary executions warned about the lack of political will to investigate, let alone prosecute, the crimes committed by the Afghan police.[148] The UN Special Rapporteur highlighted two cases of major crimes perpetrated by the Afghan police, where in spite of the scope of the incidents and the attention they received from the media, the perpetrators were not prosecuted. In one incident, the police massacred a group of men belonging to a rival tribe. The other case involved the police opening fire on unarmed demonstrators in Jowzjan Province on 28 May, 2007. As a result of the shootings, the police killed nine demonstrators and

157

wounded more than forty.[149] No-one in the government, the UN Special Rapporteur contends, showed any interest to investigate, let alone prosecute, the police officers responsible for these killings.[150]

Investigating how the Afghan authorities dealt with these two cases, the UN Special Rapporteur contended that:

local and national political interests have conspired to ensure that no effective investigation was undertaken. The technique is to let time pass until the evidence has faded and other political concerns have claimed the limelight. The matter can then be quietly filed away. The victims and their families are simply ignored.[151]

Riot control

The concern (or lack thereof) of the MoI with the building up of riot control capacity can be taken as an indicator of how committed the MoI is to the establishment of the rule of law. Starting from at least 2003, there have been a series of urban riots where the police demonstrated their inability to cope other than by shooting at the demonstrators, usually managing only to make the rioting even worse. The MoI had stated that the instructions sent from the centre to the police units specified that demonstrators were not to be shot, but lack of training in other techniques as well as of equipment left little option.[152] In reality, training in riot control started being provided in 2002, but evidently achieved little impact.[153] Training was imparted in Turkey and equipment was provided, but on arrival the trainees were dispersed to different provinces.[154]

Writing in 2006, Tonita Murray commented that:

Despite nearly five years of expensive reform efforts, and in a country almost continuously in a state of disturbance, it is startling to discover that Afghan police are inadequately trained in maintaining order and crowd control. Such control usually begins with the least coercive means and increases if needed. The Kabul rioters took two hours to reach the centre of the city from the outskirts, yet no efforts were made during that time to close off streets to divert the demonstrators from the main areas of the city. Police had little protective gear and no pepper spray, water cannon or tear gas, although some had guns, which are the last rather than the first resort for controlling mobs. There appears to have been no intelligence, no contingency plan and no leadership. Given that controlling civil disorder is a basic police responsibility even in peaceful countries, and that ample training resources are available in Afghanistan, it is a mystery that there have been no sustained efforts to train Afghan police in order maintenance and riot control.[155]

In 2006, following violent riots in Kabul, the Americans promised tear gas and water cannon equipment to the police.[156] In 2007, it was reported that the training of riot police was underway, 500 policemen in total, of which 260 were assigned to Kabul.[157] In 2008 finally the MoI was claiming to have established a unit to handle riots and violent protests, including 1,600 trained

THE AMBIGUOUS IMPACT OF REFORM

men (sixteen-week courses) and 700 more undergoing training with the aim of reaching a total of 5,000. Little equipment was available at that time, but there were 'promises' from the international community to supply it.[158] In practice, when riots occurred in October 2010 in Kabul between Hazaras and Kuchis, the riot police could not be mobilised effectively and the police once again shot demonstrators when attempting to restrain them, leading to loss of life and much controversy.[159] Overall, after 2001, Afghanistan's police used firearms in more than twenty riots.[160]

Box 5: Behaviour of police in rioting.

During the February 2004 Herat riots, seven were killed by the army and police;[161]

Four demonstrators were killed by the police during the May 2005 riots in Jalalabad;[162]

In February 2006 the police killed four protesters in Kabul and one in Maimana when demonstrations over satirical cartoons of the Prophet Mohammad turned violent;[163]

During the May 2006 riots in Kabul, fourteen people were killed, mostly by police fire;[164]

In June 2007 in Jowzjan Province, police fired on protesters demanding the removal of the province's governor, killing at least ten persons and injuring at least forty.[165]

On 10 May 2008 in Nangarhar, police fired on protesters, killing two civilians, media outlets reported;[166]

On May 23, 2008, during a protest in Ghor province, the Afghan police killed two civilians and injured seven;[167]

In August 2010 several Hazaras were killed by the police during clashes with Pashtun Kuchis;[168]

In March 2011 riots took place in Kandahar, in protest at the burning of the Quran by a Christian preacher in Florida: the police responded with firearms and killed at least sixteen. At a security meeting after the riots, 'It was decided to train a well-equipped special police to control such demonstrations in future and prevent damages to properties and civilian casualties'.[169]

Community demands and rule of law

The tendency to let communities sort out criminal matters themselves is difficult to reconcile with any concept of the rule of law. The police were always happy to leave honour crimes and family matters to the elders and the mullahs, particularly in Pashtun-populated areas, but not only there. Indeed one difference between the post-2001 period and the pre-1978 one is that from

2001 onwards even in areas of the north the police left the elders in charge: for example, in the Andarab districts and other parts of Baghlan.[170] Occasionally cases of extrajudicial executions caused the intervention of the police in the northern areas, but in general this was a rare occurrence.[171] In fact in 2006 the AIHRC reported that honour killings were on the rise, rather than in decline, although the increase in the number of killings reported to the AIHRC might have reflected the Commission's expanding coverage as much as an actual increase.[172]

According to UNODC estimates about 80 per cent of all legal cases are dealt with by the customary justice system.[173] A survey carried out by the Asia Foundation came up with similar figures. Dispute resolution in particular is almost monopolised by local notables, as opposed to state agencies.[174] The actual importance of customary justice varied from province to province, depending on local conditions. In a province like Helmand, in 2009 95–8 per cent of justice was delivered by non-state actors. At that time, coordination between police and judiciary was improving because of a massive international effort but by 2010, as a result of the increased presence of foreign troops, some judges and lawyers were being moved back to the districts, again enabling more cooperation with the police, but with little impact in terms of attracting people towards the state judiciary.[175]

Two factors contributed to the role of customary justice:

- the lack of trust and lack of outreach of Government agencies and institutions, as well as their corruption;[176]
- the presence in many cases of reputable alternatives, such as clerics, community councils and elders, or Taliban courts to provide dispute resolution.[177]

Criminal cases are often dealt with through customary law:

Jirga or Shura in rural areas also on their own initiative handle criminal cases, including murder. No participants in Shura or Jirga have been trained in the application of formal legal standards, and thus rely on traditional notions of fairness, thereby creating inconsistent standards between the formal and informal systems in the ways that defendants are treated. The adjudicators and arbitrators within the informal system often have an ambiguous understanding of the Afghan constitution, including the rights and obligations of the citizens.[178]

Nobody has seriously investigated how many criminal cases are referred to customary law. It appears to be a very large proportion in the tribal areas (mostly Loya Paktia), where enforcement capacity exists (the tribal councils can mobilise their own enforcers), as well as in the south because of the lack of government capacity:

Due to the high level of insecurity [in the Southern Region] (the existence of the U.S. military base, the concentration of Afghan government armed forces, and the insurgents), there are repeated shifts in the government leadership, especially in Kandahar. In most part of the districts, the local Jirgas are the only sources where locals

THE AMBIGUOUS IMPACT OF REFORM

can find remedies to legal disputes. In most cases, local Jirga are adjudicating both civil and criminal cases throughout the rural districts.[179]

Cases have been reported of government officials, including police, sending criminal cases to community councils and elders for resolution, an attitude which is in fact against the law:

> Government officials often send criminal cases (including murder) to the Jirga and Shura for informal resolution, rather than to the government courts. This is in violation of legislation, which bestows legal authority over criminal cases to the government judiciary, whereas civil cases may enjoy non-state local remedies if the court permits.[180]

Elsewhere the proportion is certainly lower, as enforcement is more problematic: however as we shall see, there are third ways beyond state and community enforcement. Reports about the widespread handling of criminal cases through customary law are actually quite common:

> The majority of respondents in Nangarhar, Logar, Herat, Jawzjan, and Kabul reported that most criminal offenses, especially murder in rural districts, are handled by Jirga and Shura. Often the executive branch of the government at the district level diverts murder cases from the government primary court and sends them to be solved by a local Jirga or Shura.[181]

Even in areas around Kabul, community councils were dealing with a large majority of civil and criminal cases:

> According to members of the [Kalakan district] Shura and government officials, the Shura solves 98 per cent of both civil and criminal cases. In the last four years, the Shura has already solved sixteen murder cases; this success has given the Shura a highly influential position within the district. Locals believe that it is the Shura that has brought peace and stability to the district by encouraging the armed political groups and commanders toward more cooperative efforts. The respect of the local commanders for the Shura has given the Shura the ability to create a neutral space wherein conflict can be negotiated and possibly resolved.[182]

As the passage quoted above seems to obliquely suggest, enforcement in much of the country could only be provided by local strongmen and their armed retinues. It is doubtful whether this could still be described as customary justice. This is even clearer in the case of the Khaja Du Koh district shura (Jowzjan province):

> Like other districts in Jawzjan, the system of governance and politics in Khaja Du Koh is under the direct influence of the *Junbish-e-Mili* (National Movement) political and military organizations. Jawzjan has been the stronghold of the Junbish-e-Mili led by General Abdul Rashid Dustam. Junbish enjoys influence among the organs of the central government as well as within the extended Shura system that begins at the capital of the province and spreads throughout the districts and villages. Among other

organizations, the Shura system forms the dominant system of governance and is responsible for maintaining stability and peace among the different ethnic groups. The extended Shura system is also the dominant organ wherein people seek resolution for their disputes, and the number of cases brought to the Shura and solved by it far exceeds those in the government courts. [...] The leadership of the Shura has the ear of the Junbish leadership, and receives their respect and acceptance. In most cases, the district Shura has a sound relationship with the local police forces, who to a large extent are former Junbish fighters and commanders. Each village has a representative at the district Shura, and each district Shura has a representative at the provincial Shura, which is an important consultative organ for provincial government.[183]

Similarly in the city of Shiberghan:

Within the city of Shabarghan, three districts form three separate Shura, and jointly create a city Shura that is a member of the provincial Shura. The Shabarghan Shura receives cases directly as well as cases that are sent on a regular basis by the governor's office, city court, and prosecutor's office. These cases can be either civil or criminal in nature; even family cases such as divorce are sent by the city court to the city Shura. Since the fall of the Taliban regime, the Shabarghan [sic] Shura has solved twenty-five murder cases. The Shura handles around twenty legal cases monthly, including commercial cases. [...] The absolute majority of cases, including all criminal cases, have been solved by the Shura system, which hears at least two to three cases per week. In this capacity, the district Shura has been able to bring calm among the residents and prevent infighting and the continuation of hostilities by taking the lead in solving eighty murder cases since the fall of the Taliban in 2001. The district Shura also handles traffic offenses, but family matters are often taken up within a local Shura, which provides a more private and familial environment. The Khaja Du Koh Shura has twenty members.[184]

The presence of private prisons in parts of Afghanistan is one indication of the involvement of strongmen in the administration of justice, either as enforcers of decisions taken by mullahs or elders, or as judges and enforcers at the same time:

In Kandahar, CoP Akram acknowledged 'private prisons' as a significant challenge. [...] There were unconfirmed reports of private detention facilities around Kabul and in northern regions of the country.[185]

In southern Afghanistan, arbitrary arrest, torture, and extortion are all common. Businesses are frequently seized by commanders and their owners thrown in one of many private prisons if they protest.[186]

Amnesty International received evidence that individuals linked to the ATA are holding people arbitrarily in private detention centres that are not linked to the transitional government. Different informal agencies are carrying out arbitrary detention, informed by personal or political vendettas, or are linked to extortion. [...] High ranking regional commanders are known to have private detention centres. In Kandahar city, Amnesty International learnt that reports of 'disappearances' received by the police were all related to detention of people in private places of detention.[187]

THE AMBIGUOUS IMPACT OF REFORM

The use of private prisons by Kandahar's police was witnessed by Graeme Smith during his time there.[188] The boundary between customary law and strongman's rule can be thin, not only because the latter can operate as enforcers of decisions taken by local notables, but also because:

> there are indications that this customary system of law—which varies in form and substance throughout Afghanistan—has been subverted and manipulated by local wartime and current power-holders.[189]

From a rule of law perspective, even when customary law remains relatively 'uncontaminated' by not-so-customary influences there is a clear problem of compatibility. This is certainly the case with family law, for example, or with criminal law, at the very least affirming the rule of law in parts of the country is somewhat delegitimised by the fact that implementation is not universal. The case of local dispute resolution is more controversial, but it is clear that problems arise particularly when disputes take place between communities (as opposed as to within communities). In such cases there are no undisputed mechanisms in place for resolution: the elders of the two communities have to negotiate among themselves, but communities typically are unequal in strength and in their connections with the authorities, facts which may well affect the outcome of the negotiations.

The existence of a readily available alternative to the dysfunctional state justice greatly weakened social pressure for the provision of more effective and fair justice. The Afghan case in this sense contributes to the argument that the emergence of the rule of law is a delayed consequence of the monopolisation of justice by the state and not an outgrowth of community justice.

Civilian policing after 2001 was always on the back burner, despite the pressure of some of Afghanistan's international partners. The main reason for this lack of interest in Kabul was the lack of any significant constituency exerting pressure in favour of civilian policing and, generally, in favour of a functional policing system. Some business and civil society actors were doing exactly that, but the Karzai regime did not identify them as key constituencies of its own. None of this is too surprising in the context of post-2001 Afghanistan. Certain aspects of the reform effort were however supposed to be in the self-interest of the ruling elites: centralisation in particular. Even on this front progress was modest, a fact which confirms the findings of the previous chapters with regard to the difficulty of the post-2001 Afghan state to achieve even a modest level of self-interested functionality.

10

PROVINCIAL DYNAMICS

A CASE STUDY OF HERAT

This chapter describes in detail the functioning of a provincial police system throughout different phases of the post-2001 era, how it adapted and how it was influenced by nationwide developments and political struggles. Among the reasons why Herat was chosen is that it was home to one of the most resilient of Afghanistan's strongmen, Ismail Khan. The way he organised the police in Herat offers an interesting term of comparison because his system was replaced after 2004 by a different one, managed by the MoI. In Herat the contradictions of centralisation without sufficient human resources and of extreme weakness of the political centre emerge particularly clearly.

Historical background

During Najib's rule (1986–92), the Police Academy shortened its degree programme and the training programmes became more intensive. The summer breaks were cancelled and the three-year programme was reduced to a two-year intensive programme.[1] The bulk of the police force, however, would be formed of conscripted soldiers. In Herat, the three security institutions—the army, the police and the National Security Directorate—each conscripted separately. If young men aged between seventeen and thirty-five reported to the recruitment centre voluntarily, they would be assigned to serve within the province. If the eligible men did not report to the recruitment centre and were conscripted by the government, they would be sent to a training camp in the provincial centre. After a month, the conscripts would be sent to Kabul and then assigned to different provinces.[2] A major part of the police force in Herat, therefore, would come from outside the province.

In terms of their livelihood, police officers received an average salary of around 4,000 Afghani. In addition, they were provided with food and other basic items distributed monthly. A married officer would receive monthly 40 kg of wheat, 7 kg of oil and 7 kg of sugar. Furthermore, the government had established cooperatives from which officers could buy subsidised home appliances.[3]

Police during Ismail Khan's first rule over Herat (1992–5)

One day after the collapse of Najib's regime and the fall of Kabul into Mujahedin's control on 8 Saur, 1371 (1992–3), Herat was captured by Mujahedin forces. The strongest of the Mujahedin militia faction was affiliated with Rabbani's Jamiat and led by Ismail Khan. While serving as an army captain in the Herat garrison, Ismail Khan had played a key role in an army revolt in Herat in 1357 (1979) in protest against the Russian invasion of Afghanistan.[4] After the revolt, Ismail Khan joined the Mujahedin forces and led the Jamiyat militia faction in Herat. With the fall of Herat in 1371 (1992–3) to the Mujahedin, however, Herat was divided among Ismail Khan's forces and two Shi'ite Jihadi militia factions—Hizb-i Wahdat and Hizbullah—which were supported by Iran.

For a few months after the fall of Herat into the Mujahedin's control, each militia faction used its fighters to police the area that they controlled. The two Shi'ite factions established three bases in the northern part of the city and took control of three police stations in the centre of the town. The rest of Herat—including the army bases and other police stations—came under Ismail Khan's control. For three months, these different factions patrolled the area under their control and provided basic security. Soon Ismail Khan moved against these factions and after disarming them established his full control over Herat province. He appointed his close Jihadi associates to key security posts and tried to establish a police force responsible to himself. He appointed as provincial police chief Azizullah Afzali, the leader of a rival faction within Jamiat, which he was now trying to co-opt.[5]

As in other parts of the country under Mujahedin rule, the professionalism of the police was in steep decline. Ismail Khan removed most of the professional police officers who had been trained during Najib's era from key police posts (including the command of police stations), assigned them to lower-ranking posts and replaced them with his loyal militia commanders, all of whom had not received any police training and only had experience in guerrilla warfare. Nevertheless, some remaining police officers from Najib's era provided the expertise and the professional support for the functioning of the provincial police. This period also saw an end to the long-standing state policy of appointing police officers from outside the province. The new police officers all came from Herat and were loyal to Ismail Khan.[6]

To staff the police, Ismail Khan continued Najib's conscription policy. Young men between the ages of eighteen and thirty-five were again conscripted for service. Unlike during Najib's rule, however, the conscripts were not sent to Kabul or other provinces and would serve either in Herat army garrisons, now led by Ismail Khan's militia commanders, or in heart's provincial police.[7]

In addition to providing security, the police became an instrument for enforcing Ismail Khan's conservative interpretation of Islam. For instance, although music was not banned, women were not allowed to drive. The police would stop any motor cyclist who gave a ride to women. Furthermore, the police continued to function as a paramilitary force. The police would accompany Ismail Khan's army in the battles against General Dustom and later on with the Taliban in the southern provinces as the Taliban approached Herat.[8]

On the whole, Herat's police under Ismail Khan, despite its obvious limitations, was one of the most effective and best organised in post-1992 Afghanistan (see section 2.2.3). Only in northern Afghanistan, where more professionals were retained in their jobs, did the police have greater capacity, but the political leadership there was not as keen to maintain 'law and order'.

Police under the Taliban's Emirate

As the Taliban established their rule over Herat, there were three major changes in the provincial police. First, the police as an institution collapsed as the Taliban dismissed the bulk of the police force and placed their fighters in police stations. The Provincial Police Directorate (Qumandany Amniyat) lost its long-standing key role as the head of the provincial police force. While according to formal rules of the MoI and the Afghan Police, the police stations had traditionally been accountable and reported to the Provincial Police Directorate, the Taliban's dismissal of most of the staff of the Provincial Police Directorate broke down the bureaucratic and administrative structure of the provincial police. The police stations, now manned by young fighters without any uniform and mainly from Pashtun regions, operated almost autonomously. For instance, if the Taliban in a police station arrested a man for not repaying his financial dues to his creditor, they would detain him inside the police station until the debtor's family made due arrangement for repaying the loan. The Taliban fighters occupying the police station would not create a file or record of the petition or the case. They would not refer the case to the Criminal Investigation Unit of the Provincial Police Directorate or even report to it. Although even under Ismail Khan the police stations would not always observe the formal rules and procedures, the Taliban abandoned the bureaucratic rules and procedures of the police completely.[9]

The only professional police officers, who had received official training under Najib's rule and were not dismissed by the Taliban, were working at the Passport Department and ID Issuance Department. They helped the Taliban with issuing passports and IDs. These officials no longer wore uniform either. They had to grow long beards and wore turbans and traditional Afghan clothes. The few police officials who were allowed to wear uniforms were the traffic police officers who were stationed on the streets to manage the flow of traffic. In sum, whatever little was left of a professional police force was lost under the Taliban's rule.[10]

Police during Ismail Khan's second rule over Herat (2001–4)

With the collapse of the Taliban in late 2001, Ismail Khan was able, once again, to consolidate his control over Herat. The political dynamics of Afghanistan were now different from those that had existed during his first rule over Herat. The central government, supported by the US and the international community, claimed to be the legitimate authority in Afghanistan and disdained the warlords who ruled the provinces.[11] As a result, Ismail Khan was more responsive to popular demands and tried to attain popular support in Herat, in order to consolidate his hold and make it harder for the central government to unseat him. With this aim in mind he tried to keep his subordinates under control so that they had less space for preying on the population.[12]

He adopted a three-tier strategy to govern Herat effectively. First, as during his first rule over Herat, he relied on his confidants and loyal commanders to run the government in Herat. Second, he held public sessions regularly in his office in Wilayat to receive petitions and use his personal authority and power to follow up with petitions. Third, he adopted a micro-management style and strict personal oversight of the government staff to keep them accountable. Although his strategy undermined the development of formal rules and procedures, and therefore institutions, it was effective in keeping public employees under control and limiting their predation on the population. This was true also of the police who were less predatory under his rule compared to the period after his removal as the governor of Herat.[13]

Building a loyal police force

With the fall of the Taliban, Ismail Khan soon established his control over Herat. He appointed Mama Ziya, one of his long-time militia commanders who had fought with him against the Russians, as Herat Provincial Police Chief. Sayyed Naseer Alawi, another one of his loyalists, was appointed as the chief commander of his militia forces—*Ghond Nazme Jihadi*. Headed by his son, Mirwais Sadegh, who later was appointed by Karzai as the Minister of Aviation in the central government, the Peace and Security Commission oversaw all the security and intelligence agencies in the province.[14]

Unlike his first period of rule over Herat, Ismail Khan did not implement conscription. To staff the police force, he relied on his militia commanders and their networks. He or his son, for instance, would recruit former militia commanders who had fought with them against the Soviets or the Taliban and appoint them to key positions within the Provincial Police Headquarters or as heads of police stations. These commanders would then recruit their former fighters to work as their subordinates within those police units. The relationships between the commanders and Ismail Khan as well as between the commanders and their fighters were mainly based on personal trust and loyalty.[15] As a professional police force commented:

under Ismail Khan, we had the government of uncles and nephews. The subordinates would usually call their superiors *uncle* while the superior would often call their subordinates *nephew*.[16]

Not surprisingly, even now (2011) Ziya, who served for four years as the Provincial Police Chief under Ismail Khan, is still called *Mama* (Uncle) Ziya. The terminology used within the police at the time highlighted that the relations between the superior and subordinate ranks was centred on personal loyalty and informal ties, rather than formal rules and regulations—as it will be discussed later (see sections 8.1.3 and 7.2 above on this point).[17]

Ismail Khan tried to bring the police under his control by ensuring that not only were those occupying senior police posts his own men, but also that they behaved in a disciplined way. By late 2002, all senior police officers were from the Jami'at political party and Ismail Khan's loyalists.[18] The case of Khawaja Issa is illustrative.[19] Ismail Khan appointed him as the District Police Chief in district 4, which included the commercial zone of the city and the exchange market. In early 2003, money traders complained to Ismail Khan about instances of night robberies from the exchange market. Ismail Khan put pressure on Khawaja Issa to ensure the security of the commercial centres, but the situation did not improve and the traders accused the District Police of being linked to the thieves. Ismail Khan then dismissed Khwaja Issa from his post. Khawaj Issa, however, resisted Ismail Khan's order, claiming that such an order must be issued by Mama Ziya, who was the Provincial Police Chief. Ismail Khan then went to the district police station with his own bodyguards and his effort to disarm Khawaja Issa led to a violent clash between their men. Khawaja Issa then became a fugitive and left Herat. The Khwaja Issa example sent the warning to other police officers that their survival depended on following Ismail Khan's command. As a police officer commented:

The police under Ismail Khan was more accountable since they were his own men. He knew them personally and exerted tight control over them.[20]

Command and control of the Police

Ismail Khan adopted micro-management and strict personal oversight of the police to keep them accountable and limit their predation on the population. He used his experience as a commander of guerrilla fighters in the particular context of Afghanistan, where the insurgent movements of the 1980s were weakly organised and contained weak or absent institutions. Rather than relying on formal institutions, the insurgent commander of the 1980s usually relied on direct personal supervision and oversight to control and exert his command over subordinates.

Ismail Khan had a team of confidants and very loyal commanders whom he sent to visit and evaluate the district police stations and substations. What was seen as even more important and effective was his random personal visits of the police. He often used to patrol the city in person after midnight—sometimes on horseback—to oversee the police and even his confidants, and to punish the officers who did not take their jobs seriously.[21]

A senior militia commander whom Ismail Khan had appointed to a top position within the police remembered that one night he was supposed to patrol two districts of the city overnight to monitor the police. He described the incident as follows:

When it was after midnight, I felt tired and went home to rest. Not too long after I got home, Ismail Khan called me on radio and asked me about my position. I told him that I was on my way to visit a police substation. As soon as our conversation ended, I dressed and drove with my body guards to the location I had told Ismail Khan. I was really lucky that the police substation was very close to my home and I got there only few minutes before he arrived. It was very common of him to visit the police stations or call them on radio personally in night to see if they performed their duties appropriately.[22]

Another police officer who served as a District Police Chief stated that once he was supposed to keep in detention a man against whom his neighbours had complained. Every now and then Ismail Khan's delegates visited his district police station to make sure that the man was held in the detention facility of the police station and had not been freed. When a neighbour complained to Ismail Khan that the District Police Chief kept the man in detention during the day only and set him free overnight and let him go home, Ismail Khan personally paid a few random night visits to check on the police chief and the detainee.[23]

In addition, Ismail Khan held regular public hearing sessions daily in the large hall of his office (Wilayat), where he received petitions and heard public complaints. If someone had a complaint against the police, for instance, he would personally hear the complaint and, if needed, punish the undisciplined police officer.[24] Since he held the supreme authority in Herat, he could dismiss the misbehaving officers from their posts at will or even imprison them. Many police officers who had served during his rule stated that the police were afraid to ask for bribes openly or extort from the population out of fear of punishment by Ismail Khan.[25]

Ismail Khan also tried to strengthen his control over the police by periodically rotating his police chiefs every six to twelve months. This meant that while the chiefs of district police in 2004 were often the same as those of 2002, they had been assigned to different districts. During the interviews in 2005 it emerged that many of these chiefs were not particularly happy about having been moved to a different district then their own, a fact which over time eroded their loyalty to Ismail Khan.[26]

Although Ismail Khan's personal oversight of the police made the police relatively accountable, his approach undermined formal rules and procedures

PROVINCIAL DYNAMICS: A CASE STUDY OF HERAT

as well as the development of institutions. First, although the formal rules of reporting were gradually being established and the Provincial Police Headquarters was growing into its role at the head of the provincial police, the procedures were often streamlined by Ismail Khan's orders and the reporting system and due process were not followed. The operation of the police and the role of the police in the administration of justice were secondary to Ismail Khan's orders and personal judgement rather than based on formal rules and procedures.[27]

The district police stations were required by the internal rules of the police to report regularly to the Provincial Police Headquarters. If they detained an individual for breaking the law or committing a crime, they were supposed to file a report and send the suspect and the report to the Criminal Division of the Provincial Police Headquarters. The Criminal Division would then complete the file and send it to the Provincial Attorney Directorate. Under Ismail Khan, however, these procedures were often subverted. The district police chiefs would usually report to Ismail Khan and in the case of detaining someone, the police chiefs often consulted Ismail Khan personally and followed his orders, however arbitrary they might be.[28]

One example of this was recounted by a former district police chief. One day a woman complained to Ismail Khan that her neighbour had deceived her son and taken him to Iran. Ismail Khan ordered the police chief of the district to arrest a family member of the man who had deceived the old woman's son. According to the police chief, he arrested the father of the man and then asked Ismail Khan about what he had to do. Ismail Khan ordered the police chief to keep the old man in detention until his son came back and brought the old woman's son. The police chief detained the old man in the district police station for five months until the old man's son along with the old woman's son came back from Iran. Apparently, the woman's son had gone to Iran voluntarily in order to work. Then Ismail Khan ordered the release of the old man.[29]

Similarly, the officials from the Military Court complained that under Ismail Khan the formal procedures were not observed. According to an official from the Herat Military Court:

the military and civilian courts were not separated; the official rules and procedures were not observed. Civilian cases were often sent to us since the civilian courts were overwhelmed. The offences of the police and army personnel, on the other hand, were often punished by their superior or by Ismail Khan, without referring such cases to the Military Attorney Directorate and the Military Court.[30]

Police corruption

The strict oversight of the police limited their ability to collect bribes and extort from the population, but it did not mean that corruption disappeared. Ismail Khan's reliance on personal oversight undermined the development of bureaucratic and systematic mechanisms of oversight and control. Of major significance was the underdevelopment of systematic reporting and surveillance. Since Ismail Khan had to rely on a small number of trusted loyalists to oversee the police, the extent to which his confidants could monitor and oversee the police was limited. As a result, the senior police officers could exploit the weakness of the reporting system to skim off public resources.[31] As a police officer highlighted:

> under Ismail Khan it was much harder for the police to ask bribes from the population, but the senior police officers did have a lot of *payda* [informal and mainly illegal revenue]. The few senior officers at a district police station, for instance, could collude with each other and inflate the number of personnel that they had. They kept two lists: one with the real number of the personnel and the other list including the ghost personnel. When sending the list to the provincial centre for salaries and food, they would send the inflated list and then distribute among themselves the extra money and the food they received from the centre. When Ismail Khan's men visited the police stations to check on the attendance, they would use the accurate list without ghost personnel.[32]

The underdevelopment of the system of reporting and analysis of information sent by the district police stations to the provincial centre meant that such misrepresentation could often go unnoticed and made the system vulnerable to corruption.

During his control of Herat, Ismail Khan controlled the custom revenues of Herat, which yielded as much as US$ 80 million yearly.[33] He distributed part of those revenues among his loyalists who had been appointed to top positions. They, therefore, did not have to extort from the population since they had good income while not allowing their subordinates to engage in predatory activities, either.[34] Part of the revenue was also used to equip Herat's police to a standard higher than the rest of the country, for example. All districts received some transport vehicles. By the time Ismail Khan was removed, districts away from Herat city had two to three off-road cars (a mix of Toyotas and UAZs) which were handed over to the police by Ismail Khan himself.[35] While this may have helped to contain corruption in Herat, from the point of view of the central government it was just a different form of corruption and a particularly annoying one in that it affected state revenue directly and badly.

Police in post-Ismail Khan Herat

The removal of Ismail Khan from his post as the governor of Herat just one month before the first presidential election (October 2004) abolished the system of personal rule which Ismail Khan had developed and also altered how the police operated in Herat.

With his removal, the central government gradually tried to restructure the police in Herat with the goal of ending their loyalty to Ismail Khan and transferring it into the ANP. First, all police officers had to pass through a police reform programme to remain in their jobs. Second, the central government soon took control of police appointments, gradually appointing officers affiliated with Ismail Khan's rivals or from outside Herat to senior positions within the provincial police force.[36]

Initially the new Kabul-supported governor, Khairkhwa, was cautious. Two professional policemen made their way to occupy the position of district chief, but there were specific reasons for these appointments. In Ghuryan the new chief, a professional from Paktia, had to be called in because of a tribal conflict in the district. It was decided that the CoP should be from a distant region, so that he would not get involved too much. In Enjil the previous CoP, Faiz Ahmad Azimi, fled after the removal of Ismail Khan. It was thought that a professional might have been the right choice to pacify the situation, because Faiz Ahmad was notorious for strictly enforcing 'virginity checks' and for entering houses without a warrant. The break with the past was therefore more apparent than real. Four more police chiefs of districts were transferred or appointed after the removal of Ismail Khan, in Zendajan, Pashtun Zarghoun, Kohsan and Guzara. Two of them were former jihadis linked to Ismail Khan, while the remaining two were local notables of uncertain allegiance. Rather bolder appointments were made within the Herat province police department, with some important positions being taken away from supporters of Ismail Khan, such as the chief security officer and his deputy, the commander of a city police station, the chief of airport security and the chief of Islam Qala police station, close to the main provincial custom office.[37] As we shall see, these appointments did not improve the provision of security by Herat's police.

While Ismail Khan had opposed foreign-imparted training for Herat's police, the US could now establish two police training centres: one by the Herat Airport and the other one in the Adraskan district of Herat. The Italians contributed a group of Carabinieri to train ANCOP units in Adraskan. Relying on US police trainers as well as a few Afghan experts, the training centres provided two-month courses for patrolmen and four-month courses for would-be NCOs.

Police and politics

After Ismail Khan was unseated, the provincial police became part of the central government patronage system, which drastically changed how the police operated in Herat. The central government gradually took control of appointments to the provincial police, but President Karzai's strategy was to co-opt militia factions and reward them with government jobs in order to preserve the political settlement in Afghanistan. With that aim, public offices in the central government as well as in the provinces were treated as spoils to be distributed in order to attract the support of the militia factions. The Herat provincial police was also included among the spoils. The central government gradually removed Ismail Khan's loyalists from senior police posts or transferred them to other provinces. Instead police officers or sometimes militia commanders loyal to other factions were appointed to senior police posts in Herat. The provincial police force, therefore, became factionalised. Senior police officers, sometimes within the same station, often belonged to different political factions.[38]

The best example of this practice was the re-appointment of Khwaja Issa (see section 10.4.2 above) as the police chief of Enjil district. Khwaja Issa was believed by his colleagues to lead one of the networks involved in kidnappings and was viewed to have changed the district police office into an extortion racket. One type of his predatory activities was what he classified as 'administration of justice'. If a debtor refrained from paying his debt, the creditor could go to Khwaja Issa, who would demand a share of the money—often around 50 per cent in exchange for collecting the money from the debtor. Khwaja Issa's men—now police officers—would arrest the debtor, detain him at the Enjil police headquarters and torture him until he returned the money.[39] In addition, Khwaja Issa was widely believed to be involved in kidnapping of the wealthy. As an official from the office of Herat's governor put it:

inside the police headquarters his men dressed as police. Outside the police headquarters, they would take off their police uniforms and would use their police guns for kidnapping the traders and exacting money from their families.[40]

After allegedly killing a Kandahari trader, Khwaja Issa was dismissed by Karzai from his police position, but a few months before the 2009 presidential elections he was reappointed to his post as the police chief of Enjil district, with a promotion from Lieutenant Colonel to Colonel.[41]

The diversity of the political affiliation of the police has two major consequences. First, unlike under Ismail Khan, the police were granted more impunity. Ismail Khan, as mentioned earlier, enjoyed monopolistic rule over Herat. The police were controlled by his own militia commanders who were loyal to him and under his control. As demonstrated in the case of Khwaja Issa, Ismail Khan intended to keep in senior police posts only those who were subservient to him. After the central government tried to undermine the powerbase of Ismail Khan within the police by replacing Ismail Khan's loyalists with those affiliated with other factions, the central government was unable to keep the police as accountable as Ismail Khan had been able to. These officers belonged to pro-central government political factions, whose support the central government intended to preserve. With the protection that these officers received from their political faction or patron, they enjoyed more freedom and greater impunity. The punishment of police officers or their dismissal after their involvement in predatory activities became less common. As a senior professional officer said:

in the past all police officers were Ismail Khan's people; now most of the police officers are linked to strong political factions…. The police chief in Gozara District is linked to Jamiat faction, the one in Pushton Zarghun is linked to Hazrat Mujaddidi, etc. With the support that they receive, no one is going to punish them... No matter what they do.[42]

The other consequence was that factionalism reinforced conflict and rivalry within the police and undermined the cohesion of the police force. Since the survival of police officers depended on the strength of the political factions they belonged to, police officers tried to strengthen the position of their faction within the police and MoI while undermining other factions. The factional competition within the police exacerbated mistrust and undermined cohesion and cooperation. For instance, in many cases a district police chief and his deputy belonged to different factions, and instead of working as a team, they refrained from supporting and cooperating with each other.[43]

Command and control

With the inclusion of the Herat provincial police force in the ANP (after the vetting and the American-imparted training mentioned above), the command and control system also changed and the MoI started relying on official reports sent by officers stationed in Herat and inspecting teams sent from the MoI in Kabul. The central government, however, faced major challenges in controlling the provincial police through these two mechanisms. The first challenge was the classical principal-agent dilemma. The inspecting teams who were supposed to function as the agent of the MoI enjoyed discretion and monopoly over the transfer of information from Herat to Kabul, which allowed them to abuse their authority and manipulate the information they relayed to Kabul. The spatial and temporal distance from Herat to Kabul undermined the capability of the MoI to exert the control over the police which Ismail Khan had enjoyed. Second, with the assumption of control of the provincial police by the centre, as mentioned in the previous section, the police force became dominated by numerous militia factions, whose support the central government did not want to lose. The support that police officers received from their patrons undermined the ability of the MoI to keep them accountable even when the MoI intended to do so.[44]

The MoI sent inspecting teams from each of its directorates every few months to oversee the provincial police and report to the MoI. This method, hypothetically, should have enabled the MoI to exert its control over the police in the provinces. The weakness of this method, however, is that in the absence of multiple competing channels sending information to Kabul, the inspecting team have almost a monopoly over the information relayed to Kabul and could avoid sending accurate information. The provincial police officials were well aware of this and it was in their interests to treat the inspecting teams as well as possible and earn their complicity. The teams would be taken to luxurious hotels, offered a very good reception during their visit to Herat and even be presented with expensive gifts. In return for such a reception, they would send a very positive evaluation of the provincial police to Kabul.[45]

This process exemplifies the standard principal-agent dilemma, in which the principal is not able to monitor the agent properly to ensure the accuracy of the information he receives. What helped Ismail Khan overcome this challenge to a certain extent was his proximity to the provincial police. The small size of the territory that Ismail Khan ruled allowed him to overcome the principal-agent dilemma through his own strict personal oversight of the police and his confidants whom he sent to monitor and oversee the police. In addition, the regular public hearings that Ismail Khan held in his office offered him a separate source of information, which meant that he did not have to rely solely on the reports of officers and his confidants on the performance of the police.[46]

Political economy

Ismail Khan's rule exemplified what Olson describes as 'stationary bandits'.[47] With his monopolistic control of Herat, Ismail Khan had the incentive to keep his police force accountable and limit their extraction and predatory activities in order to mobilise popular support and improve his prospect of ruling Herat. That explains why Ismail Khan tried to oversee the police strictly and punished those officers whom the population viewed as abusive and predatory.

With the factionalisation of the police, however, dynamics and incentives changed. Those who were left in control of the police force after Ismail Khan often had limited time as they did not expect to remain in power for long. For them, it was important to maximise the resources that they could extract from the population in order to channel part of those resources back to the political patron on whose support they were dependent for maintaining their current position, as well as ensuring a good future appointment.

This type of economic linkage took the form of higher-ranking officers selling lower-ranking posts. The officers started to demand from lower-ranking officers and soldiers the payment of an advance as well as regular payments in order to remain in their jobs. The lower-ranking officers and soldiers would then collect bribes from the population to make the payments to senior officers (see section 6.3 for the same system at national level). Not surprisingly, in post-Ismail Khan Herat, petty corruption within the police and police predatory activities increased drastically. Almost all ordinary citizens as well as police officers who were interviewed in Herat believed that police corruption—particularly collecting bribes from the population—had soared in post-Ismail Khan Herat.[48] As a senior police officer highlighted:

under Ismail Khan, the police did not dare ask for bribes openly. Now asking for bribes by the police has become routine and if they do not take bribes, they won't be able to keep their jobs.[49]

Another police officer stated that:

the police did not ask [for] bribes under Ismail Khan since they did not have to pay Ismail Khan to buy their posts. Ismail Khan controlled a lot of resources and was not in need of selling police posts.[50]

The dynamics of corruption in post-Ismail Khan Herat compared to the period ruled by Ismail Khan was well described by a senior attorney from Herat who argued that corruption under Ismail Khan was highly centralised. Ismail Khan appropriated the custom revenue from Herat and distributed part of it among his loyalists whom he had appointed to senior posts. He, however, kept the rest of public employees and the police disciplined and did not allow them to collect bribes from the population.[51] This resembles of course the way states behave: claim a monopoly over taxation and use that to regularise the system of extortion.

Aside from their limited time, what enabled senior police officers to demand money from their subordinates was the support they received from their political patrons. As discussed in the next section, prosecution, punishment or dismissal of the police due to involvement in corruption and extortion became less common under post-Taliban Ismail Khan. The support that the senior police officers received from their patron took the form of impunity whereas they were rarely prosecuted or dismissed from their job. Such impunity undermined the command and control of the police.[52]

Police corruption and criminal behaviour

A factor compounding the corruption initially was the suspension of Ismail Khan's top-ups of police salaries, at a time when none of the police in Herat had been trained by the Americans and therefore incorporated into the National Police, whose salaries were much higher. Among other things this resulted in massive recruitment problems. In 2005 the personnel chart was 83 per cent complete as far as officers were concerned, but only 31 per cent complete in the case of soldiers. NCOs were only marginally better off, being 41 per cent complete.[53]

An epidemic of criminal behaviour spread within the ranks of the police. The case of Khwaja Issa, discussed above in section 10.5.1, was not isolated. Senior police officers within the provincial police headquarters were also widely believed to be involved in kidnappings. Many facts made Herati people believe that the top echelons of the provincial police were involved in kidnappings. When instances of kidnappings were reported to the Security Division of the provincial police, the victims' families were told to meet the kidnappers' demand since the provincial police did not have the power to arrest the kidnappers.[54]

Even when the hideouts of kidnappers were discovered (as in the case of the father of Shirzad, one of the wealthy traders from Herat), the provincial police refrained from taking any action. In addition, after the victims' families reported the incidences to the police, the kidnappers would learn that the family had contacted the police and the details of their conversations. With the increased instances of kidnappings in 2007, public protests demanded the removal of senior police officials and instisted that proper investigations take place. In August 2007, the sons of four money traders were kidnapped. On 15 September, a group of armed men attacked Herat's exchange market in full daylight. As the wave of kidnappings intensified further, Herat provincial council, the only elected body at the provincial level, also went on strike and along with Herati parliamentarians demanded that President Karzai remove senior police officials.[55] These public protests, however, failed to bring accountability to the police or to reduce the kidnappings. Karzai at first promised to bring changes in the leadership of the Herat provincial police. Under pressure from anti-Ismail Khan political leaders in Herat, however, Karzai refrained from removing senior police officials.[56] The status quo remained.

Eventually the senior police officials, linked to Ismail Khan's rivals, were removed from their posts in Herat, but they were appointed to new posts outside Herat, and no investigation was conducted into their alleged involvement in kidnappings. On 8 April 2008, Homayun Eyni, head of the Afghanistan Special Police Force (Police 119) and adviser to the Minister of Interior, confirmed that the provincial police were linked to the criminal bands responsible for kidnappings.[57] No formal investigation was carried out, however.[58] Tarway Heydari, the main suspect, was appointed as the police chief in district 10 of Kabul.[59]

With regard to the cases of kidnappings, neither the military attorney nor the martial court carried out investigations into the alleged involvement of the police, since such cases were viewed as a national security matter and under the jurisdiction of the National Security Directorate. However, before the National Security Directorate in Herat carried out investigations into the link between the police and kidnapping bands, the central government called the suspected senior police officers to Kabul.[60]

Oversight of the police

Aside from the inspecting teams sent from Kabul, four organisations can be identified, which perform some type of oversight over the provincial police. The first two are the Military Attorney Directorate (Saronwali Nezami, SN) and the Military Court (Mahkameh Nezami, MN). The Directorate is responsible for investigating and prosecuting the cases of crimes perpetrated by the military personnel—the police as well as the army. The cases which are processed by the SN are of three types. The first comprises of cases referred to the SN by the police or the army when they discover crimes committed by their personnel. The second includes cases which may be initiated by ordinary citizens filing complaints against the police or army personnel. The third involves cases where the Detective Unit of the SN visits the police or the army and discovers crimes perpetrated by them. In any of these cases, the SN is required to complete the investigation over the case within fifteen days and send it to the Military Court.[61]

The SN, however, faced major challenges in performing its duties. First, Herat's SN is short of staff. With its staffing of fifteen, it is responsible for the cases in the whole Western Zone, which includes four provinces. According to senior officials from the SN, they lack sufficient manpower even for processing the files which were referred to them by the police.[62] The SN, therefore, rarely has the time to form Detective Units to visit the police and oversee their performance. The SN thus mainly relies on cases referred to them by the police themselves. Such cases often involved abuse of public properties such as police cars or weaponry. Surprisingly, in spite of the increased involvement of the police in extortion and bribe-taking from the population, cases of corruption are rarely referred to the SN.[63]

According to a senior official from the Military Court, the SN did not prosecute a single case of police corruption from the four provinces over one year.[64] During 2009 and 2010 the Military Court had not received any case of police corruption from Badghis province. According to the same source:

> when the Mujahedin controlled the provincial government [referring to Ismail Khan's faction], the police chiefs sent us many cases where their subordinates were accused of corruption and demanding bribes. Nowadays, however, the police chiefs rarely send us cases of corruption. It is evident that corruption exists, but I believe either the police chiefs prefer not to report such cases or there is not effective oversight of the police.[65]

Furthermore, SN officials claimed that their efforts were sometimes undermined through the threats that they received or pressure from 'the top' when trying to prosecute crimes committed by the police or the army. According to a senior official of SN, under pressure from influential political figures, they sometimes had to halt investigations and send incomplete cases to the Military Court. The Military Court would then dismiss such cases due to lack of evidence.[66] When pressure was not enough, outright intimidation could occur. The official whom one of the authors interviewed claimed that he received a threat call the same morning with regard to the case they were working on. In fact, four days later, an explosion took place outside the SN office, although the SN personnel survived the attack. In sum, as the interviews with the officials from the SN and the Martial Court indicated, these two institutions faced major challenges in overseeing the police.[67]

The third organization authorised to oversee the police is the Afghanistan Independent Human Rights Commission (AIHRC) (see also section 9.6.2 above). According to the Afghan laws, AIHRC is supposed to record and report human rights abuses including those involving the police and other security institutions. According to its officials, during the first few years after the establishment of the AIHRC, they received many petitions from citizens complaining about police corruption, torture under police custody and other human rights abuses involving the police. Over time the number of such petitions declined drastically since the AIHRC, according to these officials, was not able to effectively deal with such human rights abuses, which undermined people's confidence in the institution.[68]

The police often refused to cooperate with the AIHRC investigative teams. For instance, when they received petitions with regard to torture in police custody and went to the police stations, they faced problems with having access to the victim. The victim was either moved away from the detention facility and hidden somewhere else or the investigative teams were told that those in charge were not present at the location. More importantly, even when a team completed its investigation and found evidence of abuses of human rights by the police, the AIHRC had limited power in dealing with such cases. The AIHRC often sent letters to the police stations, demanding a change in their behaviour. The most they could do was to threaten the police chief that the AIHRC would report the instances of human rights abuses to their superior or even the MoI.[69]

The AIHRC, however, did not have the authority to file a petition in the court with regard to the cases of human rights abuses by the police. As a result, although it has helped reduce torture in custody by the police, the AIHRC, according to its own staff, has not been able to meet the popular expectations with regard to dealing with human rights abuses or other predatory activities perpetrated by the police and keeping the police accountable. Failing to meet the popular expectations has resulted in a drastic decline of petitions that citizens have filed with the AIHRC in recent years.[70]

The media hypothetically can also oversee the police through investigative reports. According to many journalists working in Herat, they did not have many opportunities to work under Ismail Khan. The only media at the time were the *Ittefaq Islam* daily newspaper and the provincial public TV channels, both controlled by the provincial government.[71] With the removal of Ismail Khan, the private media flourished—written as well as radio and TV channels. In spite of the greater freedom enjoyed by journalists, they had difficulty gaining access to information, let alone producing investigative reports. To obtain information from the police, journalists had to petition the Provincial Police Headquarters to get permission to talk to specific police officers, or they could alternatively talk to the Public Relations Office of the police. In practice, access to information was a privilege rather than a right for journalists. Journalists had to build a relationship with the police before they were offered information, and publishing critical news of the police usually has an adverse effect on building such a relationship.[72] The national media, on the other hand, have better access to information. The information about provincial police, however, does not attract much attention at the national level and leads to fewer debates and discussions on the news about provincial police.

In sum, what does the Herat case tell us? Stationary bandit Ismail Khan might have been of state-building stock, except that he was in opposition to the central government, which supported lesser strongmen in the same area. In general, a central government will never like the monopolisation of violence by regional actors as it is against its interests. The Herat model of policing was not replicable on a national scale, because it was exactly its small size that allowed a more effective supervision. However, it does highlight what makes a system of policing lacking functioning layers of supervision and external oversight work.

11

CONCLUSION

Was Afghanistan's experiment with policing under the monarchy and the first republic doomed to failure? Although the development might have seemed slow to many Afghans, there were no signs per se that the system being developed was not viable or sustainable. It was cheap to run and required modest human resources, which the country could provide. It was functional, even if imperfect and not immune from corruption and abuses. It matched the development of Afghan society: civilian policing was in its early days, as was Afghanistan's civil society.

The onset of a long series of wars in 1978 had little to do with policing, but affected it very much as the police became involved in the fighting and successive regimes all reshaped it in their image. The development of civilian policing was abruptly suspended, while paramilitarism dominated the scene. However, the leftist regime of 1980–92 and the Taliban from 1996–2001 were able to create paramilitary forces which were quite functional, even if their purposes were not those that the public of western democracies would appreciate.

What all this means in 2011 is that creating a functional police force in Afghanistan is not a hopeless task. How to explain then the fact that none of the ministers who succeeded each other at the head of the MoI after 2001 managed to lift it from its state of dysfunctionality. The resources committed to the task were by 2011, to say the least, very significant, thanks to generous help from the USA. Such persistent dysfunctionality challenges the conventional wisdom concerning state- and institution-building: there must be some reason why processes viewed by western policy makers and academics as undoubted benefits are rejected or at least not endorsed by local elites.

One factor highlighted in this book is that the constituencies of a particular regime might see an effective police force as a threat to their interests. Not every regime sees an advantage in the development of a free, independent business sector, even when that regime proclaims adherence to liberal principles, or of a burgeoning middle class. In Afghanistan, as of 2011, the provincial strongmen were still the main base of support of the Karzai regime, perhaps more then ever before.

After 2006, even within the regime some interest in the development of an effective paramilitary police became evident, because the insurgency had turned into a major threat and even the strongmen started realising that their armed retinues were no longer sufficient to afford them protection. The compromise could have been local paramilitary police forces (as opposed to a mobile one fully controlled by the centre), de facto under the control of the strongmen but re-trained and endowed with better discipline. This in fact was the direction things seemed to be moving towards from 2004 onwards, but creating a functional policing system in collaboration with Afghanistan's warlords and strongmen proved a major challenge. Few of the warlords had the ability to maintain order within their own police forces: Ismail Khan and Atta Mohammed primarily. Moreover, often they were not even on good terms with the central government. Otherwise, the strongmen proved incapable or unwilling to deploy well-organised police forces in their fiefdoms. At the same time they would mostly oppose efforts by professional police officers to achieve exactly that.

It could be argued that a certain coalition of interests, opposed to the creation of a strong central state, might then struggle even to endow the state with the minimal functionality that it needs to survive. Such elite coalitions struggle to find a formula for the creation of a state 'strong but not too much', because some of the key processes which lead to the formation of strong states are by nature resilient to control or restraint. In Chapter 1, we have highlighted how the monopoly of policing is a precondition for further evolution towards legitimate coercion, the trademark of a strong state. A ruling coalition whose self-interest goes against the monopoly of policing will therefore struggle to consolidate its hold. Among the reasons which might prevent a coalition from supporting the achievement of the monopoly of policing is a precarious political settlement, where components of the coalition do not trust each other and are uncertain about their future status within the coalition. A monopoly of policing might then be used against them one day. This seems also to have been the case in Afghanistan.

The shadow economy which engulfed Afghanistan after 2001 is of course a major reason why anything smelling of an effective police force caused allergic reactions among some of the key stakeholders in the post-2001 regime. The isolated reformers who wanted change along the lines advocated by the European and American donors could only rely on the availability of financial resources to buy the formal consent of dominant networks within the MoI for the desired changes. However, the simple lack of determined support within the MoI could have been enough to ensure the failure of ambitious and complex reforms. The fact that often there was even open sab-

CONCLUSION

otage against the reforms made the situation even more hopeless. In fact, such reforms would have struggled in any case because of their excessive ambition: the mismatch between the objectives and the poor human resources available was evident from the beginning. The politics of intervention, of international aid, of bureaucratic politics ensured that despite the evident unsuitability of the project to turn the MoI into an efficient and modern bureaucratic machine, it would continue to be pushed ahead year after year, without the consideration of alternatives.

In the end, the international demand for a system able to implement the rule of law met with the political aims of the ruling elite in Kabul to produce a hybrid system, featuring a façade of rule of law 'in the making', while behind it the trappings of a modern bureaucratic organisation were in fact used to implement a system of patronage and favour. We can describe this as 'prebendalism' in its modus operandi, or, if we stress the long-term consequences, as 'limited access orders'.

If the aim is to create a centralised state in Afghanistan, with a functional police force at its service, it might be necessary to establish a new police force from scratch, in parallel to the existing one, and gradually develop it while progressively marginalising the old police. In the current situation, taking on the village communities and providing better policing there seems a tall order: border, highways and cities are more realistic priorities. While this task is in principle feasible, as demonstrated by the historical precedents, it is difficult to imagine in the political environment of summer 2011 how this could be done in practice: where would the political impulse come from? How would the vetoes of the strongmen and of the networks be removed or bypassed?

Probably there is no alternative in the foreseeable future to parallel police systems developing in Afghanistan, with civilian policing playing a marginal role for several years to come, but with a centralised paramilitary police, legitimised by the need to fight a growing insurgency, gradually becoming the dominant force. Perhaps Minister Atmar's plan to turn part of the AUP into local police units, if politically feasible, could help delegitimise those portions of the police most affected by the influence of the strongmen. Even to implement a plan of this type, the MoI would need to resolve the problem of how to recruit better and more managerial skills, as well as to accelerate the formation of professional officers.

Because this problem is not very close to a solution, it is more than a mere academic exercise to think of an alternative, more down-to-earth and less state-building police system than the one currently planned in Afghanistan. The pre-1978 system, the Taliban's system, Ismail Khan's and Atta Mohammad's systems all have something to teach with regard to how to run a police system on the cheap and with limited human resources. Sometimes oversight can be provide by a political party (several of them) or sometimes by a social class or category (the clergy in the Taliban's time). Conceivably, this could be a task for Afghanistan's parliament, if it was given enough space and independence by the government and it was elected through a credible process. The problem with Afghanistan's current government is that it floats above society, lifted by billion of dollars of external aid. There is no constituency which is in a position to exercise oversight on it, except for the strongmen which endow the government with a modicum of influence in most provinces.

In other words, therefore, until the Afghan political system changes dramatically, there is going to be little room for a more effective policing system. Some improvement in paramilitary policing is likely to occur, because the strongmen are now (2011) willing to give some space to the police, in reaction to an insurgency that they themselves cannot contain. Perhaps, by accident more than by design, some charismatic minister or political leader will seize the opportunity for appropriating more space than originally intended by the strongmen and their allies in Kabul and create a police force which will no longer be a pawn in the hands of the strongmen. A development of this kind would in fact not be so unusual, in terms of historical comparisons. In Italy, for example, the need to fight terrorism in the 1970s led to important changes in the police and gendarmerie (Carabinieri), as well as in the judiciary, which acquired a political autonomy and a degree of professionalism they did not enjoy before.

Beyond Afghanistan, this book adds to the growing body of evidence that international intervention cannot replace internal political dynamics. Even when it manages to affect them and change the direction of development, the result is not a coherent, functional system, but a hybrid, usually incoherent, system which fulfils disparate purposes, of which the demand of western powers for a strong, efficient state which controls territory and populations while being internationally allied with them is usually the least important. These ineffective hybrids come at great cost to the coffers of the western powers, a fact which raises the issue of whether some more efficient way of pursuing western interests can be conceived.

Efficiency of western intervention aside, the development of the police in Afghanistan after 2001 suggests that the technocratic approach taken in particular by European advisers (and some others) was never going to work. As in the 1980s, it flew too high over Afghan society and politics and, should the MoI have been reshaped in its image, the result would have been once again 'splendid isolation'. While there was some scope for European models in Afghanistan's cities, the Afghan countryside needed something more down-to-earth if it had to be under some kind of government control. Here paramilitarism had no alternative, but most importantly some kind of engagement with the armed groups roaming the countryside was necessary. Otherwise, Kabul might have found itself pitted against the dominant forces in the villages. The people running the MoI were more aware of this danger and in fact often acceded in the opposite direction: appeasing armed groups, coopting them and incorporating them in a weakly supervised policeforce, in many cases resulting in their takeover of the police. The lack of a realistic model of policing on offer on the European side made this radical divergence possible: a stronger focus on a viable form of paramilitary policing could have helped the reformers at the MoI approach the armed groups in the villages from a position of greater strength and extract a better compromise.

NOTES

1. INTRODUCTION

1. This section and the next one are adapted from Giustozzi (2011).
2. Examples of how it worked before incorporation into the state are described in Tariq; Schmeidl and Karokhail; Ghosh, 158ff.
3. Reith.
4. Marenin, 127; Bayley, 40–2; Liang, 14.
5. Again see Giustozzi (2011) on this point. See also Holmes and Carothers, 4.
6. Olson.
7. Hualing.
8. On the problem of building functional police bureaucracies see Turk, 23–4.
9. Yasin, 167; Chaudhry, 69, 100, 109–10, 166.
10. See Bayley, 162–7, 178–80.
11. Hutchful, 87.
12. www.securitycouncilreport.org/atf/cf/.../Afgh%20Compact.doc.

2. BACKGROUND: HISTORY OF POLICE IN AFGHANISTAN

1. Chilton et al, 27.
2. Kakar (1979), 77ff.
3. Ibid., 36ff.
4. Ibid., 53–4.
5. Hassin, 35.
6. Gregorian, 248.
7. Hassin, 35ff.
8. Hassin, 40–1; Gregorian, 299.
9. Hassin, 41–2; interview with Gulabzoi, Kabul, October 2007.
10. Ibid.
11. Gregorian, 372.

12. Interview with Lt. Gen. Sayyed Mohammad Quddusi, Police Academy Kabul, October 2007.
13. Hassin, 49–50.
14. Gregorian, 299.
15. Hassin, 55–71.
16. Hassin, 77.
17. Hassin, 54–5.
18. Hassin, 67.
19. Hassin, 76–7.
20. Hassin, 51–3.
21. Hassin, 41–2.
22. Hassin, 51.
23. Hassin, 54–5.
24. Smith et al. (1969), 367.
25. Hassin, 75.
26. '6–8' according to Hassin, 76.
27. Hassin, 66.
28. Hassin, 70.
29. Hassin, 71–3.
30. Interview with police officer trained in the 1970s, October 2007.
31. Interview with former Woluswal governor Mohammad Aman Kazimi, London 3 June 2008.
32. Glatzer, 109.
33. Hassin, 74.
34. Interview with former minister Gulabzoi, Kabul, April 2008.
35. Smith et al. (1969), 363.
36. Azimi, 120.
37. Interview with police officer and Police Academy teachers, Kabul, 14 April 2008; Interview with former police officers Ghulam Mohammad Kamall and Khawal Shinwari, London, 19 January 2008.
38. Interview with police officer trained in the 1970s, 11 October 2007.
39. Interview with former police officers Ghulam Mohammad Kamall and Khawal Shinwari, London, 19 January 2008.
40. Interview with former police officers Ghulam Mohammad Kamall and Khawal Shinwari, London, 19 January 2008.
41. Hassin, 75.
42. Interview with police officer trained in the 1970s, 11 October 2007.
43. Afanasiev, 313.
44. Personal communication with former deputy Minister Shah Mahmood Miakhel, July 2011.
45. Walt, 152.
46. Smith et al. (1976), 366.
47. Interview with police officer trained in the 1970s, May 2006, Kabul; telephone interview with Lloyd Baron, Vancouver, September 2007.
48. Interview with former Woluswal governor Mohammad Aman Kazimi, London, June 2008.

49. Interview with police officer trained in the 1970s, October 2007.
50. Interview with police officer trained in the 1970s, May 2006, Kabul; telephone interview with Lloyd Baron, Vancouver, September 2007.
51. Kakar (1978), 205.
52. Interview with Peter Schwittek, NGO manager, Kabul, October 2007.
53. Interview with former Woluswal governor Mohammad Aman Kazimi, London, June 2008.
54. Telephone interview with Lloyd Baron, Vancouver, September 2007.
55. Interview with Peter Schwittek, NGO manager, Kabul 23 October 2007.
56. Interview with police officer trained in the 1970s, October 2007; telephone interview with Lloyd Baron, Vancouver, September 2007.
57. Fry, 238.
58. Hassin, 55.
59. Hassin, 67.
60. Hassin, 68.
61. Hassin, 54–5.
62. Hassin, 68–9.
63. Hassin, 75; interview with Ustad Zal, Police Academy, Kabul, April 2008.
64. Klyushnikov, 22–3.
65. Chilton et al, 25.
66. Interview with police officer trained in the 1970s, October 2007.
67. Smith et al. (1967), 365.
68. Interview with police officer and Police Academy teachers, Kabul, 14 April 2008
69. Hassin, 68–9.
70. Hassin, 70–1.
71. Interview with Ustad Kaliwal, Police Academy, April 2008.
72. Interview with former Woluswal governor Mohammad Aman Kazimi, London, June 2008.
73. Weinbaum, 53.
74. Walt, 152.
75. Minnott, 177–9.
76. Telegram from Kabul Embassy to Department of State Washington, 30 April 1996, EMBTEL 532 RTPD BONN 12.
77. Interview with Ustad Zal, Police Academy, Kabul, April 2008.
78. Interview with police officer and Police Academy teachers, Kabul, April 2008.
79. Interview with former Woluswal governor Mohammad Aman Kazimi, London, June 2008.
80. Azimi, 120.
81. Interview with high ranking MoI official, Kabul, May 2006.
82. Interview with Waris Waziri, formerly teacher at the Academy, London, November 2007.
83. Personal communication with Lloyd Baron, who resided in the country in the 1970s, September 2007; interview with Peter Schwittek, NGO Manager, Kabul, October 2007.
84. Interview with former MoI officer, May 2006, Kabul.

85. Interview with former police officers Ghulam Mohammad Kamall and Khawal Shinwari, London, 19 January 2008.
86. Ibid.
87. Omarzai, 60–2; interview with high ranking MoI official, Kabul, May 2006.
88. For details of the incident, see Brown.
89. Stepanov, 43–44, 55.
90. Azimi, 245; Klyushnikov, 27.
91. Interview with former police officers Ghulam Mohammad Kamall and Khawal Shinwari, London, January 2008.
92. Stepanov, 45.
93. Grinin, 69.
94. Klyushnikov, 26–7.
95. Grinin, 69.
96. Kliuchnik, 115–6.
97. Azimi, 245.
98. Giustozzi (2000), 95–7; Lozhkin, 199.
99. Interview with former police officers Ghulam Mohammad Kamall and Khawal Shinwari, London, January 2008.
100. Fedaseev, 226–8.
101. Interview with MoI official, Kabul, April 2010.
102. Giustozzi (2000), table 23.
103. Interview with former police officers Ghulam Mohammad Kamall and Khawal Shinwari, London, January 2008.
104. Stepanov, 59; Sysoev, 376.
105. Pleshakov, 122.
106. Interview with senior police officer, Kabul, April 2008.
107. Interview with former police officers Ghulam Mohammad Kamall and Khawal Shinwari, London, January 2008.
108. Alekseev, 414.
109. Interview with Gulabzoi, Kabul, October 2007.
110. Interview with former police officers Ghulam Mohammad Kamall and Khawal Shinwari, London, January 2008.
111. Stepanov, 59.
112. Interview with Gulabzoi, Kabul, October 2007.
113. Hassin, 90ff.
114. Stepanov, 56–7; Grinin, 78; Rudenko, 394.
115. Hassin, 91–2; Pleshakov, 121.
116. Hassin, 96–7.
117. Klyushnikov, 36.
118. Tsigannik, 143.
119. Tsigannik, 164; Gubinchikov, 220.
120. Interview with former police officers Ghulam Mohammad Kamall and Khawal Shinwari, London, January 2008.
121. Giustozzi (2000), 85, 97; Pleshakov, 124; Vorobiov, 335–6.
122. Fedaseev, Mushaveri, 229.

NOTES pp [29–38]

123. Bykov, 285, 287.
124. Interview with MoI official who served under Gulabzoi, April 2010.
125. Personal communications with police officers who served in the 1980s, London, Kabul and the provinces, 2005–10.
126. Tsigannik, 142.
127. Lozhkin, 200.
128. Interview with Mohammed Faridi Hamidi, AIHRC, Kabul 4 November 2011.
129. Giustozzi and Noor Ullah; interview with Gulabzoi, Kabul, October 2007.
130. Interview with Gulabzoi, Kabul, October 2007.
131. Interview with MoI official, Kabul, 27 April 2010.
132. Hassin, 116ff; interview with Sayyed Mohammad Quddusi, Police Academy Kabul, October 2007; interview with police officer trained in the 1970s, May 2006, Kabul; interview with former police officers Ghulam Mohammad Kamall and Khawal Shinwari, London, January 2008.
133. On this revolutionary legality, see Hassin, 101ff.
134. Omarzai, 60ff.
135. Interview with senior police officer with experience in the 1980s, Kabul, November 2011.
136. Interview with former senior army officer, Kabul, spring 2010.
137. Interview with Gulabzoi, Kabul, April 2008.
138. Klyushnikov, 33–5.
139. Lozhkin, 213–4.
140. Giustozzi (2000), tables 27, 28 and 29; Chilton et al., 30, 63.
141. Interview with Ustad Zal, Police Academy, Kabul, April 2008; Interview with Sayyed Mohammad Quddusi, Police Academy Kabul, October 2007
142. Interview with high ranking MoI official, Kabul, May 2006.
143. Interview with Peter Schwittek, NGO manager Kabul, October 2007.
144. Interview with police officer, Kandahar, January 2006.
145. Interviews with police officers who worked at the Provincial Police Headquarters, Herat, July 2009.
146. Interview with police officer trained in the 1970s, May 2006, Kabul.
147. Interview with Peter Schwittek, Kabul October 2007.
148. Interview with Ustad Zal, Police Academy, Kabul, April 2008.
149. Interviews with police officers who worked under Taliban's rule, Herat, July 2009.
150. Hartmann and Klonowiecka-Milart, 269.
151. Rashid (2000), 105–6; Dorronsoro, 284–5.
152. Giustozzi et al., forthcoming.

3. AFGHANISTAN'S POLICE IN 2002

1. Nojumi, 28–9.
2. Nojumi, 26; interview with Jalali, ex minister of interior, Kabul, 26 April 2011.
3. Nojumi, 26–7.

pp [38–49] NOTES

4. Interview with Chief of Police of Baghlan, Pul-I Khumri, December 2003; Nojumi, 29.
5. Interviews with UN official, senior police officers, foreign diplomats and police advisors, 2003–10.
6. Ibid.
7. Meeting with provincial CoP, June 2009.
8. Interview with Jalali, Kabul, 26 April 2011.
9. Interview with former high ranking MoI official, Kabul, April 2008.
10. Interviews with UN officials, Kabul, Kunduz, Mazar-i Sharif, Kandahar and Herat, 2003–10.
11. Ibid.
12. Françoise Chipaux, 'For the case of Zabul see Dans le plus complet dénuement, la province afghane de Zabul mène la lutte contre les talibans', *Le Monde*, 24 December 2003.
13. Personal communication with UN official, Kabul, 2003.
14. Meeting with UN official, Kabul, April 2011; interview with MoI official, Kabul, April 2011.

4. THE CHANGING POST-2001 OPERATING ENVIRONMENT

1. Interview with high ranking MoI officer, November 2010.
2. Giustozzi (2012); see also Giustozzi (2008), 187.
3. Personal communication with UN official, Kabul, April 2010.
4. Interview with former Maruf CoP, Dand, March 2005.
5. Skinner, 300
6. Phil Zabriskie, 'Dangers Up Ahead: How druglords and insurgents are making the war in Afghanistan deadlier than ever', *Time*, 13 March 2006.
7. A police station in Balkh province, according to a UN official, Mazar-i Sharif, October 2008.
8. Ann Marlowe, 'Policing Afghanistan: Too few good men and too many bad ones make for a grueling, uphill struggle, *Weekly Standard*, 22 December 2008, Volume 014, Issue 14.
9. Marlowe, 'Policing Afghanistan', cit.

5. THE UNCERTAIN IMPACT OF EXTERNAL ASSISTANCE

1. Interview with MoI adviser, Kabul, April 2011.
2. Interview with Sayyed Mohammad Quddusi, Police Academy Kabul, 10 October 2007.
3. Interview with former senior MoI official, October 2009.
4. Perito, 3.
5. Interview with MoI adviser, Kabul, November 2010.
6. Flood (2009a).
7. Serchuk, 2–3; Perito, 5.

NOTES pp [50–53]

8. Serchuk, 2–3; Perito, 5; personal communication with DoS official, Kabul, April 2011.
9. For a survey of the FDD see Waltemate.
10. Marlowe, 'Policing Afghanistan', cit.
11. Thruelsen, 87.
12. Aryn Baker, 'Policing Afghanistan', *Time*, 21 October, 2008
13. Interview with MoI adviser, Kabul, 3 October 2009.
14. See Waltemate.
15. LIBRA briefing on police in Afghanistan, London, KCL, 8 July 2009.
16. Interview with MoI adviser, Kabul, October 2009.
17. Marlowe, 'Policing Afghanistan', cit.
18. LIBRA briefing on police in Afghanistan, London, KCL, 8 July 2009.
19. NTM-A (2010a); meeting with group of NTM-A officers, 11 November 2010.
20. Cordesman (2010), 24; interview with NTM-A deputy, Kabul, October 2010.
21. Interview with MoI official, Kabul, 27 April 2010.
22. Saltmarshe and Medhi, 22–3.
23. Inspectors General, 20–1.
24. Rod Nordland, 'With Raw Recruits, Afghan Police Buildup Falters', *The New York Times*, 3 February 2010.
25. Meeting with Gen Comitini, NTM-A Kabul, 23 April 2011.
26. Interview with MoI official, Kabul, 27 April 2010.
27. '70 percent of Afghan police recruits drop out: US trainer', *AFP*, 2 March 2010.
28. NTM-A brief, 13 March 2011.
29. Interview with MoI adviser, Kabul, November 2010.
30. Secret cable by Ambassador Eikenberry, 25 Feb 2010 (INTERIOR MINISTER ATMAR DISCUSSES POLICE TRAINING, E.O. 12958).
31. 'Afghanistan, Turkey sign bilateral agreement', NATO Training Mission–Afghanistan, 13 March 2011; Meeting with MoI adviser, Kabul, 2 April 2011.
32. 'Spanish Civil Guard to train Afghan border policemen in Spain', text of report by Spanish newspaper, ABC website, 14 June 2011.
33. James Dao, 'In Mission With Afghan Police', *The New York Times*, 11 August 2010.
34. RUSI, 11.
35. Graeme Smith, 'Fired Kandahar police chief says Canadians let him down', *Globe and Mail*, 3 July 2008.
36. Interviews with senior police officers, Kabul, spring 2011.
37. Thruelsen, 86.
38. SIGAR (2010a), 5–6.
39. SIGAR (2010a), 13.
40. West, 227.
41. SIGAR (2010a), 7.
42. NTM-A (2010a); interview with foreign embassy official, November 2010.
43. Chilton et al., 40.
44. Interview with MoI official, Kabul, April 2010.

193

6. INTERNAL ORGANISATION AND REORGANISATION

1. Interview with deputy Chief of Police of Takhar, Teluqan, February 2004.
2. Ibid.
3. Dion Nissenbaum, 'U.S. forces pin hopes on new Afghan civil police', *McClatchy Newspapers*, 24 March 2010.
4. Interview with former MoI official, October 2009; interview with police officer in Teluqan, February 2004.
5. RUSI, 130.
6. Interview with foreign embassy official, Kabul November 2010; meeting with IPCB official, Kabul, 6 November 2010.
7. Meeting with MoI adviser, Kabul, April 2011.
8. Meeting with EUPOL, Kabul, October 2009.
9. Interview with UN official, Kabul, November 2010.
10. Meeting with MoI adviser, Kabul, April 2011.
11. NTM-A briefing, 13 March 2011.
12. Interview with MoI adviser, Kabul, November 2010; interview with MoI official, Kabul, April 2011.
13. Interview with foreign embassy official, November 2010.
14. Interview with MoI adviser, Kabul, November 2010.
15. Interview with MoI adviser, May 2007.
16. Cordesman (2010), 114. The perceived success of the ANCOP model was one of the sources of the inspiration for the change: GAO, 47; interview with Gen. Beare, NTM-A, 10 Nov 2010; 'Afghan Interior Ministry sets up police recruitment command', *Tolo TV*, 01/04/2010.
17. Rahmatullah Afghan, 'Recruitment body gets more powers', *Pajhwok Afghan News*, March 31, 2010.
18. Interview with Gen. Burgio, NTM-A, Kabul, 26 October 2010.
19. Interview with Canadian TF Kandahar officer, April 2010.
20. See the personal experience of a mentor Haskell, 13–4.
21. Beattie, 196.
22. Interview with Khalil Andarabi, CoP Faryab, March 2009.
23. Interview with MoI adviser, Kabul, 3 October 2009.
24. Interview with foreign embassy official, Kabul, November 2010.
25. Graeme Smith, 'Kandahar police shoot it out with new foe—themselves', *The Globe and Mail*, February 6, 2008.
26. Interview with former senior MoI official, October 2009.
27. Ahmad Umeed Khpalwak, 'Barakzai tribesmen demand removal of police chief', *Pajhwok Afghan News*, 15 June 2010.
28. Graeme Smith, 'Turmoil in the police ranks', *The Globe and Mail*, 19 April 2006.
29. Interview with Canadian TF Kandahar officer, 12 April 2010.
30. Interview with MoI officer, Herat, Kabul 15 April 2008.
31. Interview with former high ranking MoI officer, Kabul, April 2008.
32. Interview with MoI officer, Herat, Kabul 15 April 2008.
33. Wilder, 36.

NOTES pp [61–66]

34. For an example from Kandahar see Graeme Wood, 'Letter from Pashmul', *The New Yorker*, 8 December 2008.
35. Interview with international organisation analyst, Kabul, October 2010.
36. Personal communication with Martine van Bijlert, Afghanistan Analysts Network, March 2011.
37. Ferguson, 154.
38. Lefèvre.
39. Ibid.
40. Ibid.
41. 'US seeking larger Afghan village police force: report', *AFP*, October 19, 2010.
42. Human Rights Watch.
43. On the case of Shir Alam from Paghman to Ghazni see Andrew Maykuth, 'Taliban rampage in Ghazni', *The Philadelphia Enquirer*, 10 September 2006.
44. Interview with former MoI official, Kabul, April 2008.
45. Mamozai had joined Jamiat in the 1990s, after having been in Hizb-I Islami. Interview with police officer, Teluqan, May 2006.
46. 'Police told to remove Jihadi photos from vehicles', www.ququnoos.com, 3 April 2008; Wali Arian, 'Police Must Remain Neutral in the Polls: MoI', www.ququnoos.com, 29 June 2009; Amnesty International.
47. Interview with Haidar Bassir, former deputy minister, Kabul, October 2010.
48. Interview with senior police officer, Kabul, November 2010.
49. James Palmer, 'Weak Afghan police threaten NATO plan', *The Washington Times*, 28 August 2008.
50. Rosen.
51. Rayment, 92; Bishop (2007), 211; Marlowe, 'Policing Afghanistan', cit.
52. Interview with counter-narcotics official, Kabul, April 2008.
53. Marlowe, 'Policing Afghanistan', cit.
54. 'Police told to remove Jihadi photos from vehicles', www.ququnoos.com, 3 April 2008; Wali Arian, 'Police Must Remain Neutral in the Polls: MoI', www.ququnoos.com, 29 June 2009; Amnesty International.
55. Rosen.
56. Bishop (2007), 211.
57. Interview with foreign diplomat, 8 November 2011.
58. International Crisis Croup (2008), 2–3.
59. Interview with EUPOL adviser, Kabul, October 2010.
60. NTM-A briefing, 17 February 2011.
61. Meeting NTM-A officer, November 2010.
62. 'Afghan prohibition of under-age police recruitment wins UN applause', *UN News Center*, 10 May 2010; 'Police corruption remains a drag on Afghan mission for Canadian troops', *The Canadian Press*, 14 November 2007; Lal Aqa Sherin, 'Teenagers Enlist in Army, Police', *IPS*, 2 November 2009; 'Afghan ministry warns police against underage recruitment', *Tolo TV*, 21 January 2011, 1330 GMT.
63. Matthew Rosenberg, 'Afghan Army Recruits Face Tougher Screening', *Wall Street Journal*, 9 February 2011.
64. Meeting with NTM-A officer, November 2010.

65. Najib Khelwatgar, 'Afghan enforcement officers struggle with poverty, few weapons, little ammo', *Canada Press*, 18 April 2006.
66. Marlowe, 'Policing Afghanistan', cit.
67. Interview with Gen. Burgio NTM-A, Kabul, 26 October 2010.
68. West, 163.
69. Saltmarshe and Medhi, 22–3.
70. Habibul Rehman Ibrahimi, 'Police extortion fears', *Afghan Recovery Report*, No. 32, 18 October 2002; Owais Tohid, 'Cops go crooked in Kabul as pay and training lag', *Christian Science Monitor*, 3 July 2003.
71. C. J. Chivers, 'Afghan Police Struggle to Work a Rough Beat', *The New York Times*, 13 January 2008; Marlowe, 'Policing Afghanistan', cit.
72. 'Afghan police salaries paid by Canadian military', *CBC News*, 9 October 2007.
73. Bill Graveland, 'Bank cards helping Afghan police slowly shed corruption tag', *The Canadian Press*, 19 November 2008.
74. Jason Motlagh, 'Afghan police fight to survive', *Asia Times*, 28 August 2007
75. Interview of CoP of Maimana city, November 2004.
76. 'Ministry tackling drug addiction in Afghan police', *National Afghanistan TV*, 5 September 2010.
77. 'People in Afghan north voice concern over drug addiction among police', *Afghan Ariana TV*, 17 February 2011, Dari 1530 gmt 17 February 2011.
78. Elisabeth Bumiller, 'U.S. General Cites Goals to Train Afghan Forces', *New York Times*, 23 August 2010.
79. 'Need for policing charas use by cops', *Pajhwok Afghan News*, 24 March 2006; Kim Barker, 'Drug abuse an increasing problem among Afghan police, soldiers', *Chicago Tribune*, 5 October 2008; Martin Patience, 'Drug abuse hampers Afghan police', *BBC News*, 18 February 2009; Per Anders Johansen and Tor Arne Andreassen, 'Police face huge training challenges in Afghanistan', *Aftenposten*, 29 September 2008; SIGAR (2010a). 20; Marlowe, 'Policing Afghanistan', cit.
80. Dion Nissenbaum, 'Corruption, incompetence charges plague new Afghan police force', *McClatchy Newspapers*, 10 May 2010
81. SIGAR (2010a), 20.
82. Rosen.
83. GAO (2009), 25.
84. Meeting with MoI adviser, Kabul, April 2011; meeting with official on international organisation, Kabul, April 2011.
85. GAO (2009), 25; interview with Haidar Bassir, former deputy minister, Kabul, 31 October 2010.
86. Meeting with Gendarmerie officer, NTM-A, 11 November 2010.
87. David Leask, 'In some areas of Helmand, the police are your worst enemy', *The Herald*, 10 January 2007.
88. Interview with MoI adviser, Kabul, November 2010; interview with Abdul Qayuum Baqizai, Khost CoP, October 2008.
89. See for example, Scott Peterson, 'Uphill battle to bolster Afghan police', *The Christian Science Monitor*, 20 September 2007; Beattie, 82.
90. Allen, 209.

NOTES pp [68–72]

91. Beattie, 103.
92. Interview with Canadian TF Kandahar officer, April 2010.
93. Meeting with MoI officer, June 2009.
94. Interview with Abdul Qayuum Baqizai, Khost CoP, October 2008.
95. Meeting with MoI officer, June 2009.
96. James Dao, 'In Mission With Afghan Police, Issues of Trust', *The New York Times*, 11 August 2010.
97. Burdett; Cordesman (2010), 131–2.
98. Interview with analyst of international organisation, Kabul, October 2010.
99. Interview with AIHRC official, Kabul November 2010.
100. Nojumi, 22, 15. See also Saltmarshe and Medhi, 22–3.
101. Meeting with IPCB official, Kabul, November 2010.
102. Interview with foreign embassy official, November 2010.
103. Interview with Chief of Police of Baghlan, Pul-I Khumri, December 2003.
104. Interview with Zabet Tufan, former MoI officer, Mazar-i Sharif, 16 October 2007.
105. Interview with AIHRC official, Kabul, November 2010.
106. Meeting with EUPOL, Kabul, October 2009.
107. Ibid.
108. Interview with analyst of international organisation, Kabul, October 2010.
109. EUPOL.
110. Meeting with EUPOL, Kabul October 2009.
111. Interview with Gen. Burgio. NTM-A, Kabul, 26 October 2010.
112. Amnesty International, 28.
113. Personal observation, police stations in various provinces, 2003–5.
114. Paul Watson, 'Afghan Gangs on Rise', *Los Angeles Times*, 21 May 2005.
115. Interview with former senior MoI official, Kabul, October 2010.
116. Interview with foreign adviser, Kabul, October 2009.
117. Interviews with police general in Kabul and police officer in Sarobi, January 2011.
118. Interview with former MoI official, Kabul, October 2010.
119. Interview with police general, Kabul, November 2010.
120. Interview with police general, Kabul, April 2008.
121. Interview with police officer, November 2010.
122. Interview with Haidar Bassir, former deputy minister MoI, Kabul, October 2010.
123. Interview with foreign embassy official, November 2010.
124. Meeting with EUPOL, Kabul, October 2009.
125. Nojumi, 24.
126. Interview with former senior MoI official, Kabul, October 2010.
127. Interview with high ranking MoI officer, November 2010.
128. Interview with Mohammed Faridi Hamidi, AIHRC, Kabul, November 2010.
129. Interview with MoI adviser, Kabul, November 2010.
130. Interviews with EUPOL officer, October 2010.
131. Meetings with police officers in Herat, 2010

132. Interview with MoI adviser, Kabul, September 2009.
133. Meeting with NTM-A officer, November 2010.
134. Ibid.
135. Jerome Starkey, 'Allied exit strategy at risk as Afghan police run out of recruits', *The Times*, 23 October 2009.
136. Meeting with UN official, Kabul, Apr 2011.
137. LIBRA briefing on police in Afghanistan KCL 8 July 2009.
138. Cordesman (2010), 33–4, 42; Slobodan Lekic, 'NATO: Afghan attrition remains stubbornly high', *AP*, 23 February 2011.
139. Cordesman (2010), 33–4, 42.
140. Cordesman (2010), 33–4; MoD briefing, London, 11 January 2011.
141. LIBRA briefing on police in Afghanistan KCL 8 July 2009.
142. Ibid.
143. See also Skinner, 294.
144. 'Only 132 of 819 "critical" trainers are actually present for duty': Kim Sengupta, 'Afghan police corruption 'hits Nato pullout', *The Independent*, 21 November 2010
145. 'Afghan National Police adds literacy training', Combined Forces Command—Afghanistan Coalition Press Information Center, http://www.cfc-a.centcom.mil, March 3, 2006; Interview with Gen. Burgio NTM-A, Kabul, 26 October 2010.
146. Katharine Houreld, 'Afghan police learn to shoot, patrol—and read', *Associated Press*, 22 November 2010.
147. NTM-A brief, December 2010.
148. Email communication with CPT-A. Heather Coyne NATO Training Mission-Afghanistan/CSTC-A Camp Eggers.
149. Wilder, 4.
150. Interview with Gen. M. Wakeel Akbari, MoI chief of personnel, Kabul, April 2011.
151. Skinner, 297; Luis Martinez, 'Attrition, Illiteracy Big Challenges in Afghan Security Growth', *ABCNews.com*, 23 August 2010.
152. 'Afghan minister says 90 per cent of police recruits illiterate', Aina TV, 5 March 2011, in Dari, 1430 GMT.
153. SIGAR (2011), 61.
154. Katharine Houreld, 'Afghan police learn to shoot, patrol—and read', *Associated Press*, 22 November 2010.
155. Matthew Green, 'Afghan drive to stop poaching of police recruits', *Financial Times*, 25 January 2010.
156. Marlowe, 'Policing Afghanistan', cit.
157. Carol J. Williams, 'Standing Up for Order in Kabul Takes Nerve and a Tough Hide', *Los Angeles Times*, 21 May 2002; Murray (2007), 116–7; personal observation, Kabul, 2007–10.
158. SIGAR (2010b).
159. NTM-A (2010a).
160. 'Residents in Afghan Kandahar criticize lauding of police', Afghan Ariana TV, 16 February 2011, in dari 1530 gmt.

161. 'Afghan officials contradict NATO on attack', *UPI*, 1 July 2011.
162. Interview with MoI adviser, Kabul, October 2009.
163. Rosen.
164. 'Afghan army, police need motivation to protect country—minister', Tolo TV, 9 March 2011, in Dari 1330 gmt.
165. See for example, police chief Khodaidad in Bala Buluk (Farah): Bilal Sarwary, 'Bribery rules on Afghan roads', *BBC News*, 29 July 2008.
166. Matthieu Aikins, 'The master of Spin Boldak: Undercover with Afghanistan's drug-trafficking border police', *Harper's Magazine*, December 2009.
167. Interview with former senior MoI official, Kabul, October 2010.
168. Interview with MoI official, Kabul, April 2010.
169. SIGAR (2010a), 19–20.
170. 'Kidnappers' gang busted in Samangan', *Pajhwok Afghan News*, 29 July 2008.
171. 'Crime by Afghan police rises "ten-fold" since 2002', *Kabul Weekly*, 1 July 2009.
172. Pratap Chatterjee, 'Policing Afghanistan: Obama's New Strategy', *CorpWatch*, 23 March 2009.
173. See for example Richard A. Oppel Jr., 'Corruption Undercuts Hopes for Afghan Police', *The New York Times*, 8 April 2009.
174. 'Drivers face police bribes on new road', www.ququoos.com, 19 June 2008, on the kabul-Jalalabad highway; Soraya Sarhaddi Nelson, 'Despite New Highways, Afghans Drive at Own Risk', *NPR—World News*, 16 March 2008; 'No end to police corruption on Herat-Kandahar highway', *Pajhwok News Agency*, 9 January 2008.
175. Interview with police officer in Herat, 2010.
176. Personal communication with consultant working for the British government, London, January 2011.
177. UNDP (2010d).
178. Integrity Watch Afghanistan.
179. UNODC (2010), 22ff.
180. 'Afghan official says local police chiefs will be punished for failing in duty', Tolo TV, 13 February 2011, in Dari 1330 gmt.
181. Personal communication with UN officials and government officials in Kandahar, 2005.
182. 'Policemen Arrested For Sexual Assault In Western Afghanistan', *Pajhwok Afghan News*, 20 July 2005.
183. 'Police replaces highway personnel on Mahipar route', *Pajhwok Afghan News*, 29 August 2006.
184. 'Policemen detained for involvement in robberies', *Pajhwok Afghan News*, 5 January 2007.
185. *Cheragh*, 18 January 2007.
186. M Reza Sher Mohammadi, 'Police suspend 35 'kidnap' officers', www.ququoos.com, 28 June 2008.
187. Jon Hemming, 'Afghan police chiefs sacked for negligence', *Reuters*, 28 July 2007.
188. *Cheragh*, 1 August 2007.
189. '10 police officers detained on embezzlement charges', *Pajhwok Afghan News*, 26 November 2007.

190. '10 policemen disarmed, arrested in Kandahar', *Pajhwok Afghan News*, 18 November 2007.
191. 'Policemen detained for involvement in robberies', *Pajhwok Afghan News*, 5 January 2007.
192. *Arman-e Milli*, 28 June 2007.
193. Brian Hutchinson, 'Three Afghan police sentenced for raping father and son', *Canwest News Service*, 23 February 2008.
194. Soraya Sarhaddi Nelson, 'Despite New Highways, Afghans Drive at Own Risk', *NPR—World News*, 16 March 2008.
195. M Reza Sher Mohammadi, 'Police suspend 35 "kidnap" officers', www.quqnoos.com, 28 June 2008.
196. 'No end to police corruption on Herat-Kandahar highway', *Pajhwok Afghan News*, 7 January 2008.
197. 'Herat police arrest four more of their own', www.*Quqnoos.com*, 29 November 2008.
198. 'Policemen jailed for selling police car', www.quqnoos.com, 23 November 2008.
199. '50 Policemen Fired in Herat, Western Afghanistan', *TOLOnews*, 30 July 2010.
200. 'Drivers using western Afghan road complain about extortion by police', *Tolo TV*, 21 January 2011.
201. 'Afghan border police chief on trial over drug smuggling', *AFP*, 2 August 2010.
202. Interview with Gen. Nuristani, MoI head of personnel, Kabul, October 2007.
203. Ibid.
204. 'Police chief in Afghan west detained, accused of drug trafficking'. Text of report by Afghan independent Tolo TV on 23 June 2010.
205. 'Senior Afghan Interior Ministry official detained on charges of abusing office', *Tolo TV*, 28 July 2010.
206. 'Police chief in Afghan west detained, accused of drug trafficking', *Tolo TV*, 23 June 2010.
207. Ibid.
208. 'Another police officer arrested for drug trafficking in Afghan Nimroz Province', *Afghan Islamic Press News Agency*, Peshawar, in Pashto 1255 gmt 12 March 2011.
209. 'Afghan police extort money from drivers on southwest highway', Kandahar TV, 3 February 2011, in Pashto, 1615 GMT.
210. Docherty, 121.
211. Docherty, 134.
212. Tootal, 35.
213. Bishop (2009), 50.
214. Bishop (2009), 105.
215. Scott, 175.
216. Bishop (2007), 108.
217. 'People in Afghan northern village complain about police mistreatment', Noor TV, 13 June 2011, in Dari, 1300 GMT.
218. Interview with foreign embassy official, November 2010.
219. Matthieu Aikins, cit., 57–8.
220. Paul Watson, 'Afghan Gangs on Rise', Los Angeles Times, 21 May 2005.

NOTES pp [83–90]

221. International Crisis Group (2008), 6.
222. Interview with police officer, Teluqan, May 2006.
223. West, 186–7.
224. Interview with district CoP in Herat, April 2008.
225. Wilder, 13.
226. LIBRA briefing on police in Afghanistan, London, KCL, 8 July 2009.
227. 'Drivers face police bribes on new road', www.quqnoos.com, 19 June 2008, on the Kabul–Jalalabad highway; Soraya Sarhaddi Nelson, 'Despite New Highways, Afghans Drive at Own Risk', NPR—World News, March 16, 2008; 'No end to police corruption on Herat–Kandahar highway', Pajhwok Afghan News, 7 January 2008.
228. Interviews with police officers, Herat, November 2010.
229. Interviews with truck drivers, Herat, November 2010.
230. Ibid.
231. Ibid.
232. Ibid.
233. Interviews with truck drivers and merchants, Kabul, March 2011.
234. Interviews with police officers and truck drivers, Kabul and Mazar-e-Sharif, March 2011.
235. Interviews with a police officer, Herat, March 2011.
236. Interviews with truck drivers and merchants, Herat, March 2011.
237. Interviews with truck drivers, Herat and Kabul, November 2010 and March 2011.
238. Interviews with truck drivers, Herat, November 2010.
239. Interviews with truck drivers, Herat, March 2011.
240. Interviews with truck drivers, Herat, November 2010.
241. Shaw, 6, 18, 92, 199, 207.
242. Tom Coghlan, 'Profits are vast but only the big fish survive', *Daily Telegraph*, 8 February 2007.
243. Scott Baldauf, 'Afghan police heavily involved in drug trade', *The Christian Science Monitor*, 12 June 2006; Aryn Baker, 'Policing Afghanistan', Time, 21 October 2008.
244. Meeting with UN official, Kabul, April 2011.
245. Interview with foreign embassy official, November 2010.
246. West, 186.
247. Rachel Morarjee, 'An Afghan province where heroin rules and police look the other way', *Financial Times*, 13 April 2006; Miles Amoore, 'Chief: drug smuggling cops can't be removed', www.quqnoos.com, 24 March 2008.
248. Balkh TV, Mazar-e Sharif, 4 July 2004, in Dari, 1825 GMT.
249. Anuj Chopra, 'Afghanistan's embryonic police', ISN Security Watch, 30 July 2007.
250. Daphne Benoit, 'Colonel Razziq: 'Godfather' of the Afghan border', AFP, 13 October 2009; Rajiv Chandrasekaran, 'Afghan colonel vital to U.S. despite graft allegations', Washington Post, October 3, 2010; Matthieu Aikins, cit., 60

251. Graeme Smith, 'Afghan officials in drug trade cut deals across enemy lines', Globe and Mail, 21 March 2009.
252. Interview with former high ranking MoI official, October 2006.
253. Personal communication with UN officials, Kunduz, 2003–4.
254. Paul Watson, 'The Lure of Opium Wealth Is a Potent Force', *Los Angeles Times*, 28 May 2005.
255. Interview with police officer, Teluqan, May 2006.
256. Rahim Faiez, '100 Afghan drug police killed last year', *Associated Press*, 24 March 2008.
257. GAO (2010).
258. Telephone interview with Nick Lockwood, former British adviser, 28 February 2011.
259. Meeting with UN official, Kabul, April 2011.
260. Personal communication with American officers, Kabul, September 2011.
261. Interview with MoI official, Kabul, April 2011.
262. Interview with police officer, Teluqan, May 2006; interview with police officer, Kandahar, January 2006; interview with former provincial governor, March 2009; interview with former Chief of Police of Afghan town, August 2004; interview with police officer, Teluqan, February 2004; interview with CoP of Afghan province, December 2004; interview with CoP of Afghan district, December 2004.
263. Interviewed in Kandahar, 2005.
264. Interview with CoP of Herat, December 2004.
265. Interview with Gen. Ehwaz, Chief of Police Training Centre, Kunduz, March 2004; interview with former senior MoI official, October 2009.
266. Meeting with UN official, April 2008.
267. UNDP (2008, 2009, 2010a, 2010b, 2010c).
268. Interview with MoI adviser, May 2007.
269. Interview with foreign embassy official, November 2011.
270. Meeting with International Police Coordinating Body official, Kabul, November 2010; meeting with NTM-A officer, Kabul, November 2010; interview with Police General, Kabul, November 2010.
271. Interview with foreign embassy official, November 2011.
272. Interview with former MoI official, Kabul, October 2009.
273. Interview with Haidar Bassir, former deputy minister, Kabul, October 2010.
274. Interview with MoI official, Kabul, April 2011.
275. Ibid.
276. Cordesman (2010), 120.
277. Skinner, 296.
278. Interview with foreign embassy official, November 2010.
279. Meeting with UN official, Kabul, April 2011.
280. Interview with MoI official, Kabul, April 2010.
281. International Crisis Group (2008), 13.
282. Meeting with EUPOL official, Kabul, April 2011.
283. Meeting with NTM-A officer, November 2010; interview with Haidar Bassir,

former deputy minister, Kabul, 31 October 2010; meeting with EUPOL official, Kabul, April 2011.
284. Meeting with NTM-A officer, November 2010.
285. Interview with high ranking MoI officer, Kabul, November 2011.
286. NTM-A (2010a).
287. Interview with foreign embassy official, November 2010; meeting with MoI adviser, April 2011; meeting with EUPOL official, Kabul, April 2011.
288. Meeting with EUPOL official, Kabul, April 2011.
289. Ibid.
290. UNAMA northern region Daily Report, 62, 1 June 2003.
291. For a case in Farah see Aryn Baker, 'Policing Afghanistan', *Time*, 21 October 2008; see also Nojumi, 25.
292. Nojumi, 25.
293. Alston, 29.
294. 'Karzai reshuffles police commanders after Afghan protest', *Agence France Presse*, 16 March 2005.
295. Graeme Smith, 'Officer arrested, probe launched after rampage against civilians', Globe and Mail, 24 January 2007.
296. 'Police hand in glove with smugglers in looting minerals', *Pajhwok Afghan News*, 21 December 2007.
297. Mohammad Reza, 'Afghan city on strike over crime', *AFP*, 11 March 2008.
298. Interview with foreign adviser, Kabul, November 2010.
299. Meeting with EUPOL official, Kabul, April 2011.
300. Personal communication with foreign diplomat, Kabul, April 2009.
301. Interview with former MoI official, Kabul, 26 October 2010.
302. Ministry of Interior, (2010/11); meeting with NTM-A officer, November 2010; meeting with EUPOL official, Kabul, April 2011.

7. RECRUITMENT AND RETENTION

1. Interview with Haidar Bassir, former deputy minister, Kabul, 31 October 2010.
2. Thruelsen.
3. Interview with police officer, Teluqan, February 2004.
4. Interview with Gen. Ehwaz, head of police training centre, Kunduz, March 2004.
5. Interview with government official in Herat, December 2004.
6. UNAMA source, June 2004.
7. Interview with MoI official, Kabul, October 2007.
8. Interview with former high ranking MoI official, Kabul, April 2008. On Mojaddidi, see Giustozzi and Orsini.
9. Interview with former minister Ali Jalali, Kabul, April 2011.
10. Interview with police officer trained in the 1970s, 28 May 2006.
11. Interview with Gen. Nuristani, MoI head of personnel, Kabul, October 2007.
12. Interview with former deputy minister Abdul Hadi Khalid, Kabul, October 2010.
13. Personal communications with police officers around Afghanistan, 2003–10; Interview with Gen. Nuristani, MoI head of personnel, Kabul, October 2007.

14. 'Former Afghan jihadi figures sit exam to join army, police', *Herat TV*, 22 June 2011, in Dari 1630 GMT.
15. Interview with Gen. Nuristani, MoI head of personnel, Kabul, October 2007.
16. Interview with foreign embassy official, Kabul, November 2010.
17. Interview with CoP, Kabul, November 2010.
18. Interview with Abdul Qayuum Baqizai, Khost CoP, October 2008.
19. Interview with NTM-A officer, Kabul, October 2010.
20. 'Officials say 72 per cent of police in Afghan north illiterate', *Ariana TV*, 7 January 2011.
21. Personal communication with ISAF official, October 2011.
22. Marlowe, 'Policing Afghanistan', cit.
23. Interview with Gen. Ehwaz, head of police training centre, Kunduz, March 2004.
24. Personal communication with UN official, Kabul, 2008.
25. Meeting with MoI foreign adviser, Kabul, April 2011.
26. 'Northern Afghan police chief escapes suicide bomb attack', *Pajhwok news agency*, 10 June 2011.
27. Interview with former collaborator of Atta Mohammed, 22 October 2008; interview with Afghan journalist, October 2008; interview with UN officials, Mazar-i Sharif, October 2008; Ahmad Kawosh, 'Crime Wave Alarms Balkh Residents', *Pajhwok Afghan News*, 3 June 2010.
28. Interview with former minister Ali Jalali, Kabul, April 2011.
29. Interview with Mohammed Faridi Hamidi, AIHRC, Kabul, November 2010.
30. ISAF source, Kabul, September 2011.
31. Wilder, 40.
32. Interview with former deputy minister, Kabul, April 2008.
33. Interview with former deputy minister, Kabul, October 2009.
34. Wilder, 39–42.
35. Wilder, 40; Rachel Morarjee, 'Diplomats claim Afghan appointments mark setback', *Financial Times*, 12 June 2006.
36. Tom Blackwell, 'Kandahar's police chief in denial: residents', *National Post*, 23 October 2008.
37. 'Police to begin night patrol in Kabul', *Pajhwok Afghan News*, 12 June 2006; interview with Afghan community leader, Kabul, 2006.
38. 'Afghanistan Reshuffles Police Command, Sacks 4 Senior Officers', *AFP*, 4 February 2009; Nadene Ghouri, 'Afghanistan: Law and Order Policing Kabul James Bond style', *PBS Online—Frontline*, 15 April 2009.
39. Thruelsen, 84; interview with ICG analyst, Kabul, 25 October 2010.
40. NTM-A (2010b); meeting with foreign adviser to MoI, Kabul, April 2011.
41. Meeting with foreign adviser to MoI, Kabul, April 2011.
42. Interview with former high ranking MoI official, Kabul, October 2009.
43. Personal communication with official of international organisation, Kabul, April 2011.
44. 'Afghan minister says 90 per cent of police recruits illiterate', Aina TV, Kabul, 5 March 2011, in Dari, 1430 GMT.
45. Meeting with senior MoI official, MoI Kabul, April 2011.

NOTES

46. Joseph.
47. Interview with former high ranking MoI official, Kabul, October 2006.
48. Meeting with MoI officers, Kabul, November 2010.
49. Personal communication with official of international organisation, Kabul, November 2010.
50. NTM-A (2011).
51. Interview with former high ranking MoI official, October 2006.
52. Meeting with UN official, Kabul, April 2011.
53. Personal communication with American officers, Kabul, September 2011.
54. Personal communications with former HDK members, 2003–10.
55. Personal communication with official of international organisation, Kabul, April 2011.
56. Interview with former deputy minister Hilaluddin Hilal, Kabul, 8 October 2006.
57. Meeting with foreign adviser to the MoI, September 2009.
58. Meeting with senior MoI official, MoI Kabul, April 2011.
59. Meeting with foreign adviser to MoI, Kabul, April 2011; meeting with UN official, Kabul, April 2011.
60. Interview with Gen. Nuristani, MoI head of personnel, Kabul, October 2007.
61. Interview with former high ranking official, Kabul, October 2006.
62. Interview with high ranking official of MoI, Kabul, April 2008.
63. Interview with high ranking officials, Kabul, April 2008.
64. Interview with high ranking official of MoI, Kabul, October 2009.
65. Ibid.
66. Ibid.
67. Meeting with former senior MoI official, Kabul, April 2011.
68. Interview with former high ranking official of MoI, Kabul, April 2011.
69. Interview with former high ranking officials of MoI, Kabul, October 2009 and October 2010.
70. Interview with former minister Ali Jalali, Kabul, April 2011.

8. THE ULTIMATE TEST OF FUNCTIONALITY: THE PARAMILITARY DIMENSION

1. Amnesty International (2003), 8.
2. UNAMA Daily Report, 20 May 2003.
3. For a case in then relatively quiet Chahardarah, see Candace Rondeaux, 'A Ragtag Pursuit of the Taliban', *Washington Post*, 6 August 2008.
4. Amnesty International, 28.
5. NTM-A (2010a).
6. Interview with foreign embassy official, Kabul, November 2010.
7. Saltmarshe and Medhi, 22–3.
8. 'Police commander in Afghan east says circles within government impeding police', Ariana TV, 16 February 2011, in Dari, 1530 GMT.
9. Meeting with NTM-A officer, Kabul, November 2010.
10. LIBRA briefing on police in Afghanistan, London, KCL, 8 July 2009.
11. Interview with police officer trained in the 1970s, Kabul, 28 May 2006.

12. GAO (2009), 25.
13. Interview with foreign embassy official, Kabul, November 2010.
14. 'U.S-funded National Police Command Center opens Dec. 16', Combined Forces Command—Afghanistan, 17 December 2006.
15. Interview with Haidar Bassir, former deputy minister, Kabul, October 2010.
16. Interview with MoI officer, Kabul, November 2010.
17. Alston.
18. Interview with foreign adviser in Kabul, November 2010.
19. NTM-A, Programs Weekly Assessment (as of 4 February 2011).
20. NTM-A briefing, 12 February 2011.
21. Meeting with foreign MoI adviser, Kabul, April 2011.
22. Meeting with international organisation official, Kabul, April 2011.
23. Meeting with NTM-A officers, 11 November 2010.
24. 'Afghan police complete command, control exercise', NATO News Release, 30 November 2010.
25. Interview with foreign embassy official, Kabul, November 2010.
26. Meeting with NTM-A officer, November 2010.
27. Meeting with APPRO researcher, Kabul, 29 October 2010.
28. LIBRA briefing on police in Afghanistan, London, KCL, 8 July 2009.
29. Mohammad Ilyas Dayee and Zainullah Stanekzai, 'Helmand: derided police turn over new leaf', *Afghan Recovery Report*, No. 286, 26 March 2008. Not everybody agrees with this characterisation of Andiwal.
30. See 'Musa Qala residents want no police in the district', *Pajhwok Afghan News*, 16 December 2007; also interview with former senior police officers in Kabul, November 2010 and April 2011; personal communication with British official formerly serving in the Lashkargah PRT, November 2010.
31. LIBRA, cit.
32. Meeting with Gen. Azizi, CoP Paktia, London, June 2009.
33. Interview with foreign embassy official, Kabul, November 2010.
34. Interview with police officer, Kandahar, January 2006.
35. Interview with foreign embassy official, Kabul, November 2010.
36. Ibid.
37. 'Suicide bomber kills Afghan police chief, 2 others', *The Associated Press*, 11 March 2011
38. Personal communications with diplomats and ISAF officials, November 2010.
39. Meeting with UN official, Kabul, April 2011.
40. Interview with provincial police officers, Herat, August 2009.
41. Interview with provincial police officers, Herat, Nov–Dec 2010.
42. Ibid.
43. 'Afghan ministry to probe footage showing police handing over weapons to Taleban', *Afghan Aina TV*, 26 September 2009.
44. Carlotta Gall and Waheed Wafa, 'Plot to kill Afghan leader was inside job', *New York Times*, 1 May 2008.
45. Joanna Wright, 'Changing the guard—Efforts continue to resurrect Afghan police force', *Jane's Intelligence Review*, 16 October 2008.

46. ISAF sources, July 2011.
47. Meeting with foreign MoI adviser, Kabul, April 2011.
48. Flood (2009b).
49. LIBRA, cit.
50. 'Police let Taleban take us away: freed Afghan', *AFP*, 10 December 2007.
51. Eric Schmitt, 'Afghan Officials Aided an Attack on U.S. Soldiers', *New York Times*, 3 November 2008.
52. Aryn Baker, 'Policing Afghanistan', *Time*, 21 October 2008.
53. Interview with UN official, Kabul, October 2010.
54. West, 124.
55. Interview with Canadian TF Kandahar officer, April 2010.
56. Kiley, 228.
57. Interview with foreign embassy official, November 2010.
58. Saltmarshe and Medhi, 22.
59. Interview with high ranking MoI official, Kabul, November 2010.
60. Ibid.
61. Interview with Gen. Nuristani, MoI head of personnel, Kabul, October 2007.
62. Interview with police officer, Kandahar, January 2006.
63. Interview with high ranking MoI official, November 2011.
64. Tootal, 106; Bishop (2007), 187; Rayment, 76, 92.
65. British officer cited in Ferguson, 68.
66. Scott, 175.
67. Harnden, 102.
68. Bishop (2007), 238.
69. Bishop (2009), 50; Bishop (2007), 149.
70. Harnden, 486.
71. West, 186.
72. Interview with former government official, Kabul, March 2009.
73. *Tolo TV*, 12 December 2010.
74. Jason Motlagh, 'New Afghan police terrorized by Taliban', *Washington Times*, 10 August 2007.
75. 'Forty Afghan police flee checkpoints with weapons after not paid in full', *Pajhwok News Agency*, 30 March 2006.
76. Tootal, 205; Rayment, 95.
77. '12 Afghan police involved in robbery surrender to Taliban', *Xinhua*, 3 August 2006.
78. Carlotta Gall, 'Troops in Afghan District Find Anger at Lax Government', *New York Times*, 18 September 2006.
79. '5 cops killed in internecine clash; 4 kidnapped', *Pajhwok Afghan News*, 30 July 2007.
80. 'Commander among three policemen slain by colleagues', *Pajhwok Afghan News*, 1 September 2007.
81. 'Defections hit Afghan forces', *Aljazeera.Net*, 15 October 2008.
82. '5 policemen killed by colleagues in S Afghanistan', *Xinhua*, 26 November 2008.
83. 'Security round up: Afghan police join the Taliban', www.ququoos.com, 30

December 2008; 'Dozens of Afghan policemen arrested for helping Taliban', *DPA*, 30 December 2008.
84. 'Cops join forces with Taliban', *Pajhwok Afghan News*, 25 January 2010.
85. Rod Nordland, '25 Afghan Police May Have Joined Taliban', *The New York Times*, 18 February 2010.
86. 'Policemen join Taliban in Afghan east', *Ariana TV*, 18 February 2010.
87. 'Senior Afghan policeman held over planting bombs', *BBC News*, 8 February 2010; 'Afghan police commander arrested in bomb ring', *Reuters*, 7 February 2010; 'While a police commander begins to operate against government!', *Hasht-e Sobh*, 8 February 2010.
88. 'Police officer kills 5 fellow police in Afghan east', *Aina TV*, 15 June 2010.
89. Julius Cavendish, 'Afghan police unit defects after cutting deal with the Taliban', *The Independent*, 3 November 2010.
90. *Pajhwok Afghan News*, 7 June 2011.
91. Interview with foreign MoI adviser, Kabul, October 2009.
92. Interview with Canadian TF Kandahar officer, April 2010.
93. Interview with foreign adviser, Kabul, October 2009.
94. Personal communication with foreign diplomats in Kabul, April 2011.
95. Interview with Canadian officer, April 2010.
96. On models of 'policing on the cheap' see Giustozzi (2011).
97. Nojumi.
98. Interview with foreign embassy official, London, November 2011.
99. Interview with former governor, Kabul, March 2009; interview with former district Mohammad Aman Kazimi, London, 3 June 2008.
100. Hartmann and Klonowiecka-Milart, 287.
101. Personal communication with Martine van Bijlert, Afghanistan Analysts Network, March 2011.
102. Nojumi, 29.
103. Ibid.
104. Interview with former high ranking MoI official, Kabul, April 2008.
105. Interview with former high ranking MoI official, Kabul, October 2010.
106. Interview with BBC journalist, Herat, December 2004.
107. Chilton et al., 70.
108. Interview with former Khost CoP, November 2010.
109. Marlowe, 'Policing Afghanistan', cit.
110. Saltmarshe and Medhi, 22.
111. Alston, 30–1.
112. Interview with former deputy minister, Kabul, April 2008.
113. See Giustozzi (2008b).
114. Murray, 116–7.
115. Interview with former deputy minister, Kabul, April 2008.
116. Interview with Abdul Qayuum Baqizai, Khost CoP, October 2008.
117. Chilton et al., 45.
118. Noor Khan, 'Afghan minister seeks end to private "militias"', *Associated Press*, 30 June 2009.

119. Interview with former deputy minister, Kabul, April 2008.
120. NTM-A briefing, 17 February 2011.
121. Marlowe, 'Policing Afghanistan', cit.
122. Ibid.
123. Eltaf Najafizada and James Rupert, 'Afghan Police's Lack of Guns and Gas Shows U.S. Exit Plan Flaw', *Bloomberg*, 1 September 2010.
124. 'International Forces Deny Funding Afghan Militia', *Afghan Crisis Report*, 27 July 2010; Team—Af15, Afghan Local Police In Zeer-E-Koh Valley, Human Terrain assessment, Regional Command West, ISAF, August 2010; Gran Hewad, 'When the police goes local; more on the Baghlan ALP', Afghan Analyst Network, 4 March 2011.
125. 'ANP Tests National Reporting System', *Enduring Ledger*, June 2009.
126. Interview with EUPOL officer, Kabul, October 2009.
127. Meeting with foreign MoI adviser, Kabul, September 2009.
128. Meeting with APPRO researcher, Kabul, October 2010.
129. Ibid.
130. Eltaf Najafizada and James Rupert, 'Afghan Police's Lack of Guns and Gas Shows U.S. Exit Plan Flaw', *Bloomberg*, 1 September 2010.
131. Marlowe, 'Policing Afghanistan', cit.; SIGAR (2010), 17.
132. Interview with senior police officer, Khost, October 2008.
133. 'Unserviceable Police Vehicle Disposition' in NTM-A, 'Programs Weekly Assessment' (5 January 2011).
134. Interview with foreign embassy official, Kabul, November 2011.
135. Marlowe, 'Policing Afghanistan', cit.
136. SIGAR (2010), 19ff.
137. Meeting with UN official, Kabul, April 2011.
138. Interview with foreign embassy official, Kabul, November 2010; interview with Gen. Beare NTM-A, 10 November 2010.
139. 'Unserviceable Police Vehicle Disposition', cit.
140. NTM-A (2010a).
141. Ibid.
142. NTM-A briefing, 13 March 2011.
143. NTM-A (2010a).
144. Interview with MoI official, Kabul, April 2011.

9. THE AMBIGUOUS IMPACT OF REFORM

1. Rashid (2008), 142.
2. Interview with former high ranking MoI official, Kabul, October 2010; interview with MoI officials, Kabul, April 2008.
3. Interview with former high ranking MoI official, Kabul, April 2008.
4. Rahimullah Samander, 'Senior Police Official Ousted', *Afghan Recovery Report*, 63, 21 February 2005.
5. Interview with former minister Ali Jalali, Kabul, 26 April 2011.

6. Yaqub Ibrahimi, 'National Police Secure Northern Roads', *Afghan Recovery Report*, 151, 6 December 2004; Pamela Constable, 'Afghan Militias Cling To Power in North', *Washington Post*, October 28, 2003.
7. Ahmad Nahim Qadiri, 'Government curbs northern warlords', *Afghan Recovery Report*, 79, 16 November 2005.
8. Interview with former MoI official from Panjshir, Kabul, March 2005.
9. Chilton et al. p. 35.
10. Interview with former high ranking MoI official, Kabul, October 2006.
11. N. C. Aizenman, 'Afghan Interior Minister quits after complaining of graft', *The Washington Post*, 28 September 2005.
12. Personal communication with UN official, Maimana, spring 2009.
13. Interview with police officer, Kandahar, January 2006.
14. Interview with police officer in Teluqan, February 2004.
15. Danish Karokhel, 'Kabul faces provincial problem', *Afghan Recovery Report*, No. 69, 29 July 2003.
16. Interview with MoI official, Kabul, April 2010.
17. Matthieu Aikins, cit. 60.
18. Sayed Yaqub Ibrahimi, 'Afghan police part of the problem', *Afghan Recovery Report*, 218, 7 June 2006.
19. Bashir Babak and Sayed Yaqub Ibrahimi, 'When cops become robbers', *Afghan Recovery Report*, 1 May 2005.
20. Interview with police officer, Kandahar, January 2006.
21. Interview with UNPOL liaison officer, Kabul, November 2003.
22. This paragraph is based on interviews carried out in Faryab in November 2004, with police officers and UN officials.
23. This paragraph is based on interviews carried out in Kandahar in 2005 with police officers, UN officials and government officials.
24. Interview with CoP Daman, March 2005.
25. Interview with police officer in Kandahar, February 2005.
26. Interview with Dand CoP, March 2005.
27. Interview with Jalali, Kabul, April 2011.
28. Personal communications with UN officials, Kabul, 2008–11.
29. Interview with senior police officer, Kabul, November 2010.
30. Interview with former senior MoI official, Kabul, October 2010.
31. Interview with foreign adviser to MoI, Kabul, October 2009.
32. Murray (2007), 114.
33. Interview with former high ranking official, Kabul, October 2009.
34. Interview with former high ranking MoI official, October 2006.
35. Interview with foreign adviser to the MoI, Kabul, October 2009.
36. Interview with former high ranking official, Kabul, October 2010.
37. Interview with UN official, Kabul November 2010.
38. Meeting with foreign adviser to MoI, September 2009.
39. Interview with foreign adviser to MoI, Kabul, October 2009.
40. LIBRA, cit.; meeting with CoP, June 2009.
41. Meeting with foreign adviser to the MoI, September 2009; interview with former MoI senior official, Kabul, October 2009.

42. Meeting with former minister Hanif Atmar, Kabul, April 2011.
43. Interview with MoI official, Kabul, April 2010; interview with former high ranking MoI official, Kabul, October 2009; interview with former high ranking MoI official, Kabul, October 2010.
44. Meeting with foreign MoI adviser, Kabul, September 2009.
45. Interview with former high ranking MoI official, October 2010.
46. Personal communication with foreign ministerial adviser in Kabul, September 2010.
47. Archie Mclean, 'Honest Afghan cop a rarity in corrupt force', *Canwest News Service*, 15 February 2009; Jane Armstrong, 'A Few Good Men', www.payam-aftab.com/en/category/print.php?nid=3036, 7 February 2009; interview with Canadian TF Kandahar officer, April 2010.
48. Dion Nissenbaum, 'Corruption, incompetence charges plague new Afghan police force', *McClatchy Newspapers*, 10 May 2010.
49. Marlowe, 'Policing Afghanistan', cit.
50. Richard Lardner, 'Friction among Afghans looms as challenge in south', *The Associated Press*, 22 July 2010.
51. Interview with Canadian TF Kandahar officer, April 2010.
52. Personal communication with NATO officials and officers, Kabul, April and September 2011.
53. Interview with high ranking MoI official, Kabul, November 2010.
54. Interview with analyst of international organisation, October 2010.
55. Ibid.
56. Interview with foreign embassy official, Kabul, November 2010; EU sources in Kabul, September 2010.
57. Interview with former high ranking MoI official, Kabul, October 2010.
58. Interview with CoP, November 2010.
59. Personal communication with M. Atkins, London, August 2011.
60. NTM-A (2010a); interview with foreign adviser to MoI, Kabul, November 2010.
61. NTM-A (2010a).
62. Meeting with UN official, Kabul, April 2011.
63. NTM-A (2010a).
64. Ibid.
65. Ibid.
66. Meeting with NTM-A officer, November 2010; interview with UN official, Kabul, November 2010; interview with high ranking MoI officer, November 2010.
67. Interview with former high ranking MoI official, Kabul, October 2010.
68. Interview with foreign adviser to the MoI, May 2011.
69. NTM-A (2010a).
70. Ibid.
71. Ibid.
72. Interview with foreign adviser to the MoI, Kabul, October 2009.
73. Cordesman (2010), 121.
74. Interview with Gen. M. Wakeel Akbari, chief of personnel, Kabul, April 2011.

75. Flood (2009a). On the British position, see Burdett.
76. Friesendorf; Cordesman (2010), 131–2.
77. Meeting with former Minister Hanif Atmar, Kabul, April 2011.
78. 'Female police in Afghanistan', 61ff.
79. Mark Sappenfield, 'Female cops test traditional gender roles in Afghanistan', *The Christian Science Monitor*, 7 January 2009.
80. 'Female police officer shot dead in Afghan south', *Islamic Press News Agency*, 6 March 2011, Peshawar, in Pashto, 0610 GMT.
81. Murray (n.d.), 19.
82. Wilder, 11.
83. Interview with Carabinieri officer, Herat, October 2009; interview with APPRO researcher, Kabul, October 2010; personal communication with UN official, Kabul, 2009.
84. Interview with Carabinieri officer, Herat, October 2009; interview with APPRO researcher, Kabul, October 2010.
85. Ibid.
86. Ibid.
87. Murray (n.d.), 19.
88. Interview with APPRO researcher, Kabul, October 2010.
89. Interview with APPRO researcher, Kabul, October 2010.
90. Meeting with APPRO researcher, Kabul, October 2010.
91. Interview with Carabinieri officer, Herat, October 2009; interview with APPRO researcher, Kabul, October 2010.
92. Interview with APPRO researcher, Kabul, October 2010.
93. Interview with Carabinieri officer, Herat, October 2009; interview with APPRO researcher, Kabul, October 2010.
94. Zafar Shah Royi, 'Interior minister: We need the presence of women', *Hasht-e Sobh*, 6 March 2011.
95. Murray (2007), 116–7.
96. Meeting with APPRO researcher, Kabul, October 2010.
97. Interview with senior NTM-A officer, Kabul, October 2010.
98. Interview with APPRO researcher, Kabul, October 2010.
99. LIBRA briefing on police in Afghanistan KCL, 8 July 2009.
100. Meeting with APPRO researcher, Kabul, October 2010; interview with MoI adviser, Kabul, October 2009; interview with AIHRC official, Kabul, November 2010.
101. GAO (2009).
102. Meeting with former minister Hanif Atmar, Kabul, April 2011.
103. Wilder, 5–6.
104. Interview with analyst of international organisation, Kabul, October 2010.
105. Gretchen Peters, 'Law lessons for Afghan police', *The Christian Science Monitor*, 7 January 2003.
106. Sayed Salahuddin, 'Body Formed to Teach Human Rights to Afghan Police', *Reuters*, 30 April 2003; personal communication with UNAMA official, June 2004; DoS (2008).

107. Interview with Dr Hekmati, ex-NDI, Mazar-i Sharif, 22 October 2008.
108. DoS (2009).
109. Amnesty International, 30.
110. International Crisis Group (2008), 14.
111. LIBRA, cit.
112. Meeting with International Police Coordinating Board official, Kabul, November 2010.
113. Interview with foreign embassy official, November 2010.
114. Interview with Heather Coyne, NTM-A, Kabul, November 2010.
115. NTM-A (2010a).
116. Interview with foreign MoI adviser, Kabul, October 2009; Hartmann and Klonowiecka-Milart, 271.
117. Hartmann and Klonowiecka-Milart, 269–70.
118. Hartmann and Klonowiecka-Milart, 276, 278–9.
119. Hartmann and Klonowiecka-Milart, 280–1.
120. Wilder, 50; Hartmann and Klonowiecka-Milart, 287.
121. On the British position, see Burdett.
122. 'Afghan Attorneys Teaching Afghan Police "'rule of Law'"', *Military-world.net*, 1 March 2010.
123. Mina Habib, 'Police armed and dangerous in Afghanistan', *Bellingham Herald*, 21 March 2011.
124. Richard Norton-Taylor, 'Afghan police failings fuelling Taliban recruitment, say UK army chiefs', *The Guardian Online*, 3 June 2010.
125. Interview with Mohammed Faridi Hamidi, AIHRC, Kabul, November 2011.
126. Amnesty International, 35.
127. See for example, *Arman-e Melli*, Kabul, 13 December 2005.
128. Juliet O'Neill, 'Some Afghan police seemed like thugs, report says', *Canwest News Service*, 8 May 2010.
129. Emmanuel Derville, 'A Kandahar, la guerre sans fin', unpublished AFP report, 4 February 2011.
130. A case of a mullah tortured and eventually killed in custody in Khakrez of Kandahar is reported in Allen, 23.
131. Smith (2011), 303.
132. AIHRC.
133. Amnesty International, 39.
134. Nojumi, 23.
135. 'Many Afghans being detained unlawfully—UNAMA', *Pajhwok Afghan News*, 17 November 2009.
136. International Crisis Group (2008), 7.
137. Nadene Ghouri, 'Afghan police: Corrupt and brutal, and still not fit for purpose', *The Guardian*, 6 November 2009.
138. Rosen.
139. Interview with AIHRC officer, Kabul, November 2010.
140. DoS (2008).
141. Ibid.

142. Ibid.
143. Ibid.
144. Ibid.
145. Ibid.
146. Ibid.
147. Ibid.
148. Alston.
149. Ibid.
150. Ibid.
151. Ibid.
152. Shoib Safi, 'Laying Down the Law', *Afghan Recovery Report*, No. 38, 29 November 2002.
153. Jason Krawczyk, 'Afghan National Police Is Taught Riot Control', 20th Public Affairs Detachment CENTCOM, 17 August 2002.
154. Interview with former minister Ali Jalali, Kabul, April 2011.
155. Murray (2007), 122.
156. 'Police to begin night patrol in Kabul', *Pajhwok Afghan News*, 12 June 2006.
157. Interview with foreign MoI adviser, May 2007.
158. Ahmad Khalid Mohid, 'Police not equipped to control riots: Bashary', *Pajhwok Afghan News*, 11 May 2008.
159. Interview with foreign MoI adviser, Kabul, November 2010.
160. Meeting with Gen. Manan Farahi, MoI, Kabul, 19 April 2011.
161. Declan Walsh, 'Seven die as move to oust Afghan city's warlord prompts riot', *The Guardian*, 13 September 2004.
162. Randeep Ramesh, 'Four dead after anti-American riots erupt in Afghanistan', *The Guardian*, 12 May 2005.
163. DoS (2008).
164. Carlotta Gall, 'Convoy crash sparks Kabul riots', *International Herald Tribune*, 29 May 2006.
165. DoS (2008).
166. DoS (2009).
167. Ibid.
168. 'Kabul Riots Were No Surprise', *Killid*, 21 August 2010.
169. 'Situation in Kandahar discussed after deadly riots', *Pajhwok Afghan News*, 6 April 2011.
170. Interview with former deputy minister Hilaluddin Hilal, 8 October 2006; interview with Chief of Police of Baghlan, December 2003.
171. For a case in Badakhshan involving a mullah and the stoning to death of a woman see 'Afghan arrest mullah, five others for killing woman accused of adultery', *The Associated Press*, 30 April 2005.
172. 'Afghanistan: Honour killings on the rise', *IRIN*, 15 September 2006.
173. UNODC (2007).
174. Asia Foundation.
175. LIBRA, cit.
176. See USAID, 45–6.

177. See USAID, 46.
178. USAID, 12.
179. USAID, 18.
180. USAID. 11–2.
181. USAID, 45.
182. USAID, 19.
183. USAID, 22–3.
184. Ibid.
185. DoS (2004).
186. International Crisis Group (2003).
187. 'Afghanistan crumbling prison system desperately in need of repair', ASA, Amnesty International, 11 July 2003, 41.
188. Smith (2011), 303.
189. Miller and Perito, 10.

10. PROVINCIAL DYNAMICS: A CASE STUDY OF HERAT

1. Interview with lead trainer, Herat Police Training Centre, Herat, 12 March 2011.
2. Interviews with ex-police officers and ex-police conscripts, Herat, November 2010.
3. Interviews with political analysts, Herat, June 2010.
4. Ibid.
5. Interviews with police officers and political analysts, Herat, June 2010. For more details on this period, see Giustozzi (2009).
6. Interviews with police officers who served under Najib and Ismail Khan, Herat, June–September 2010.
7. Interview with an official from Herat Police Training Center, March 2011.
8. Interview with police officer who served under Ismail Khan, Herat, March 2011.
9. Interviews with police officers who served under the Taliban, Herat, November 2010.
10. Interviews with police officers who served under the Taliban, Herat, November 2010.
11. Dietl.
12. Interview with a Member of Parliament from Herat, Herat, August 2009.
13. Interviews with police officers who served under the Taliban, Herat, November 2010.
14. Interview with a political analyst, Herat, September 2009.
15. Interviews with provincial police officers, Herat, June–September 2009.
16. Interview with a former provincial police officer, Herat, November 2010.
17. Author's own observation.
18. Interview with a senior police officer from Regional Police Headquarters, Herat, August 2009.
19. The story of Khawaja Issa was narrated by many provincial police officers, Herat, July–September 2009.
20. Interview with a senior police officer from Regional Police Headquarters, Herat, August 2009.

21. Interviews with police officers who served under Ismail Khan, Herat, August 2009.
22. Interview with a former militia commander who served as a senior police officer under Ismail Khan, Herat, 21 July 2009.
23. Interview with a former district police chief who served under Ismail Khan, August 2009.
24. Interview with a political analyst, Herat, September 2009.
25. This point was confirmed in almost all interviews with provincial police officers, Herat, June–September 2009.
26. Interviews with police officers in Herat city and the districts, 2005.
27. Interview with a senior police officer, Herat Regional Police Headquarters, Herat, November 2010.
28. Ibid.
29. Interview with a former district police chief, Herat, September 2009.
30. Interview with official from Herat Military Court, Herat, September 2009.
31. Interviews with provincial police officers, Herat, August 2009.
32. Ibid.
33. Rashid (2008).
34. Interview with a senior attorney and former government official, Herat, August 2009.
35. Interviews with police officers, Herat, 2005.
36. Interviews with a political analyst and provincial police officers, Herat, June 2009.
37. Interviews with police officers, Herat, 2005.
38. Giustozzi (2004).
39. Khwaja Issa's 'administration of justice' is well-known in Herat and was brought up not only by many of the police officers interviewed, but even by ordinary Heratis.
40. Interview with a government official, Herat, July 2009.
41. Interview with a Herati parliamentarian, Kabul, September 15, 2009.
42. Interview with a senior police officer, Herat, August 2009.
43. This point was made by many professional police officers, Herat, June–September 2009.
44. Interviews with provincial police officers, Herat, June–September 2009.
45. Interview with a senior police officer and former director of Provincial Police Guest House, Herat, 7 September 2009.
46. On the issue of the functioning of patrimonial regimes and the historical sources of institution-building as a strategy of state consolidation, see Giustozzi (2011).
47. Olsen.
48. Interviews with police officers and ordinary citizens, Herat, June–September 2009.
49. Interview with a senior provincial police officer, Herat, September 2009.
50. Interview with a provincial police officer, Herat, August 2009.
51. Interview with senior prosecutor, Herat, July 2009.
52. Ibid.
53. Interviews with police officers, Herat, 2005.

54. Interview with an official from Provincial Security Directorate, Herat, July 2009, and confirmed in many other interviews.
55. Interview with two Members of Parliament from Herat, Herat, August 2009.
56. Interview with a Member of Parliament from Herat, Herat, August 2009.
57. *Herat Daily News*, 8 April 2009.
58. Confirmed in interviews with officials from Herat Military Attorney Directorate and Martial Court, and Herat Security Directorate.
59. Interview with a senior police officer, Herat Regional Police Headquarters, August 2009.
60. Interview with an official from National Security Directorate in Herat, Herat, September 2009.
61. Interview with a senior official from Herat Military Attorney Directorate, Herat, September 2009.
62. Ibid.
63. Ibid.
64. Interview with a senior official from Herat Military Court, Herat, September 2009.
65. Ibid.
66. Interview with a senior official from Herat Military Attorney Directorate, Herat, September 2009.
67. Ibid.
68. Interviews with officials from AIHRC Regional Office, Herat, July 2009.
69. Ibid.
70. Ibid.
71. Interviews with local journalists, Herat, August 2009.
72. Ibid.

REFERENCES

Afanasiev, M.B. (1999) 'Tri god v Kabul', in *Internatsional'naya Missiya*, Moscow.
AIHRC (2009) 'Causes of torture in law enforcement institutions', Kabul.
Alekseev, G.A.(1999) 'Posle vyvoda OKSB', in *Internatsional'naya Missiya*, Moscow.
Allen, Nick (2010) *Embed: With the World's Armies in Afghanistan*, Stroud: Spellmount.
Alston, Philip (2009) 'Report of the Special Rapporteur on extrajudicial, summary or arbitrary executions: Addendum Mission to Afghanistan', New York: General Assembly, A/HRC/11/2/Add.4, 6 May.
Amnesty International (2003) 'Afghanistan: Police reconstruction essential for the protection of human rights', AI Index: ASA 11/003/2003, London, March.
Azimi, Nabi (1998), *Urdu wa siyasat*, Peshawar.
Bayley, D. H. (1985), *Patterns of Policing*, Fredericksburg: Rutgers.
Beattie, Doug (2008) *An Ordinary Soldier*, London: Simon & Schuster.
Bishop, Patrick (2007) *3 para*, London: Harper.
─────── (2009) *Ground Truth*, London: Harper.
Brown, Katherine (2011) 'The Day Embassy Kabul Forever Changed: Remembering the 1979 Assassination of Adolph "Spike" Dubs and The Dismantling of the American Civilian Mission in Afghanistan', *Small Wars Journal*, 14 February.
Burdett, Rohan (2010) 'Police reform in stabilisation: the Afghanistan experience', Afghan COIN Centre, United Kingdom, September.
Bykov, V.F. (1999) 'Pod bagramom', in *Internatsional'naya Missiya*, Moscow.
Carothers, Thomas (1998), 'Rule of Law Revival', *Foreign Affairs*, vol. 77, no. 2.
Chaudhry, M. A. K. (1997), *Policing in Pakistan*, Lahore: Vanguard.
Chilton et al. (2009), *Evaluation of the Appropriate Size of the Afghan National Police Manning List* (Tashkil), Kabul: IBF International Consulting.
Cordesman, Anthony H. (2010) 'Afghan National Security Forces: what it will take to implement the Isaf strategy', Washington: CSIS, July 12.
─────── (2011), 'Can Afghan Forces be Effective by Transition? Afghanistan and the Uncertain Metrics of Progress: Part Five', Washington: CSIS.
Dietl, Gulshan (2004) 'War, peace and the warlords: the case of Ismail Khan of Herat in Afghanistan', *Turkish Journal of International Relations*, Vol. 3, No. 2&3: pp. 41–66.

REFERENCES

Docherty, Leo (2007) *Desert of Death*, London: Faber & Faber.

Dorronsoro, Gilles (2005), *Revolution Unending*, London: Hurst.

DoS (2004) 'Country Reports on Human Rights Practices—2003', Bureau of Democracy, Human Rights, and Labor, U.S. Department of State, Washington.

——— (2008) '2007 Country Reports on Human Rights Practices', Washington: Bureau of Democracy, Human Rights, and Labor, March.

——— (2009) '2008 Country Reports on Human Rights Practices', Washington: Bureau of Democracy, Human Rights, and Labor, March.

EUPOL (2009) 'Overview of EUPOL significant activities', Kabul, September.

Fedaseev, Iu. G. (1999) Mushaveri, in *Internatsional'naya Missiya*, Moscow.

'Female police in Afghanistan' (1970) in *Police on Public Service*, 2nd Edition, Kabul: Royal Afghan Ministry of Interior, pp. 1–112.

Ferguson, James (2008) *A Million Bullets*, London: Bantam Press.

Flood, Derek Henry (2009a) 'At the Center of the Storm: An Interview with Afghanistan's Lieutenant General Hadi Khalid—Part One', *Terrorism Monitor* Volume: 7 Issue: 27.

——— (2009b) 'At the Center of the Storm: An Interview with Afghanistan's Lieutenant General Hadi Khalid—Part Two', *Terrorism Monitor* Volume: 7 Issue: 28.

Friesendorf, Cornelius (2011) 'Paramilitarization and Security Sector Reform: The Afghan National Police', *International Peacekeeping*, Vol. 18, No. 1, February 2011, pp. 79–95.

Fry, Maxwell J. (1974), *The Afghan Economy*, Leiden: Brill.

GAO (2009) 'Report on Progress toward Security and Stability in Afghanistan', Washington, January.

——— (2010) 'Report to Congressional Addressees: Afghanistan Drug Control Strategy Evolving and Progress Reported, but Interim Performance Targets and Evaluation of Justice Reform Efforts Needed', Washington, March.

Ghosh, Srikanta (1987), *Law Enforcement in Tribal Areas*, Calcutta: Law Research Institute.

Giustozzi, Antonio (2000) *War, Politics and Society in Afghanistan*, London: Hurst.

——— (2004) 'Good' state vs. 'bad' warlords? A critique of state-building strategies in Afghanistan', Crisis States Programme, Development Research Centre, LSE.

——— (2008) 'Bureaucratic façade and political realities of disarmament and demobilisation in Afghanistan', *Conflict, Security & Development*, no. 2, 2008.

——— (2008) *Koran, Kalashnikov and Laptop*, London; Hurst.

——— (2009) *Empires of Mud*, London: Hurst.

——— (2011) *The Art of Coercion*, London: Hurst.

——— (ed.) (2012) *DDR: Bringing the State Back in*, Farnham: Ashgate.

Giustozzi, Antonio et al. (forthcoming), 'Shadow justice', Kabul: IWA.

Giustozzi, Antonio and Orsini, Dominique (2009) 'Centre-periphery relations in Afghanistan between patrimonialism and institution-building: The Case of Badakhshan', *Central Asian Survey*, March, pp. 1–16.

Giustozzi, Antonio and Noor Ullah (2006) 'Tribes and warlords in southern Afghanistan', London: Crisis States Research Centre (LSE).

REFERENCES

Glatzer, Bernt (2002) 'Centre and periphery in Afghanistan: new identities in a broken state', *Sociologus*, Winter 2002.

Gregorian, Vartan (1969) *The Emergence of Modern Afghanistan*, Stanford: Stanford University Press.

Grinin, V.A. (1999) 'Dnevnik mushavera tsarandoya provintsii Kabul', in *Internatsional'naya Missiya*, Moscow.

Gubinchikov, F.V. (1999) 'V 1982om v afganistan ne voshly', in *Internatsional'naya Missiya*, Moscow.

Harnden, Toby (2011) 'Dead men risen; the Welsh Guards and the real story of Britain's war in Afghanistan', London: Quercus.

Hartmann, Michael E. and Klonowiecka-Milart, A. (2011) 'Lost in translation: legal transplants without consensus-based adaptation', in Whit Mason (ed.), *The Rule of Law in Afghanistan*, Cambridge: Cambridge University Press 2011, pp. 266–300.

Haskell, David J. (2009) 'The Afghan National Police: turning a counterinsurgency problem into a solution', Thesis, Monterrey: NPS, December.

Hassin, Shah Mahmood (1984) *The Ministry of Interior in History*, Kabul: State Printing House.

Holmes, Stephen (2003), 'Lineages of the Rule of Law', in Maravall, J. M. and Przeworski, A. (eds), *Democracy and the Rule of Law*, Cambridge: Cambridge University Press.

Human Rights Watch (2011) 'Just Don't Call It a Militia', New York.

Hualing, Fu (2005), 'Zhou Yongkang and the Recent Police Reform in China', *Australian and New Zealand Journal of Criminology*, vol. 38, no. 2, pp. 241–53.

Hutchful, Eboe (2003), 'Pulling back from the brink: Ghana's experience', in Cawtra, Gavin and Luckham, Robin (eds), *Governing Insecurity*, London: Zed Books.

Inspectors General (2006), 'Interagency Assessment of Afghanistan Police Training and Readiness', Washington.

Integrity Watch Afghanistan (2010) 'Afghan perceptons and experiences of corruption: a National survey 2010', Kabul,.

International Crisis Group (2003) 'Afghanistan: the problem of Pashtun alienation', Bruxelles, 5 August.

——— (2008) 'Policing in Afghanistan: Still Searching for a Strategy', Bruxelles.

Joseph, Richard A. (1988) *Democracy and Prebendal Politics in Nigeria. The Rise and fall of the Second Republic*, Cambridge: Cambridge University Press.

Kakar, Hasan (1978) 'The Fall of the Afghan Monarchy in 1973', *International Journal of Middle East Studies*, Vol. 9, no. 2 (April, 1978), pp. 195–214.

——— (1979) *Government and Society in Afghanistan*, Austin: Texas University Press.

Kiley, Sam (2009) *Desperate Glory*, London: Bloomsbury.

Kliuchnik, V.T. (1999) 'Puteshestvie 1358 god', in *Internatsional'naya Missiya*, Moscow.

Klyushnikov, A.S. (1999) 'Pyat' trudnykh let', in *Internatsional'naya Missiya*, Moscow.

Lefèvre, Matthieu (2010) *Local Defence in Afghanistan*, Kabul/Berlin: Afghanistan Analyst Network.

Liang, His-Huey (1992), *The Rise of Modern Police and the European State System from Metternich to the Second World War*, Cambridge: Cambridge University Press.

Lozhkin, I.E. (1999) 'Na zashite revolutsii', in *Internatsional'naya Missiya*, Moscow.

REFERENCES

Marenin, Otwin (ed.) (1996), *Policing Change, Changing Police: International Perspectives*, New York: Garland Press.

Miller, Laurel and Perito, Robert (2004) 'Establishing the Rule of Law in Afghanistan', Washington: USIP.

Ministry of Interior (2010/11), 'Anti-corruption police', Kabul: Policy and Strategy deputy Ministry, General Department of Policy.

Minnott, Janice (2008) *Letters from Kabul 1966–8*, Trafford.

Murray, Tonita (2007) 'Police-Building in Afghanistan: A Case Study of Civil Security Reform', *International Peacekeeping*, Vol. 14, no. 1, January, pp. 108–26.

——— (n.d.) 'Report on the status of women in the Afghan National Police', Ottawa: CANADEM/Canadian International Development Agency.

Nojumi, Nejat et al. (2004) Afghanistan's Systems of Justice, Medford: Feinstein International Famine Center, Youth and Community Program, Tufts University.

NTM-A (2010a), '90 Day Assessment', Kabul, 1 October.

——— (2010b), 'Assessment of Minister of Interior, H.E. Bishmullah Khan Mohammadi's First 100 Days in Office', Kabul.

——— (2011), 'MoI year in review', February 2011.

Olsen, Mancur (2000) *Power and Prosperity: Outgrowing Communist and Capitalist Dictatorships*, New York: Basic Books.

Omarzai, Gen. (2004), *Nights in Kabul*, Peshawar: Peshawar University

Perito, Robert M. (2009) 'Afghanistan's Police', Washington: USIP.

Pleshakov, V.V. (1999) 'Vspomin, tovarish', in *Internatsional'naya Missiya*, Moscow.

Rashid, Ahmed (2000), *Taliban*, London: Tauris.

——— (2008) *Descent into Chaos*, London: Allen Lane.

Rayment, Sean (2008) *Into the Killing Zone*, London: Constable.

Reith, Charles Edward Williams (1952), *The Blind Eye of History: A Study of the Origins of the Present Police Era*, London: Faber.

Rosen, Nir (2010) 'Something from Nothing', *Boston Review*, January/February.

Rudenko, N.F. (1999) 'Mne chasto snitsya Afghanistan', in *Internatsional'naya Missiya*, Moscow.

RUSI (2009) *Reforming the Afghan National Police*, London.

Saltmarshe, Douglas and Abhilash Medhi (2011) 'Local Governance in Afghanistan A View from the Ground', Kabul: AREU, June.

Schmeidl, Susanne and Masood Karokhail (2009), 'The Role of Non-State Actors in "Community-Based Policing"—An Exploration of the Arbakai (Tribal Police) in South-Eastern Afghanistan', *Contemporary Security Policy*, 30:2, pp. 318–42.

Scott, Jake (2008) *Blood Clot*, Solihull: Helion & Company.

Serchuk, Vance (2006) 'Cop Out: Why Afghanistan Has No Police', Washington: American Enterprise Institute for Public Policy, 17 July.

Shaw, Martin (2006) 'Drug trafficking and the development of organized crime in post-Taliban Afghanistan', in *Afghanistan's Drug Industry*, ed. By D. Rittenberg and William Byrd, Wien: UNODC.

SIGAR (2010b) 'Action needed to improve the reliability of the Afghan security force assessments', Washington.

REFERENCES

———— (2010a) 'Audit-10–11: Security/ANSF Capabilty Ratings', Washington, June 29.

———— (2011), 'Report to congress', 30 January.

Skinner, Marcus (2008) 'Counterinsurgency and State Building: An Assessment of the Role of the Afghan National Police', *Democracy and Security*, Vol. 4: no. 3, pp. 290–311.

Smith, Graeme (2011) 'No justice, no peace: Kandahar 2005–9', in Whit Mason (ed.), *The rule of law in Af-ghanistan*, Cambridge: Cambridge University Press.

Smith, H. H. et al. (1967) *Area Handbook for Afghanistan*, Washington: US Government Printing Office.

———— et al. (1969) *Area Handbook for Afghanistan*, Washington: US Government Printing Office.

———— et al. (1976) *Area Handbook for Afghanistan*, Washington: US Government Printing Office.

Stepanov, P.A. (1999) 'Moi vospominaniya ob Afganistane', in *Internatsional'naya Missiya*, Moscow.

Sysoev, V.L. (1999) 'Myshaver shuravi', in *Internatsional'naya Missiya*, Moscow.

Tariq, Mohammed Osman (2008), 'Tribal Security System (Arbakai) in Southeast Afghanistan', Occasional Paper no. 7, London: Crisis States Research Centre (LSE).

Thruelsen, Peter Dahl (2010) 'Striking the Right Balance: How to Rebuild the Afghan National Police', *International Peacekeeping*, Vol. 17: no. 1, pp. 80–92.

Tootal, Stuart (2009) *Danger Close*, London: Murray.

Tsigannik, F. (1999), 'Otbetstvennoe zadanie', in *Internatsional'naya Missiya*, Moscow.

Turk, Austin T. (1982), *Political Criminality: The Defiance and Defense of Authority*, Beverley Hills: Sage.

UNDP (2008) 'Law and Order Trust Fund for Afghanistan, (LOTFA-Phase IV) (Afghan Calendar 1386) 01–04–2007/31–03–2008 Annual Project Report', Kabul.

———— (2009) 'Afghanistan Law and Order Trust Fund for Afghanistan (LOTFA: Phase IV & V), Annual Project Report (Afghan Calendar 1387)', Kabul.

———— (2010a), 'Afghanistan Law and Order Trust Fund for Afghanistan (LOTFA)- Phase V 2nd Quarter Project Progress Report (April-June, 2010)', Kabul.

———— (2010b) 'Afghanistan Law and Order Trust Fund for Afghanistan (LOTFA)- Phase V, Annual Progress Report (2009)', Kabul.

———— (2010c) 'Afghanistan Law and Order Trust Fund for Afghanistan (LOTFA)- Phase V, 1st Quarter Project Progress Report (2010)', Kabul.

———— (2010d) *Police Perception Survey—2010: The Afghan Perspective*, Kabul.

UNODC (2007) 'Afghanistan: Female Prisoners and Their Social Reintegration', New York/Vienna.

———— (2010) 'Corruption in Afghanistan: Bribery as reported by the victims', Kabul.

USAID (2005) 'Afghanistan rule of law project', Washington.

Vorobiov, V. (1999) 'Segodnya o bylom', in *Internatsional'naya Missiya*, Moscow.

Yasin, Mohammad (1999), *District and Police Systems in Pakistan*, Lahore: Vanguard.

Walt, Gen. (1972), 'The global context: Report', in *World Drug Traffic and Its Impact on US Security*, Hearings before the subcommittee to investigate the administration of the Internal Security Act and other security laws of the Committee on the judiciary, United States Senate, ninety-second Congress, second session, part 4, Washington; US Government Printing Office.

Waltemate, Sascha (2011) 'Focused District Development. Turning Point for Police Building in Afghanistan?', Duesseldorf: Institute for Foreign and Security Policy.

Weinbaum, M. G. (1980), Legal Elites in Afghan Society, *International Journal of Middle East Studies*, Vol. 12, no. 1 (August), pp. 39–57.

West, Bing (2011) *The Wrong War*, New York: Random House.

Wilder, Andrew (2007) 'Cops or Robbers? The Struggle to Reform the Afghan National Police', Kabul: AREU, July

INDEX

Afghan Anti-Crime Police (AACP): creation of, 56
Afghan Independent Human Rights Commission (AIHRC): 151–2, 155; refusal of police personnel to cooperate with, 180; remit of, 179; report on increase in honour killings (2006), 160
Afghan Local Police (ALP): 56, 62, 117, 119–20; focus of, 56
Afghan National Army (ANA): 65, 85, 89, 117, 156; conflict with ANP, 68–9; Operation Coordination Center-Province (OCCP), 68; Operation Coordination Center-Region (OCCR), 68; roads controlled by, 88
Afghan National Civil Order Police (ANCOP): 59, 74, 97, 131, 146; creation of, 56, 137; deployment to Marjah (2010), 143; drug abuse amongst personnel of, 67; literacy rate amongst personnel of, 75
Afghan National Police (ANP): 82–3, 111, 123, 156, 173, 177; conflict with ANA, 68–9; mobile battalions, 137; resources devoted to combating insurgency activity, 41; suspected collusion of personnel with Taliban, 122; US oversight over, 50; use of uniforms by ANAP personnel, 62

Afghan National Police Strategy (ANPS): aims of, 154
Afghan New Beginnings Programme (ANBP): DIAG database, 41
Afghan Police Incident Reporting System (APIRS): 130
Afghan Public Protection Force (APPF): 62–3, 147; establishment of (2009), 56
Afghan Social Outreach Programme: launch of (2008), 62–3
Afghan Uniformed Police (AUP); 62, 69, 117, 147, 185; distrust of ANCOP, 143
Afghanistan: 2, 10–12, 15, 21, 24, 41, 48, 59, 111, 169, 183, 185; Badghis, 62, 120, 179; Baghlan, 39, 61, 63, 101, 113, 117, 125, 160; Balkh, 15, 22, 69, 101, 136–7; borders of, 39, 85; Civil War (1928–9), 18; Derzab, 123; Dikundi, 92; Farah, 85, 120; Faryab, 12, 92, 101, 135–7; Ghazni, 16, 92, 122–3, 156; Ghor, 103, 120, 159; government of, 47, 62, 133, 152; Helmand, 40, 50, 60, 68, 74, 80, 82, 90, 118, 121, 123, 144; Herat, 15, 22, 34, 40, 61–2, 71, 81, 83–5, 88, 95, 99, 120, 126, 128, 135, 148, 159, 161, 165–8, 172–3, 175–81; Jowzjan, 157,

225

INDEX

159, 161; Kabul, 14–15, 17, 23, 25–6, 32, 34–5, 39–40, 47, 58, 68–70, 73, 80–1, 83–4, 88, 90, 96, 99–100–1, 104, 111, 115–16, 125–6, 128, 133, 136–8, 146, 148, 151, 154, 158–9, 161, 165, 175, 178, 186; Kandahar, 12–13, 15, 17–18, 27, 40–1, 50, 60, 63, 67, 76, 81, 88, 92, 95, 101–2, 104, 113, 116, 121, 123, 125, 128, 137, 139–40, 143, 153, 155–6, 162–3; Kapisa, 40, 123; Katawaz, 16; Khost, 18, 63, 92, 100, 126, 129; Kunar, 81; Kunduz, 15, 29, 90, 99–100, 119; Laghman, 40; Logar, 16, 40, 52, 95, 161; Mazar-i-Sharif, 34, 84, 88; Nangarhar, 22, 40, 67, 70, 113, 118, 148, 159, 161; Nimruz, 82; Nuristan, 16, 92; Operation Enduring Freedom, 1, 128; Paktika, 32, 92; Panjshir, 27, 40, 61; Panshir valley, 39; Parwan, 25, 40, 60–1, 101; Sar-e Pol, 83; Shamali, 16; Soviet invasion of (1979–89), 26, 168; Takhar, 24–5, 39, 90–2, 99, 105, 112, 136; Uruzgan, 40, 60, 63, 92, 117, 156; Wardak, 40–1, 63, 81–2, 123; Zabul, 40, 92, 112

Afghanistan Analyst Network: 2

Afghanistan Border Police (ABP): 11, 17, 19, 89, 91, 97, 147, 155; corruption in, 83, 99, 121; defection of personnel to Taliban, 123; lack of discipline in, 65, personnel of, 78, 81, 90, 99, 104, 109, 113, 116, 130, 137

Afghanistan Compact: provisions of, 11

Afghanistan Special Police Force: personnel of, 178

Ahmadzai, Esmatullah: 112

Alawi, Sayyed Naseer: 168

Ali, Hazrat: 113; CoP of Nangarhar, 70

Alikozai: 140

Amanullah, King: military forces of, 18; reign of, 14

Amarkhel, General Aminollah: commander of Afghanistan Border Police in Eastern Afghanistan, 116

Amin, Hafizullah: 24–8; supporters of, 26

Amnesty International: 115, 152, 155, 162

Andarabi: 39

Andarabi, Khalil: 101, 113

Andiwal, Mohammad Hussein: 118

Asia Foundation: 79

Asos, Sultaeddin: 27

Atmar, Mohammad Hanif: 94, 96, 109, 146, 150; Afghan Minister of Interior, 52, 56, 58, 90, 141; background of, 71

Auxiliary Police (ANAP): criticisms of, 62; formation of (2006), 62; use of ANP uniforms by, 62

Azfali, Azizullah: 166

Azimi, Faiz Ahmad: 173

Bank of Afghanistan: 70

Barakzai: 140

Bassir, Haidar: 112

Beg, Mutalleb: CoP of Takhar, 90

British Broadcasting Corporation (BBC): 120

Bulgaria: 30

Canada: 58, 123, 153

China: police reform in, 9

Civilian police: 3, 146–7; characteristics of, 4

Corruption: 20, 38, 139, 144, 179; extortion by police personnel, 21; impact of personal oversight on, 171–2; in ABP, 83, 99, 121

Criminal Investigation Department (CID): 58, 69, 130; offices of, 71, 80; personnel of, 80

Czechoslovakia: 30

Daud, Mohammed Daud: 58, 101; assassination of (2011), 101; bodyguards of, 90; Chief of the Northern Zone, 105, 119; Deputy Interior Minister for Counter Narcotics, 119; Governor of Takhar, 62, 109

INDEX

Defence of the Revolution: 29
Directorate of Census Data and Personal Registration: 17
Disarmament Commission: DIAG database, 41
Disarmament, Demobilisation and Reintegration (DDR): of militias, 113; programmes of, 139
Dostum, General Abdul Rashid: 34, 137, 161, 167
Dubs, Adolph: kidnap and murder of (1979), 25; US Ambassador to Afghanistan, 25
DynCorp International: 49; training courses provided by, 139

European Union Police Mission (EUPOL): 70, 96; approval of Patrolmen Basic Program of Instruction (2011), 51; marginalisation of, 51–2; sponsorship of mobile units, 58
Eyni, Homayun: head of Afghanistan Special Police Force, 178

Federal Republic of Germany (West Germany): 22; mobile communications technology sourced from, 19
Focused District Development (FDD): 51, 142; aims of, 50; implementation of (2007), 50

Gendarmerie: 17, 21, 27; characteristics of, 4–5
German Democratic Republic: 30
Germany: 152; advisors from, 49; government of, 147
Ghana: corruption in police force of, 10
Gulabzoi, Sayed Mohammad: 27–8, 37, 142; Afghan Minister of Internal Affairs, 29, 31; family of, 29
Guzar, Amanullah: alleged connection to criminal activity, 104; CoP of Kabul, 104

Habibi, Hashim: 138–9; allies of, 137

Hazara: 106–8, 118, 137, 142, 144; conflict with Kuchis, 159; introduction into police force (2009), 61
Heydari, Tarway: 178
High Police Commission: establishment of, 103
Hizb-i-Islami: 39, 112; former members of, 63
Hizb-i-Wahdat: 102, 166; Khalili faction of, 40
Hizbullah: 166
Hotak, Ghulam Muhammad: 63
Hungary: 30

Illegal tolls: 84, 89; systems used in collection of, 88; variations in, 85
Independent Directorate of Local Government (IDLG): 62–3, 125; establishment of (2007), 56
India: British Raj, 22
Integrity Watch: 79; police access survey, 80
Interim Criminal Procedure Code (ICPC): Italian sponsorship of, 153; provisions of, 153–4
International Covenant on Civil and Political Rights (ICCPR): 9
International Security Assistance Force (ISAF): 42, 62–4, 76–7, 79, 95, 121–2, 128, 130; mentors provided by, 131; military personnel of, 52
Iran: borders of, 85
Islam: conservative interpretation of, 167; Qur'an, 159; *zakat*, 83
Issa, Khwaja: 169, 177; CoP of Enjil district, 174
Issa, Mohammed: head of police, 23
Italy: Carabinieri, 148, 173; sponsor of ICPC, 153

Jalali, Ali Ahmad: 105, 114; Afghan Minister of Interior, 103, 135; resignation of (2005), 136
Jamiat-i Islami: allies of, 135; factions of, 166; members of, 102

227

INDEX

Jones, Terry: burning of Qur'an by (2010), 159
Junbesh: 39
Junbesh-i Milli: 102, 144; supporters within police force, 109
Jurat, Din Mohammad: 135

Kabul Conference (2010): 145
Karmal, Babrak: 27–8; administration of, 26
Karzai, Hamid: 109, 113, 118, 136, 142–3, 145, 178; administration of, 163, 184; allies of, 40; attack on (2008), 120; attempted co-option of militia factions, 173; interim administration of, 34; proclamation of amnesties for deserters from police force, 66; President of Afghanistan, 101; reappointment of disgraced generals (2006), 103–4
Khakrizwal, Mohammad Akram: background of, 101; corruption during tenure of, 139
Khalid, Assadullah: Governor of Kandahar, 60
Khalid, Abdul Hadi: 56, 99, 105
Khalq: 24–6, 136; Pashtun presence in, 30
Khan, Habibullah: reign of, 13
Khan, Ismail: 61, 101, 126, 165–6, 169–71, 176, 180, 184–5; ideology of, 167; reliance on personal oversight, 171–2; supporters of, 62, 174
Khan, Mohammed Daoud: 14, 19, 22–3, 31, 37; President of Afghanistan, 19; police procedure reforms under, 20; supporters of, 24
khassadars: 13
Khel, Sayyed: 61, 125; CoP of Baghlan, 63
Kingdom of Jordan: 52
Kotwali Cadet School: 14
Kuchi: 118; conflict with Hazaras, 159; Pashtun, 159

di Lampedusa, Tomasi: *Gattopardo*, 12

Law and Order Trust Fund (LOFTA): personnel of, 93; support for payment systems, 92

Maoism: influence of, 19
Massud, Ahmad Shah: 40, 63; Afghan Minister of Defence, 39
Military Attorney Directorate (SN): 178–9; Detective Unit, 178–9; shortage of staff, 179
Military Court (MN): 178–9; personnel of, 179
Military Professional Resources, Inc. (MPRI): mentorship programmes of, 53
Militias: 5, 28–9, 101, 130, 144, 173; anti-Taliban, 99; DDR of, 113; CIA-recruited, 104, 128; Shi'ite Jihadi, 166
Ministry of Defence: transfer of Border Affairs to, 27
Ministry of Enforcing Virtue and Preventing Vice: creation of, 35
Ministry of Finance (MoF): 48; corrupt practices in, 92; personnel of, 92–3
Ministry of Interior (kotwali): 13
Ministry of Interior (MoI): 14–15, 21–4, 26–9, 31, 33, 38–40, 47–8, 52, 55–6, 58–60, 62–3, 66, 68, 71–7, 93, 96, 100, 103, 105, 107, 112–13, 115, 118, 124–6, 130, 139, 141, 147–8, 150, 152, 165, 175, 180, 183, 185–6; alleged role of personnel on Kabul Serena Hotel (2008), 120; Census Department, 17; Department for National Public Security, 135; ethnic group representation in, 107–8; Family Response Unit, 148–9; gendarmerie component of, 28; incorporation of Public Security Ministry, 14; internal affairs department, 94; involvement of personnel in drug trade, 89; National Command Centre, 55; National Threat Assessment (2008), 53; payment system reform in, 67; Property Directorate, 18;

INDEX

Recruitment Command, 59; shortage of personnel experience by, 97; sphere of influence, 28; staff of, 16; structure of, 14, 19, 55–6, 91–2, 119; transport battalion, 131–2
Ministry of Justice: personnel of, 146
Ministry of Women Affairs: reports of rape by Afghan police personnel, 156
Mohammad, Khan: 116–17; CoP of Kandahar, 101, 139; targeted for assassination, 101
Mohammadi, Bismillah Khan: 78, 96, 104–6, 108, 111, 143–5, 149, 154; Afghan Minister of Interior, 52, 58, 119, 131; introduction of new Act of Duty (2010), 65–6; tour of provisional inspections (2010), 93
Mujahidin: 166; infiltration into state apparatus by members of, 28

Najibullah, Mohammad: 28, 32, 34, 165
National Directorate of Security (NDS): 41, 62, 69, 102, 165; jurisdiction, 178; limitations on information gathering procedures, 127
New Zealand: Special Forces, 77
Noor, Atta Mohammed: 184–5; bodyguards of, 102; Governor of Balkh, 90, 101–2, 137; leader of Jamiat-i Islami, 102
Noor, Siddiq: 109
Noorzai, Yunis: 113; head of ABP, 109, 130
North Atlantic Treaty Organization (NATO): 52, 75, 77–8, 154; Training Mission-Afghanistan (NTM-A), 51–2, 58–9, 66, 74–5, 76, 90, 93–4, 104, 106, 131–2, 154
Nuri, Shah Jahan: 112–13; death of (2011), 112
Nuristan: 108
Nurzai, General Malham: arrest of (2010), 82

Office of Security Cooperation-Afghanistan: 51, 76, 142; Capability Milestones (CM), 76; created by US DoD (2005), 49; renamed CSTC-A (2006), 49

Pakistan: borders of, 39; decay of policing in, 9; Quetta, 83
Paktiawal, Ali Shah: sacking of (2009), 104
Panjshiri: 135, 140, 143–4; allies of, 40; formation of, 39; supporters of, 40
Parchami: 24, 26–7; presence in Sarandoi, 27; purged from teaching staff at Police Academy, 24
Pashtun: 62, 100, 106–8; Barakzani, 60; conflict with Uzbeks, 137; Kuchis, 159; level of presence in Afghan police force, 23; level of presence in Khalqis, 30; Noorzai, 60; territory inhabited by, 18, 34, 60, 143, 159, 173
Peace and Security Commission: 168
People's Democratic Party (HDK): ideology of, 109; members of, 26, 28
Police Academy: 24, 32, 58, 95, 103, 106, 111, 122, 138, 146; attempted re-launch of (1997), 34; degree programme of, 22, 165; faculty of, 23, 48; required attendance for NCOs, 75; trainee induction level (2007), 48
Police and Kotwali School: 14
Popolzai: 140
Provincial Attorney Directorate: 171
Provincial Police Directorate: 167; Criminal Investigation Unit, 34, 167, 171

Qanuni, Yunis: 40; Afghan Minister of Interior, 39, 140, 143
Qapiq, Abdul Mahmood: Afghan Attorney General, 153
Qati, Matiullah: CoP of Kandahar, 104; death of, 204
Quick Reaction Force: 135–6; personnel of, 135

Rabbani, Burhanuddin: 109; administration of, 35, 39, 99

229

INDEX

Rahman, King Abdur: 14, 19; family of, 13; reign of, 13, 18
Rawlings, Jerry: President of Ghana, 10
Republic of Afghanistan (1973–8): 14; estimation of number of police force size, 19
Revolutionary Council: members of, 26
Russian Federation: 118; weapons sourced from, 38

Sadat: 106, 144
Sadegh, Mirwais: 168
Sarandoi: 25–6, 28; Academy, 30; presence of Parchami in, 27; staffing levels of (1979), 25
Sayydkhel, Maulana: alleged criminal activity, 101; targeted for assassination, 101
Shah, Nadir: 14, 19
Shah, Timur: 131
Sharif, Amin: 112
Shirzai, Gul Agha: 60; Governor of Nangarhar, 139
Smith, Graeme: investigation of torture of civilians by Afghan police personnel, 155
Soviet Union (USSR): 17, 27, 32, 109, 116; advisors from, 30–1; Invasion of Afghanistan (1979–89), 26, 168; training of personnel in, 99
Spain: government of, 52
Special Inspector General for Afghanistan Reconstruction (SIGAR): criticisms of CM rating system, 53
Specialised policing: development strategies, 6–7
State Intelligence Agency (KhAD): 29
Surkhi Parsa riots (1979): 25
Switzerland: government of, 147

Tajiks: 106–7, 109, 141, 144; territory inhabited by, 40
Taliban: 34, 37, 66, 68, 157, 160, 167–8, 177, 185; defection of personnel to, 123; fall of (2001), 38, 55, 78, 115, 120–2, 137, 168; infiltration of territory by, 127; insurgency activity, 1; members of, 63; opposition to, 39, 99, 102, 111; recruitment strategies of, 154; targeted assassination campaigns of, 101; territory controlled by, 129, 167
Taraki, Nur Muhammad: supporters of, 26
tazkira: establishment of, 13
Terakhel, Mullah: 126
Turkey: 14, 52

United Arab Emirates (UAE): 52
United Kingdom (UK): 58, 141; Birmingham, 14; government of, 80; military of, 121–2
United Nations (UN): 101, 103, 113, 117, 121, 141; Assistance Mission to Afghanistan (UNAMA), 66, 72, 79, 95, 104, 126, 140–1, 150, 156; criticisms of ANAP, 62; Department of Safety and Security (UNDSS), 126; Development Programme (UNDP), 79, 92–3, 153; Office on Drugs and Crime (UNODC), 80, 160; Special Rapporteur on extrajudicial, summary or arbitrary executions, 157–8
United States of America (USA): 22, 61, 168, 173, 177, 183; advisers from, 111; Central Intelligence Agency (CIA), 104, 128; Department of Defense (DoD), 47, 49–50; Department of State (DoS), 23, 49–50, 103; Drug Enforcement Administration (DEA), 91; government of, 20, 49, 150; military of, 50, 83, 121, 130, 146
Uzbek: 106–8, 141, 144; conflicts with Pashtun, 137; presence in government in, 109–10

Wardak, Abdul Rahim: Afghan Minister of Defense, 40
Wardak, Brig. Gen. Sayed Aziz: arrest of (2010), 120

INDEX

Warsaw Pact: advisors from, 30
Watanjar, Mohammad Aslam: Afghan Minister of Interior, 26
World Trade Organization (WTO): 9

Zarar, Ahmed Moqbel: 105–6, 111, 140–1, 143–4; Afghan Minister of Interior, 56; background of, 140
Zia, Ahmad: 112
Ziya, Mama: background of, 168; Herat Provincial Police Chief, 168–9
Zurmat, Azim: 25